West with the Rise

West
with the Rise

Fly-fishing across America

JAMES BARILLA

University of Virginia Press • *Charlottesville and London*

University of Virginia Press

© 2006 by the Rector and Visitors of the University of Virginia

All rights reserved

Printed in the United States of America on acid-free paper

First published 2006

9 8 7 6 5 4 3 2 1

LIBRARY OF CONGRESS CATALOGING-IN-PUBLICATION DATA

Barilla, James, 1967–

 West with the rise : fly-fishing across America / James Barilla.

  p. cm.

 ISBN 0-8139-2537-1 (cloth : alk. paper)

 1. Fly fishing—United States—Anecdotes. 2. Barilla, James, 1967– I. Title.

 SH463.B37 2006

 799.12′4′0973—dc22   2005024389

For Nicola and Brook

Contents

Setting Out

We are mostly water, moving through channels, pounding through rapids in the chest, seeping like a spring rain through the soil of our muscles and the bedrock of our bones, into the aquifers that drain back to the heart. I'm sitting in a cafe overlooking the Sawmill River in western Massachusetts, watching it cascade down the ledge of an old millworks where they used to manufacture bobbins for the sewing industry and now sell used books. Only the waterlogged scraps of the old millrace have withstood the power of the water to have its way. Spume drifts up into the boughs of the hemlocks and sparkles as it catches the sun.

It's a sublime spot for a cup of coffee and conversation, but for me the tumbling water is more than a setting for something else. I have come here, alone, to river watch. I must look strange, perched in my chair and staring like a heron in search of a meal, while all around me people chat and sip and turn pages. As usual, I am wondering about what is beneath; what is living in those golden spaces where one strand of current swallows another, where the falling water folds upon itself and swirls away into the depths of a pool. I watch the river, but just watching is never enough.

What drives me to fish? Why stand for hours in cold water, making repetitive motions with a graphite stick, scanning the air for one kind of insect and swatting another on the nape of my neck?

Sometimes the answer lies in the intricacies of one river. Every spring, rivers like the Sawmill swell as the snow melts and tear trees loose from the hillsides. When the surge recedes, a deep pool is shallow, a shallow stretch has been scoured out, a bank has been undercut, a tree thrown across the current. The same river is never the same. But the imagination is migratory; like warblers in the spring or salmon in the sea, it always returns to the same stretch of woods or water, while in between those journeys home it roams across continents and seas.

I'm at a restless point in my life. I'm thirty-four years old. My wife, Nicola, and I have been talking about having kids for several years now. It hasn't happened. Now we are talking to the fertility specialists, and they are talking IVF, in-vitro fertilization. Watching the river circulate through its pools, I recall sitting in the waiting room at the doctor's office in an upscale suburb of San Francisco with the other unfortunate couples, the women stoic, the men ill at ease, knowing some painful revelation was waiting on the other side of the door. We tried not to look at each other. A large saltwater fish tank filled one wall of the room, and we watched the clownfish and puffers circle the glass in a lurid parade. They were undoubtedly meant to calm us, but something about their perseveration along the walls of their cage made me all the more breathless.

The doctor was brisk, walking the fine line between empathy and not getting our hopes up. He told us the technology has raced ahead since the first "test-tube baby" was born almost twenty years ago. These days they induce the ovaries to produce multiple eggs at once. They harvest them through a needle inserted into the abdominal cavity, and they take a semen sample from me. The technicians select the most vigorous sperm and inject those individually into each egg in a process called intracytoplasmic sperm injection, or ICSI. The fertilized eggs develop in a special medium for several days; then the specialists pierce the protective coating of several eggs to assist them in "hatching." They load two or three eggs into syringes tipped in delicate tubing and plant them in the uterus. The rest they freeze for later use, and hope nature will take over.

"You've got some time to think about it," the doctor said, summing up. There were pictures of his daughters on his desk. "But if you were to decide to proceed, it would be best to start soon. The sooner the better, as far as those eggs are concerned."

I've been in a state of heightened anxiety ever since. Acronyms, technicians in scrubs, syringes, and special growing mediums—this is not how I expected parenthood to begin. For years I've heard about people getting pregnant accidentally: the slightest miscalculation and nature will jump into action. Artificial has always meant the means to prevent making babies, not to create them. How far into the realm of the unnatural am I willing to go to fulfill the biological imperative to reproduce? The sudden intrusion of the body and its biological imperatives into my sense of our life makes me queasy. This is what your body is for, one voice says, and another rebels, refuses. I have reveled in the frenzy of mayflies at dusk, the salmon surging into the mouth of their natal stream, without ever confronting the reason they risk everything— reproduction. Now sperm cells wriggle like microscopic elvers in my imagination, on their way upstream to the promised egg. They're inside me, waiting to begin their journey. But it's a trip they will not make; or at least, it won't be the one they have been programmed to pursue.

The artificial and the natural: wading into the river is the way I reconcile the desire to participate in the natural world with the paradoxical desire to remain outside it, the way I confront the incongruity of the river's ecological systems and the artifice of feather and hook, the way I find my place as an individual human being in the community of species. I have already endured the climax of the hyper-real—at the lab, I was handed a small plastic cup with a lid and pointed, awkwardly, to the bathroom. There, in the company of several urine samples and the idle chatter of the technicians on the other side of a stainless-steel window, I was told to produce a semen sample. It will go on like this, I know—the boundaries of the private, mysterious body falling away before the inquisitions of reproductive science. My own role will be marginal—I won't be the one injecting the gonadatropin (garnered from the urine of pregnant women) into my lower abdomen twice a day, or enduring the ultrasound explorations of my insides every week. I will watch, and support. Perhaps it is this lack of participation that brings the vision of a long fishing trip to mind, a chance to seek the heart of these questions of human creation before I have to stand aside and watch the monitors while everything happens.

A fishing expedition is partly a process of remembering who we were, and partly an exploration of who we have become. One trip has haunted me since childhood. It begins with the storied waters of the East and heads west to places I read about when I was a kid, reading Nick Lyons's accounts of fishless days on Catskill rivers and tramping with Robert Traver through the backwoods of Michigan. I devoured Ernest Schwiebert's description of matching hatches on spring creeks in the Paradise Valley—that sounded like paradise to me. If you grow up fishing the tiny, amber pools of eastern mountain brooks, then the wavy blue lines on a map are a dream of big water. Before you've learned to drive, you've made the watershed journeys in your mind, crossing ridges, the Berkshires, the Appalachians, the Black Hills, the Bighorns, the Bitterroots, the Cascades, the Sierra, stopping all along the way to test the waters.

An exercise in escapism, a period of reflection, a chance to reconcile mind and biology—whatever the reasons, leaving was hard. Nicola said it was fine for me to go. I could tell she didn't mean it. What would we do? She would have to wait with the unanswered question, going to work, watching television in the evenings, mired in routines that wouldn't answer anything, while I wandered across the country. She'd had a test a couple weeks before in which a barium dye is injected into the uterus so the shape of the reproductive system can be viewed on a screen. The fallopian tubes should have been clearly visible, but only one appeared. The other was blocked. We learned from our doctor that the ovaries do not alternate their production of eggs; one side may produce for years, then quit and let the other side take over. My news wasn't great either—the abundance of little gametes was on the low side of normal, and their motility, their friskiness, was also on the low side. So we knew the source of our predicament: we could wait for years while egg after egg traveled hopelessly down the blocked tube and the sperm swarmed on the other side. To me this blockage was metaphoric: we had shared a vague dream of our future, and now we were confronting a barrier that separated shared fantasy from individual biology, my body from hers. Motion was my balm; she coped by staying put.

How is fishing the cure for restlessness? Nicola wanted to know. Would I be safe? Would I come back? The only answers I had were illogical. Ultimately, I wanted to go away so I could come home, wiser, prepared for the journey ahead. I packed my gear. I flew east. I bought a truck with a cap on the back. I started to dream of rivers, and going home.

The Biting Kind of Fly

When I thought about where to start my journey, one place came immediately to mind. It wasn't the place where I had first cast a fly, or even the stream where I had fooled my first fish, although those occasions weren't too far away in place and time. On Mormon Hollow Brook I realized that my fly rod was not like my skateboard or my Dungeons and Dragons dice or even my baseball glove, all of which would eventually wind up under my bed or in a cardboard box in the garage. I would keep using that fly rod year after year, and mark the passage of time by the rivers I had fished. Fishing was permanent.

I decided the best place to begin this journey would be the very spot where I had renounced everything to do with fly-fishing and sworn I would never pick up a rod again. I was nine years old, and I had pushed my way through a tangle of hemlocks and mountain laurel to stand near the brink of a foam-flecked brown torrent. It was April, not the height of blackfly season in New England, nor really even the start of mosquito season, and the deerfly season was still in its earliest stages, all of which meant almost nothing, since they were all present in an innumerable and constantly replenished horde. It didn't matter how many I killed; it didn't matter that I had slathered myself with so much repellent that I stank like a paper mill; they came back like the living dead, absolutely fearless and lusty. I stood with a shroud of blackflies dancing around my shoulders, one occasionally scrambling into my ear, or up my nostril, or down my sleeve, or up my pant leg, while the deerflies spun in tight loops around my head, looking to snarl themselves in my hair. Weaving about my face, a chorus of mosquitoes whined nasally about how hungry they were.

Worse, I needed to concentrate, and I needed my hands, because I had a monumental mess in front of me. There are two lessons one learns early on in fly-fishing. The first is that any branch, bough, limb, or leaf is absolutely dying to get hold of your fly and will almost never lose a tug of war. Second, your line, the rocks, your feet, and the water will conspire to tangle your line in the most elaborate snarls imaginable. To untangle such knots requires the skills of a weaver and the patience of a Buddha. To untangle such knots in the presence of a biting insect swarm requires what I've come to recognize as the insect dance, a spasming, shoulder-scrunching, and head-lolling series of sufferings. The jaw remains clenched, except when the victim spits forth a stream of vile language and threats. You don't want to meet someone like this; relentless bugs are known to drive people, like moose, into rampages. More important, you don't want to be someone like this.

I had a nine-year-old's patience for the situation, which is to say, not much. I bit the fly off my leader, pulled it down through the guides, and began weaving the end back and forth through the loops, all the while doing the insect dance. Tugging one loop created another. Untwisting one strand twisted another. The snarl didn't seem to get any smaller; it just changed shape. Finally I couldn't take it any more. In a burst of gesticulating madness, I loosened the reel from the rod, took the line in hand like a lasso, and swung the reel around and around over my head, battering it against tree trunks as I howled something like "Arrraghhhh!!!" Then I let it go, watching the big tangle of fluorescent line sail up into the branches and down into the ferns, where the reel landed with a thud.

"That's it!" I screamed, by which I meant I'd had it with vindictive tree branches, lost flies, and most of all with bugs! I ran out of the woods with the swarm in pursuit, jumped on my bicycle, and rode home, done with fishing forever.

I was done with fishing for three days, which is a long time when you're nine. My bug bites healed. I went to school; I watched cartoons in the afternoon after the soap operas finished; I read science fiction before I went to sleep. I began to see my line just sitting there in the ferns, unused, buried by snow in the winter, or picked up and carried away by some other fisherman. What bothered me most, however, what I ultimately couldn't bear, was knowing that the brook kept right on flowing without me and would keep its secrets. That underwater realm would remain unknown to me. I started fishing from pool to pool in my sleep.

I kept my oath until the third afternoon after school, when I told myself that nobody else had heard it but me, and if I felt like breaking it, that was my business. I got on my bike and pedaled down to Perry Farm Road, forced my way back up through the undergrowth, and found my line in the ferns. The bugs were waiting for me too, of course, but they didn't have long to feed. I wrapped the line up into a big handful around the spool, knots and all, and hustled out of there. At home I sat down on the porch where I had some room to spread out, and after an hour I had untwisted the final loop and pulled it out into a miraculous straight line. I bent the spool back into shape as best I could, so that even if it did move like a wobbly hubcap, it would coil line. I was ready to fish again.

Twenty years later, the road to Mormon Hollow Brook is the washed-out semblance of a streambed itself, studded with boulders and carved by gravel bars that have recently seen flowing water. A sign nailed to the trunk of an oak says "Road Closed" in faded orange paint. I squeeze my mountain bike between the two concrete pylons and proceed with caution down the steep ridge to the brook, clutching my rod case and the brakes.

I'm wary of this place. The last time I was here, on a bright and blustery day in January, I hiked upstream to an ancient beaver pond. I recall exulting in the absence of bugs, and I got so giddy that I neglected to take care. Not far from where I'd once flung my reel in disgust, I leaned out over a steep, frozen bank to scan the depths for trout. The frozen hemlock duff gave way, whisking me off my feet and plunging me down through a thin layer of ice into water up to my waist. The pool was frigid enough to burn my thighs scarlet, but I was so shocked to be floundering for a foothold that I didn't really notice the cold until I hauled myself out. Then I felt it like the hand of a cadaver. I could feel it tightening as I sprinted back to my bike and pedaled furiously up the hill. By the time I got home, my jeans were frozen into tubes of cardboard, and it took a lot of kneading by the woodstove before the life returned to my legs.

The stream is flowing clear but high for July, each pool the dark amber of a strong cup of tea. The state forestry people have been thinning out the hemlock along the bank, leaving the silver birch and ash. I put down my bike by the bridge, and sure enough the bugs catch up with me, not so much the blackflies but the deerflies now in a veritable swarm, as if my head were the nucleus of some dense metal with hundreds of whizzing electrons in orbit. I reach up and with a casual sweep of the arm snatch two of the red-eyed demons right out of the air.

Despite the urge to squeeze my fist tight, I don't crush the life out of them immediately. My streamside vengeance is always the same: I toss the offenders into the water and see what happens as they float away.

What happens this time is disappointing. Where many a hatchery trout lurked in the past, there's no sign of habitation. The violent splash I long for never comes; not even a minnow leaps through the sunshine to pounce on the victims. My tormentors drift downstream and out of sight.

This part of Massachusetts, with its tannic streams and granite bedrock, is one of the hardest hit by acid rain, and I don't know if the hatchery even stocks here anymore because of it. A lack of stockies isn't necessarily a bad thing; there were always native fish in this brook, skinny and black as licorice sticks, and I would be happy to find that they have taken over the stream. But I'm also afraid of discovering that nothing at all swims here now.

I choose a deer-hair caddis, barbless, big enough to drop like a meal that doesn't come along often. Small green frogs launch themselves into the water as I step down among the rocks, and the damselflies of these waters, black-winged, bodies a metallic green, dance from rock to rock ahead of my feet. I place my steps cautiously, making sure the stones can bear my weight, half-expecting a misstep to trip me up.

Hidden in the ferns at the head of a promising pool, I work my knees over the knobs of a root, feel the damp ooze into my sleeves as I elbow into the gravel for a cast. I rise up onto my haunches, pinch the hook between my fingertips, and pull the rod tip back until it's taut, scrutinizing the deadly angles of the branches and rocks.

Finally I let the fly spring from my fingers. A moment of delectable anticipation passes as it lands near the froth of its intended target and curls into a drift.

"Perfect," I gasp to myself, a gleeful certainty rising in my bones.

The fish respond to my fly as if it were a bomb tossed into a crowded street. The water churns as fish bolt every which way for cover, their bodies making an audible thump against the stones. I pull in my fly, muttering to myself that at least there are still fish in the stream. I can't blame midwestern smokestacks for going fishless.

Slowly the physical memory of my days here seeps into the fishing. I've been fishing wide-open spaces for too long, have gotten too accustomed to standing upright and whirling my line through the air with impunity. It won't work here—I can't saunter to the brink of a pool and expect the fish to remain calm. I will have to do more than get down on my hands and knees and waddle like a raccoon if I want to catch these trout. I'll have to slow down, remember the way the nine-year-old took every motion slowly, painfully slowly.

Fishless, I reach the beaver dam, the scene of my soaking the winter before. It's a dreary place, hemlocks filtering out all but a few tawny bars of sunlight, the water black and still as a puddle of molasses. It's enough to summon Ophelia's ghost, singing mournfully as she floats downstream. Her song should be a warning to get out before something unpleasant happens, but I'm no Romantic poet, I'm a fisherman, and the gloom makes me hopeful at first. Crouched in a grotto among the hemlocks, for the first time I feel hidden from the vigilant, underwater eyes. Even the water's apparent lifelessness encourages me: I imagine the bottom as a streamside version of the deep-sea floor, where desperate, starving trout lurk like anglerfish, ready to gobble anything that moves.

Confirmation of my folly comes soon enough. In a new version of past frustrations, my line winds up snarled in a knot of amazing complexity, encompassing several treetops and a stump downstream. When I stand up for the inevitable tug of war, I discover that my sneaker has also been snared in a loop. I have to slip off the shoe to free my foot, and my one-legged balancing act drives the fish into a frenzy of fear. The pool erupts with their wakes, and Ophelia begins to wail.

I'm hanging from a branch like a chimpanzee, picking at a tangle of needles while the sweat stings my eyes and the deerflies seek revenge in my hair, when a diabolical voice whispers a familiar enticement: *You could cut your losses by cutting your line.* Cut the line and leave it draped across the branches, hike out into the sunshine, forget all this hassle. It would be so easy.

"Forget it," I tell myself. The same old madness is lurking here. Monofilament I can part with; people leave snarls of nylon in branches everywhere. But you won't find fly line festooning the streamside vegetation, because fly line, with its supple skin, is the angler's long and delicate proboscis, testing the waters like a butterfly's tongue. Cutting one's line means more than an end to fishing for the day—it's a desperate act, a self-inflicted wound. I reach for another handful of twigs.

When I've got my leader back, I decide it's time to hunt less elusive quarry for a while. Fishing like a nine-year-old is hard work; I'm spent. I climb up over the dam into a surprisingly humid afternoon that makes me squint at first, as if I've just crawled out the mouth of a cavern. The sun shimmers over a green tureen of swamp grass. I find what I'm seeking among the gray skeletons of drowned trees—blueberries ripe and swollen with the rains. They can't get away! Some are powder blue, some dark as midnight—I try them all. They're all sweet, with the same tannic astringency that darkens the streams.

I could quite happily slumber away an hour here, and I even consider a patch of soft needles beneath an old white pine as just the spot. But I'm not sure who might come along to wake me up. Someone else has been here, and left a rather large pile of scat to mark the spot. Stained blue, of course. A raccoon? It looks bigger. I decide to head back downstream.

Below the bridge, the brook is different. On every stream there are gaining reaches and losing reaches, places where the groundwater wells up through the gravel to widen the stream and places where it recedes and draws the stream down with it. Perry Farm Bridge marks the start of a gaining reach as well as the boundary of the old farm, now a forest again. Maple and ash crowd the banks, mountain laurel grows in abundance, and deer trails wind through the mazes of glossy leaves. Take a few steps into these woods and the road disappears—the sound of falling water offers the best sense of direction. The water itself changes here, becomes less like black tea and more like green, and there is suddenly more of it bouncing over the rocks.

There have always been more fish below the bridge too, or at least they have always been easier to catch, and today is no exception. The earlier lessons in wariness serve me well, and although I cannot help but make a bough-shaking ruckus as I fight my way through the mountain laurel, the trout respond not by fleeing but by snatching my fly. When I coast them along the surface, it's as if I've drawn forth some glowing remnant of yesterday's sundown; a fragment of star-spangled night shines in my hand. It's hard to imagine fish like these jouncing along in a hatchery truck tank. They're small enough, and spindly enough, and elaborate enough in the head and jaw, that they might just be natives.

I'm tempted to believe my last fish—the one that explodes from the shadows under Saxton's Bridge like a bass hitting a plug—is a native. It's almost dark enough, almost jeweled enough. But it's a good eleven inches long, and plump. It's not impossible to find a trout this big in this brook, but it is impossible to find a native that looks this good. A native of this size should look like the son of snapping turtle, a snarling grandfather hauled from the moonshine depths of some backwoods holler, all ears and beak and yellow teeth. This fish is movie-star sleek, too stylish to be true. But I'm grateful for the delusion, and for a graceful way to end the day.

The trout holds by my foot after I slip out the hook, a gesture I could read as a portent of a fish-filled journey to come. Then it shakes itself and drifts back into the shadows.

The Old Party Spot

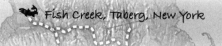

Fish Creek, Taberg, New York

A name like Fish Creek sounds promising. Of course, there are lots of Fish Creeks. Some have plenty of bullheads; others are paradise if you like fishing for smallmouths. I've even visited several Trout Brooks, only to find that times have changed since trappers prowled the wilderness that is now the patch of scrub behind the strip mall. So when I find the blue filament of Fish Creek on the map, I'm encouraged but not elated to learn that this local Opening Day favorite is not far away. Everybody's favorite in April is often nobody's favorite in July.

I've come back to East Syracuse, the scene of my inauspicious introduction to trout fishing. The first trout I ever saw were swimming in the parking lot of the Big M supermarket, their lives raffled away for charity. For two dollars you could climb onto the scaffolding that surrounded the glass tank and dunk a line into the frothy water. One of the fish had a hundred-dollar bill tied to it somehow, and a number of grim-faced men were hunkered over the water looking for it before they cast. I took my place among them, small and uncertain, while my mother watched with the groceries down below.

"One time," my mother said. Among the bubbles from the air pumps I could see gray shadows circling the glass. I dropped my line. The lure swung around the tank, then popped to the surface.

"Okay. That's it."

I handed the rod to the barker. It was the beginning of a life of imagining lots of fish, and capturing few of them.

Fish Creek flows on the fringe of familiar terrain for me, but finding it is not easy. It isn't the Mississippi, a body so broad you can feel the pull of it on the surrounding hills and a pointed finger can send you there down almost any road. The fact is I have a hell of a time finding it, having never seen it in my life. I follow what I think is it, a trickle that splashes down through front yards into the center of town. I try to allow the locals some slack by imagining this ditch in the full force of a spring freshet, but still, it isn't worth casting over now.

A sultry haze hangs over the afternoon, and here I discover that my truck's lack of air-conditioning is going to wring the patience from my brow. I'm trying to keep my back from sticking like a wad of stale gum to the seat when I see the sign: Ice Cream.

"Thank God," I say, pulling up in front of the antique façade of the U.S. Mercantile Hotel. I hop up the slouching stairs to the marble counter of an old soda fountain where a big fan cools a row of green vinyl stools.

A teenage couple is alone inside, idling away the doldrums of the afternoon by flicking through the pages of a glossy magazine. They hide it under the counter when the screen door slaps shut behind me.

"Sorry," I say. I feel like I'm intruding, but their eager faces tell me not to worry; they've been waiting all afternoon for somebody to wander through that door.

"Do you guys know the way to Fish Creek?"

They shake their heads. "But I can call my brother," the boy says, tightening down the brim of his backwards baseball cap. "He used to fish a lot."

While he's on the phone there's a commotion outside, and the sound of many small frantic feet.

"It's the campers," the girl hisses, as if to warn me that a band of hostile savages are on the threshold and that I had better flee to the cellar. "You'd better order quick."

The door opens and in they file, thirty kids ravenous for ice cream crowding around my knees with pleading eyes.

"Get in line!" the counselor barks, trying to sound older than he is, and he motions them all to get behind me. The boy takes one look at the horde, slams down the phone without a good-bye, and grabs his scoop from the water pail.

"My brother says it's right here; we're right next to it."

"You mean that little brook across the street?"

"No, down the street. You can see the bridge from the steps."

I can hear impatient little voices behind me, trying to nudge me along. *Hey, no pushing!* I want to say, hearkening back to some elementary school lunch-line memory. I want to ask if the brother mentioned any favorite spots. Was he a fly fisherman, by any chance? I can see, however, that this isn't the time. The little savages have me outnumbered. With his scoop poised in a declaration of urgency, the boy demands to know my order. I should order a cone. Instead, we all wait while the metal shaker blends a malt.

"Whipped cream! Whipped cream! Under there!"

The bother I've caused ends with a blast: like a snow-making machine, the whipped-cream canister shoots a tornado of white stuff all over the counter.

I sit in a booth and watch the elation of ice cream unfold. Pure pleasure blooms on small faces as the cones are handed down; pure anguish reigns over the next in line.

Two boys at the end of the line lean their faces in front of the fan and let the wind whisk through their hair. Nicola and I haven't really discussed adoption. We know the options: everything from paying someone to provide their eggs to traveling to China to take away unwanted baby girls. There is a thriving market in infants, although older kids wind up with few willing takers. Somehow, the idea of taking in a child who is not our own, while admirable, doesn't fit our dream. We've read that the fetus recognizes the mother's voice while it's still in the womb, that if you tap the mother's belly, the baby will answer with a tapping of its own. How much of that would we miss?

Deep down, I think we're obsessed with passing on our genes. We both believe in nature too much to rely completely on the nurture side. I fear that at some point I won't recognize any part of myself in an adopted child, that some willful stranger will arise in the youngster we have raised, to repudiate us. Of course, the child as parental reflection is a fairly narcissistic idea, one that genetic offspring are busy refuting all the time. It would be better to relinquish the belief in genetic determinacy, if it were possible.

One of these kids could be like me. They would like ice cream, but they would also like to scamper after fish. I wouldn't mind having a sidekick like that.

"I'm having cookies and cream," one boy says. "Or maybe peanut-butter cup. Or maybe double-fudge ripple."

The line is still nudging forward when I finish.

I cross the bridge and catch a glimpse of riffles and gleaming water and children wobbling over rocks barefoot. The creek is bigger than I thought, with plenty of lively water.

"Trout!" I declare, as if receiving my own long-awaited ice-cream cone, and step on the gas.

I have to get a license. Inside the living-room half of a modular home, an older woman reclines behind a broad expanse of mahogany veneer, while a young couple sits stiffly by the door. There is finance in the air.

"Can I help you?" the woman says, and before I can reply two kids come running out from the other room clutching crayons and pieces of paper.

"See, Grandma! See!" They shove and shake their drawings in her face, trying to get her to look at theirs first. This is always how it goes—I see one kid who's cute, who makes me think that would be fun, and then another tyro arrives to terrify me. What's worse, these two are the spitting image of my youthful sister and me—cranky, bored, and ready to rumble. If my kids get my genes, I'm finished.

"Nice, nice, now put those down right here so Grandma can see them." Grandma pats the desk, then points me to the other room.

I nod to the couple to suggest that I might have to squeeze past them and make a sideward pirouette to avoid any contact with their knees, noticing as I pass that the floor is covered with lengths of overlapping shag carpet that must serve as sales samples. It occurs to me that some-one could trip on these, and I'm imagining the grandmother fracturing a hip on her way to the bathroom when my own foot catches the edge of a powder-blue square.

Staggering forward, my arms outstretched like a demented boogey-man, I somehow manage to keep from falling flat on my face. The couple tuck themselves into fetal positions as I flail past, while the kids run into the other room, suddenly petrified by the stranger.

"You okay?" the grandmother asks me. The man releases a startled cough and the woman smoothes her thighs. My cheeks burning, I say sure. "You go on in there. Don't mind those kids."

I find them clutching their mother behind another desk, the taller one pressed to the crook of her neck, his head knocking her executive glasses aside, the other burrowing into the pillow of her shoulder.

"Timmy, you and Alicia go play in the other room," she says.

They don't move. Timmy shakes his head no, and Alicia grabs a tighter handful of sleeve.

Would I want one of these? The commitment. The demands. The need for a life of one's own, for space. What if I regretted it? Eighteen years until they can go off to college and vote. That's a long time.

"Why don't you go draw Mommy a pretty picture?"

They both shake their heads. No way. Their mother offers me an exasperated smile.

"Come on, you two," she says, and motions for me to sit down as she leads them out of the room. I sit and look at photos of Timmy and Alicia smiling on her desk. She comes back briskly.

"Boredom," she says, and clicks on her typewriter.

She doesn't know about fishing, but she does know the creek itself is hard to reach.

"I'm talking two hundred feet down, and steep, most places. The only other bridge crossing is on private land. They used to let people fish there, but I heard they posted it. People down there partying all hours of the day and night, until they finally said enough is enough. The liability. Shame, though, for you."

I wave to Timmy and Alicia as I leave. They're drawing again. I make out what appears to be a clumsy monster in a cowboy hat on Timmy's page. His fangs are purple and so are his claws, but his eyes are blue, like mine.

Just as the woman warned me, the stream heads off into a ravine while the road sticks to the flat expanse of cornfields. I soon lose sight of it, along with any hope that I might just park and slide down an embankment. Fortunately, I find that the bridge she mentioned is posted, but not against fishermen.

"Fishermen parking only. All others will be towed," the signs read. There are a couple of cars parked beneath them in the giant borrow pit studded with mummified cigarettes and emerald shards of beer bottle, the relics of parties past.

I'm happy to enjoy my privileged status, until I notice two guys eyeing me from the bridge. They're clad only in cut-offs, and they aren't fishing. One of them blows a plume of smoke in my direction, straddles the guardrail, and tosses his butt aside. He stands watching the water with the sun on his tanned shoulders while I get out my waders and string the line through the guides of my rod. I'm trying to squeeze my foot into a sneaker when his splash echoes in the concrete chambers beneath the road. The other guy has taken his place, looking down and rubbing a bicep.

I lock up and walk over to get a look at the creek. Before I can reach the bridge and offer a greeting, the second swimmer flicks down his cigarette and jumps. I watch him accelerate and disappear, his cigarette still smoldering on the tarmac.

The smell of the water wafts up to me, mingled with the aromas of hot tar and tobacco, a smell I have never been able to define as only algae, or rocks, or fish. Just as the sea has its own tang of brine and all that lives and dies within its waters, so the bigger rivers exhale their own peculiar breath as they pour over the rocks. I lean out and breathe in this airborne spume while the guys tread water far below.

"Man, that water's cold!" one of them yells. They are clambering out as I arrive on the bank. I stand staring at the graffiti under the bridge, layer upon layer of it, and not just the usual scrawl of profanity, but paintings, bizarre bathing-beauty caricatures, and distorted mushroom heads splashed across the cement like a giant comic-book page. Some guerrilla artist has been at work out here while everyone else slurped beer and swam. The men pick their way past me, shivering and barefoot over the stones, leaving me alone with the pool.

The collision of stone and water is obvious here. The creek has been gnawing for centuries on the ledge that leans over the pool. Springs leak out between pages of slate and cascade through moss and ferns into the indigo depths below. It's not so obvious, however, where the trout might be holding. I bounce my tan caddis off the jagged slate and let it wind and drift among the currents. I tug it back in short strips as if it were struggling to take off. I let it flutter in the spray where the springs disappear. I let it drown and swim it through the shadows. Nothing replies.

At first I blame the swimmers for putting the fish down. What right-minded fish would risk coming to the top for a bite when a fleshy torpedo could smack the surface at any time? But my toes tell me otherwise as I wade downstream. What's too cold for comfortable swimming is still too warm for trout to feed in the afternoon. Had the water been right for fishing, neither of those guys would have taken the time to splutter anything about how cold it was; they would have raced for shore, blue-lipped and gasping. I swirl my hand around. It feels like classic smallmouth water.

In the next run, I find the proof I'm looking for: a bronze shape that sways in the current and rises to tiny possibilities, just like a trout. Like many trout, it ignores my offerings, and I lose hope quickly.

Right now I should confess a reluctance, even a laziness on my part, when it comes to fishing nymphs. When I open my fly box at the start of a day, rain or shine, I reach for dry flies. I cast those dries until my patience wears thin or the sun goes down, and hopefully I find a stretch where the fish are willing to appreciate my efforts—otherwise I go home fishless. I am enamored of the rise, and I lack the faith to believe that a trout will take a nymph if I can't see it happen. A friend of mine once rationalized it succinctly: "I don't fish nymphs because I don't have to." He lives in Montana, where in my experience, he's right. Maybe you only catch five fish instead of twelve, but that's still plenty for me.

It's a slightly different story two thousand miles to the east, where the snowpack melted four months ago and the nights are likely to be sultry. I stand at the top of a magnificent run, water tumbling over rocks and swirling into another deep pool. Here I inhale the earthy tonic of the streambed willows, which still fails to rouse me, and I offer a few lackluster drifts. I'd be willing to wager that if I hung around until the dusk settled and bats appeared, I'd get fifteen minutes of frantic dry fly-fishing here. But the rest of the day's fishing is likely to be nothing more than a workout for my forearm. I know I should put on a nymph, but I could wind up hanging around here while the chilly Delaware bubbles with rises. Miles of river, miles of road ahead—my mind is zooming onward. The freedom to move only feels real when I'm moving. Picturing the mating flights of phantom duns get me reeling in my line, quickly.

Two more guys have appeared on the bridge. They salute me with upraised beer cans.

"Catch any?"

I make excuses. It's too early and too warm.

"Try right there," one guy says, mimicking a cast. "C'mon, I want to see you catch one."

They're waiting for me at the top of the bank. The first to approach is still jiggling his wrist in a false cast, laughing with the jaunty bravado that I've encountered in veteran salesmen. He has eyes that remind me of harmless jellyfish.

Trailing a bit behind, his companion regards me with a raptor's intensity from the shade of a baseball cap. The hollows under his cheekbones are creased and brown, making his chin resemble an old apple core.

"I've seen them pull fish as long as your leg out of here," the first one says, setting his imaginary hook into a lunker's throat. His lips, under a fringe of sandy moustache, are disconcertingly sensuous. "Right off this bridge. You the one with the Mass. license plate?"

I nod. I could get into the trip, but the whole idea is too intimate to explain to other men. I don't think they've come to this swimming hole to hear about my parenting anxieties. The three of us glance at each other and scuff our feet and look down at the water flowing past, safe within the bounds of outdoor camaraderie but sensing also the volatility of our differences. With their snuff-swollen lower lips and black T-shirts, they seem to me like an older, less wholesome version of the Dukes of Hazard, like the Duke boys might have looked had they been passing a joint and tossing beer cans out the window of the General Lee.

Who knows what kind of weirdo I seem to them, with baggy brown waders wrapped around me like trash bags, stuffed into a rotting pair of running shoes and secured at the waist with a bungee cord? I have two hats on my head, one a cobalt-blue Foreign Legion cap that drapes 30 SPF fabric around my neck, the other an oilskin sombrero tamped down on top to keep the rays off my face. Add in dark sunglasses, and I look like a cross between an astronaut and a Skid Row lunatic. I wear the hats because I don't like sunscreen, and since I had a skin cancer sliced from the side of my nose at the tender age of twenty-five, I have to do something to keep the afternoon sun off my face. Of course, they have no way of knowing that, and they're too polite to ask me why I'm out in public with two hats on my head. After all, I might reply that it's to protect my head from the laser beams that aliens are shooting down from outer space, and then where would we be?

"You come way out here just to fish?"

I take off my sunglasses so they can see the sanity in my eyes. I say I was visiting family around here.

"This used to be a huge party spot," the salesman says, spreading his forlorn arms and waving his beer to convey the vastness of the scene.

"This whole place would be lined with cars on a day like this. There'd be twenty people on this bridge waiting to jump. Partying here all night long. You should have seen the girls here too. Oh man, there were honeys all over the place."

He's poised to continue this description but lets it lapse when his friend tugs the brim of his baseball cap to indicate that he'd like to speak for the first time. The words come out raspy, like it's been a while since his voice box has seen use.

"I don't know where they all went. I was just down at the other bridge looking around, and there's nobody down there but young kids. Course, I was a young kid myself when I used to party up here. Hell, that was ten years ago, if you can believe it."

He shakes his head and clears his throat.

"Need a cigarette."

It occurs to me that these men might be fathers, which makes them seem more forlorn than before. Imagine the salesman getting home from work and his daughter clasping his leg just above the knee. Imagine this gaunt figure shooting hoops with his son in front of the garage. Then picture them here, escaping into the scene of their lost youth. I suppose the pursuit of other women is one way to deal with the quandary of parenthood. There's probably some limbic, sociobiological command center that instructs the male body to search out alternative mates as a response to infertility, or the encroachment of middle age. A natural reaction? Perhaps it is natural to want to run away. Perhaps we're all just primal primates. But this heartless, pheromone-driven vision of nature doesn't appeal to me. I'm here in search of trout, not the beer-inflamed ardor of my teens.

"He's right," says the first guy, starting in again. "The ladies are gone. Too many beer cans, that's what the cops said. Spoiled a good thing, like they always do."

Because I cannot have children naturally, the arbitrary nature of evolution has become disheartening. According to the natural order of things, I'm not meant to be fruitful, while others are apparently meant to multiply like rabbits. I have begun to notice, with a mixture of envy and alienation, the couples with children they don't want, the parents who don't have time for kids, the parents who have too many little faces pleading for attention. But I've also begun to recognize a kind of longing for liberation in the eyes of some men. They want to be left alone. They want to be back in the game, in pursuit of the unknown again, and I think, thank goodness I'm not pushing that double stroller. I love the unknown too, but not the arbitrary. Fishing proceeds according to a series of rules, and fidelity, faith in the presence of trout when none are rising, intimate knowledge of the river's ecology become the guide to fulfillment. You never know what will happen on a particular day, but you know the rules of the game.

To Nicola, however, this trip must seem like a dalliance with the freedom of the arbitrary, a prelude to a possible ending. Who knows what kind of characters I will meet on my random course? She can undoubtedly picture me at a party spot with guys like this, beer in hand, eyes scoping the terrain for quarry. "Wouldn't it be easier if you were with someone else?" she asked several times before I left. "You wouldn't have to deal with all of this." Of course not, I told her. This isn't your problem—it's ours. Let me get used to the idea of having kids. Let me get used to the idea of not having kids. Because we always had these conversations at home, the doctor's office, that scene of much discomfort, came to seem like a place of solidarity, the place where we renewed our vows by facing our arbitrary reproductive fate together. That's where we have been closest recently. There is comfort in going against nature.

They tell me I should go up to Point Rock Reservoir and fish where the creek comes out below the dam—that's where all the fish are. They have a buddy who limits out up there all the time on worms. They're probably right. The coolest water must be below the dam, and the trout have probably gone there in search of it.

"You want a cold one?" The salesman nods toward their car. "Plenty more in the cooler."

I wonder for an instant what it would be like to spend the evening shooting the bull with these two characters, but I'm too restless at the thought of new water, and I'm afraid that at some point I might see them parenting. I tell them I have to drive, and I pull down the gate so I can peel off my waders. I see them standing on the bridge, gazing at the empty beach, as I drive away.

Getting Intimate with the Truck

I drive south on the interstate as thunderclouds gather overhead. Just south of Syracuse I catch up with them, and the rain batters the highway. Near Binghamton I leave them behind, a bruise in the rearview mirror, and turn to the east on the road to New York City. The lush green ridges of the Catskills belie the existence of skyscrapers at the other end. The storm has swept through ahead of me, and now a mist rises from the asphalt and hangs over the valley, full of hovering midges and twirling caddis when the road bends down to the river. They spatter the windshield, and I have to squirt and wipe with the blades again and again just to see the logging trucks bearing down on me.

It gets dark and a crescendo of katydids and crickets rises over the rumblings of the engine. I see a misty figure merged with the riffles at Hale's Eddy, insects swarming around him, and the Delaware here looks as broad and wild as any scene in the West. I curse myself for leaving Fish Creek before the evening rise, just so I could drive and yearn along the Delaware. The thunderclouds circle around and punctuate the sky with lightning, and I'm drawn into the deluge again.

Finally I reach the turn for Peaceful Valley Campground and splash through a series of puddles to the camp store. The rain has stopped, but lightning still flashes, and I catch sight of rolling fields dotted with campers that pop like frosted light bulbs, then disappear. Thunder rumbles over a ring of mountains whose misty shoulders seem to loom closer in the dark. Somewhere among the dripping leaves of the forest the river flows by along the road. I park near the only tent in sight.

There's a flashlight zooming around the inside of the tent, and some unhappy campers inside. A little girl's voice sounds near tears. "Mommy, it's all wet where I am." An exasperated mom voice says, "Well move over toward Jimmy." "He won't let me. He keeps kicking me." "Jimmy, let her move over there." A petulant boy's voice: "It's wet over here too." A booming bark from Dad: "That's enough out of both of you." Silence. The light scans over the ceiling and flicks out, but the rustle of feet against nylon continues in the search of dry ground.

IVF gets you thinking about your own worst traits. You get past the point where you actually see children in your immediate future, and then you have to think really hard about whether you, as a particular exemplar of maledom, should be reproducing. You remember what you were like to your younger siblings—the jealousy, the anxiety, the tendency toward tantrums. Kicking my sister in a wet tent—that was the least of my early sins. Now those social propensities begin to seem less random, begin to seem like part of a genetic matrix that technology is on the verge of controlling. Right now they can pluck a cell from an eight-celled embryo and tell you if it has any genetic defects. They can also tell you the sex, although nobody has gone that far yet. It isn't that far from the day when you will be able to pass on the best of yourself and avert the worst.

I've made up my mind: my inaugural night will be spent in the back of the truck. I bought the truck, a blue Ford Ranger, from a contractor who said he'd driven it mostly on the highway. It looked to be in pretty good shape for a high-mileage vehicle: no signs that he'd driven over boulders with a load of concrete. I took a test drive, and I also tried stretching out in the back. It had a cap that curved upward near the door, so I didn't feel too claustrophobic, at least on that sunny afternoon. It also had a six-foot bed, which meant I could just fit if I lay down diagonally.

I take out the cooler, and the lockbox that came with the truck but won't fit under the cap, and the duffel bag full of Nicola's books that my parents want out of their attic, and the two twenty-pound barbells I took from my mother's house so I wouldn't get flabby on the road, and by the time I'm done I've worked up quite a sweat. I have supper—a bowl of raisin bran, some prewashed salad leaves, and a pair of artichoke hearts from a jar, while sitting under the candle lantern on the unlatched gate. It starts to drizzle, and I shut myself into the back of the truck and blow up my sleeping pad. The spot seemed flat when I parked, but now gravity tells me it isn't so, that I'm parked on the shoulder of a swale. I have two screened slits to ventilate my cell, which are too small to let out the steam of my breath and too big to keep out the no-see-ums. If I lie out on the sleeping bag, the tiny bugs strike blood and I itch insanely. If I lie under the bag, I'm steamed like a frankfurter. I close the screens and moan while the rain patters the roof.

At some point I must slip into dementia, for I rouse myself in the midst of a cool, foggy morning with the robins twittering in the trees.

It feels like it could be just after dawn, or it could be two in the afternoon. I wipe my face with a groggy fist and lean forward to peer out the window. The dewdrops of my own stale breath rain down on me, and I look in horror at the shelf below the window—it's covered with mouse turds! Time to get up.

It's seven thirty, and by the looks of it I'll make the morning rise, since the mist hasn't burned off. I shove everything back into the truck and drive down to the bridge. I know I'm too sleep-addled to be doing this. I should be dunking my face in cold water and tracking down a cup of coffee. Instead I try to pull my fly rod out from the jumble of stuff I've heaped on top of it—the new one, the one I used for the first time on Fish Creek. I left it rigged up with the reel hanging out the end of the case so I could jump out and hit the evening rise on the Delaware in a jiffy. This is not a recommended procedure. My old rod is in there too, along with two pieces of an old wool sock I had cut in half and wrapped in duct tape to cushion the rods in their travels from California to Massachusetts. Maybe it's the cling of the duct tape. Or maybe it's the weight of the bag of paperbacks that has fallen on top of the case. The rod won't come out, and when I tug it a little harder—not too hard, but a little harder—it emerges broken, with the tip hanging on the line near the fly. I rub my haggard forehead in disbelief at this stroke of early-morning stupidity. My new rod. The start of the trip. Never caught a fish. I'm distraught. Thinking doesn't come easy under the circumstances.

Now you've done it, you doggone nincompoop!

It's the voice of my inner critic, the guy I envy in some ways and detest in others, who always speaks up at the worst times. I'll call him Montana Slim, because his unwelcome, buzzardly presence always reminds me of a brief but humiliating encounter with an unpleasant character in Missoula. Nicola and I were walking home by the old train station, holding hands, and apparently we looked too much like lovebirds for the pair of gaunt, sunburned desperadoes who followed our strolling from the shade of their battered ten-gallon hats. As we got close, the nastier of the two spat a gob of tobacco juice onto the curb beside his boots.

"She's a lot better lookin' than you are, Slim."

I turned to find his sunburnt gullet working with disparaging laughter, like a vulture trying to force down a gobbet of rotten meat. He'd found a good place to poke me; I was feeling insecure about us, and about myself as a young, not very assertive, man. Nicola pressed my arm to let me know that I shouldn't stop and dignify him with an answer, but the bewilderment on my face only made him cackle more as we hurried past without replying.

Calling my inner critic Montana Slim is the way I can deliver some semblance of retribution, since it's the name of the withered cowboy who shares Sal Paradise's ride across the plains in Kerouac's tale. This Montana Slim's moment in the spotlight comes when he stands to relieve himself from the side of a speeding flatbed truck, only to wind up drenching himself while the others laugh.

I walk into "Al's Landing" looking like a broken-hearted bum. The fact that it's there, and open so early, should be signs of hope, but I'm too keen on disaster to notice. I'm hoping they might sell some sticks of tip epoxy, and maybe I'll be able to use my jackknife, my toenail clippers, and some matches to get the tip back on there again. I'm expecting Al, but the door jingles and a young woman with short brown hair emerges from other rooms where she was probably eating breakfast over a newspaper. I lay my busted rod down on the counter and stammer something—a lie, in fact—about how I broke it when my fly got caught in a tree and I tugged too hard. I'm too embarrassed to tell the truth.

"That happens," she says, rolling up a flannel sleeve. "Sometimes they just go."

She lights a candle and says there's no guarantee on the surgery she's about to perform.

"You do this often?" I ask while she fishes out a brand-new tiptop from the display case and begins to heat it up with the candle and a pair of needle-nose pliers. I can't believe gross negligence such as mine can be more than one-of-a-kind.

"You'd be surprised," she says. "People come in here with all kinds of trouble."

The rod looks stubby, its elegance marred, but functional nonetheless.

The word "trouble" jogs my memory of an awkward time. The last time I fished this river I was sixteen, selling Japanese food at a bluegrass festival that filled the campground and going fishless in the evenings. I also had a crush on the woman who was working with me. I tried to hide it, and blundered around, spilling things, trying not to look at her.

"If only you were ten years older," she liked to say. "When you get older, watch out!"

Al helped me out; he gave a fly that worked. I caught a couple fish. I felt a little better.

"How's the fishing?" I ask, mostly just to fill in the wait, when what I really want to ask is, "Where's Al?"

"The fishing's great. I'd bet money there's some rising out there right now. Right in front of this bridge."

The thought of rising trout a scant ten yards from the door turns my attention back to the present, which is a relief. The more I think about myself at that age, the more I cringe.

"Yeah. You wouldn't think there'd be fish right next to a bridge, but we don't see enough people for it to matter. It's been a great year for fishing and a terrible year for business. We've had all this rain, and then when it drops people are doing something else. Me, I wouldn't just take up golf, but some people do. They just don't, you know, have enough conviction or something."

I feel even more sentimental about the unappreciated fly shop on the river that doesn't get enough pressure, and guilty because I'm secretly thinking, *Ha, nobody else but me! Nobody else but me!*

She says they could be taking little slate duns, about size 18, but if she were me, she'd tie on a big Wulff Adams and fish the pocket water downstream where they don't have as long to look at it.

"They're easier to fool down there," she says, which probably reflects an appraisal of my fishing prowess. "That's just me, though. I don't like to work too hard," she says, before I can take offense.

I buy stuff I don't need and hurry out the door. Sure enough, there are trout rising in the slick water above the bridge. The river meanders through a long slough, past downed trees and banks of undulating weeds and mud pushed aside by floods. It falls into murky troughs along the shore where the current seeps along, slow as a lagoon. It looks like prime pickerel water, but this is frigid water from the bottom of Pepacton Reservoir. Trout in pods of three and four are surging through the back-wash of the side channels to engulf disabled duns. Some are hefty enough that their descent makes the sound of a wave against a tethered boat.

At the back of the fly shop, overlooking a bend where the rises are particularly furious, an old man sits on a deck outside a sliding glass door, in a wheelchair. His hair is long and gray, and the ridge of his nose holds thick glasses in place. A tracheotomy tube curls around to his throat, secured with bandages. He's watching the trout rise, silent. It must be Al. I wonder how long this illness has kept him off the water. Does he imagine a trip like mine? He must know this river almost like he knows his children.

Melancholy thoughts do battle with hyperactive visions of trout on the line, and lose. I hustle the line through the guides and tie on a little blue-winged olive parachute that I'm fortunate enough to find in my box. On my first cast across to where the willows drape over the bank, the trout rises. I miss the strike. I cast and let the fly drift—it refuses. It rises around my fly, pointedly snubbing me.

A few small duns flutter past me, but I don't see any drifting down with the current. I decide to switch to an emerger, which is supposed to drift along like a nymph that's struggling to hatch. I can't claim to have designed this fly with that purpose in mind, however. In my fly box, when parachutes lose their hackle they become emergers. "Use it 'til you lose it" is my motto. This ancient, battered wisp of olive with a scruffy bit of wing below the eye would be perfect here, except that I have my doubts about the hook. It still looks flimsy after I pinch it smaller between my fingers. I have a vague memory of this fly as exceedingly attractive and thoroughly unreliable, but it's the only one I've got.

The fish rises again to my first cast. I have him on long enough for the line to tighten, and then it falls slack. I strip in the fly and find the hook bent open. I should cut this veteran off my line and I know it, but I don't have anything else. I tell myself to play the next fish softly.

There's a decent fish working along the bank above me. I let the emerger wash along the swaying fringes of grass. On the second cast, the trout responds with a casual inspection, tilting to the side and pondering the fly. Then its snout parts the surface and plucks my tidbit from the current.

Normally I would respond to this suspense the way I react to those horror movies when the psycho finally attacks, with a cathartic spasm of all nerves firing at once. But by now I've already jangled away my jitters with the first two rises, and I raise my wrist so the line straightens just past limp. The fish feels the jab of the hook nonetheless and breaks for deeper water. I let the line play out through my fingers with minimal resistance, but as he darts for the other bank, the hook pulls out, bent open once more.

I try every other small scrap I can offer. They all receive disdainful looks, until finally I break down and clip the hackle and tail off my little blue-winged dun. I hate to speed up the natural process by which trout teeth rip the hackles off the body, but under duress the worst is possible. Immediately a small brown rises, and I joyously haul him right in without fear. As if to thwart any further success, a flock of mallards swoop down over my head and land, squabbling, almost on top of me.

"You'll get no bread crusts from me, you bastards," I mutter at them as they paddle downstream. They quack in protest.

Following their progress, I find a crowd gathered on the bridge to watch me. Once again a guy is imitating my false casts, while others point and chuckle. More people are walking up to join them, carrying canoe paddles and paper-bag lunches. I don't mind Al watching me fish, although I'm not so sure he finds himself fishing vicariously through me. It probably isn't easy, watching an incompetent like me flail the water, knowing you could do it a lot better.

"Looks like your Norman Rockwell painting just got spoiled," I hear someone in the group say as a kayaker rounds the bend and passes through my pool.

Al has wheeled himself back inside. I never waved. I reel in and duck under the bridge and head down into the next pool, far enough away that I can't hear my audience anymore. The first patch of blue sky is widening over the mountains. I wade across the shallow mouth of (yet another) Trout Brook and fish a narrow, hemlock-lined run of pocket water reminiscent of the bridge pool on Fish Creek.

In the slack behind a squat, current-defying boulder, I manage to fool another small brown. To release it, I have to brace myself against the rock whose surface is encrusted with the husks of long-hatched stoneflies, crayfish body parts, and the chalk of old bird turds. The sun bursts through the clouds and the fish go down immediately. Suddenly I'm exhausted and staring vacantly at my hand gleaming in the water and the hypnotizing sparkle of the rapids. Like this morning's spinners, I'm spent.

I make myself two peanut-butter-and-jelly sandwiches and pour milk into a bowl to drink—I've forgotten to bring cups. There's no shade in the big field, just steaming mud puddles. This trip is not supposed to be about sleep, or the lack of it, but already I'm beginning to realize that the questions of where I lay my head and how well I slumber will become obsessions. Big life questions are all well and good, my body is telling me, as long as I'm full and rested. Deprive me, and you will suffer. My mind fixates on a single question, demanding to know how the gypsies would deal with this camping on soaked ground, over and over again like an irritating, irrational mantra. I don't know anything about the particulars of a gypsy caravan, but in a pinch they might get creative and fix a lean-to out of the picnic table, my fly-rod case and the back of the truck.

I sit in my camp chair under this makeshift yurt and shut my eyes. A breeze flutters across my face, and the light ripples through the blue nylon of the ground cloth. *This is pleasant,* I tell myself. *This is how the gypsies would do it.* I close my eyes, only to awaken to the ground cloth flapping in my face like a frantic wing. The storm clouds patrolling the valley have sent down a gust and collapsed my shelter on top of me. For a strange moment everything is loud and jostling, and I fight with my arms like a drowning man in choppy blue seas. Then the wind subsides, and I extricate myself and sit blinking in the sudden brightness. The gypsies, I know, would be laughing.

It's like a greenhouse inside the truck cab, a steaming tribute to solar power, so I unravel my bath towel and my raincoat and prop them up with the visors to block out the front window. I shut my eyes, and in spite of the heat and the tendency of flies to find their way in and batter themselves against the glass, I fall asleep.

The sun is receding when I wake up. My watch says it's after five, and I wanted to eat dinner and tie a bunch of blue-winged olive emergers before going back to the river. I figure I need a hot meal to keep up my strength and use up the food in the cooler, so I dig out my stove.

Mistakes made when traveling often lead to unexpected encounters. My blunders have already led me to the kindness of the woman in the fly shop, and now the stove is going to force me out into company again because the fuel bottle is empty. This would not be a problem since I have a gallon of white gas with me, but I've forgotten the funnel I need to pour the gas into the bottle without turning myself into a gas-soaked rag.

At the camp store they have fuel, lantern bulbs, even a stove, but no funnels. I'm about to give up, but the woman behind the desk says she'll radio Dave—he'll know what to do.

"I'm on my way over there," he crackles on the receiver, and a minute later I hear his golf cart splash through the puddles. He comes in like a whirlwind, revved up and swaggering, deeply tanned, hands swollen like a contractor's, grinning.

"What's the problem?" he says, with an accent straight out of the boroughs of the city.

I tell him I can't cook dinner because I don't have a funnel.

"C'mon," he says, "you need a funnel, I got a funnel. Come with me."

He tells me to take a seat beside him in the cart while he takes his beer out of the cradle. "Where's your beer?" he says, and I say I guess I forgot that too.

"All right, hang on. You want a filter, we got a filter."

He tears off behind the barns into a gravel pit lined with school buses.

"I just got done boiling fifty lobsters. You get yours?"

No, I say, I didn't know about it.

"Aww, shit, you missed out. We had corn, salt potatoes, the whole bit for ten bucks. It's quite a trip cooking that many lobsters, I'll tell you." We careen through a muddy lake of a puddle and break from the road across the slick grass. He asks me where I'm from, and I say California, and he says, "Jesus, you're shitting me? What the hell you doing way out here? I'll bet you don't get service like this out there. Door-to-door filter service, thank you very much."

I say I'm fishing my way across the country, and he nods and tells me his buddies got up at four thirty in the morning and fished through the campground and caught fifteen trout, not a one of them under fourteen inches.

"What were they using?"

"What were they using?!!! A fishing pole! What were they using! Give me a break, buddy!"

We enter a junkyard under the trees where dead '70s cars are rusting away. There are cannibalized tractors and truck beds sliced from their cabs, and in the midst of this jumble stands a Wayne school bus, spray painted a dull green. We pull up here.

"I lived in here for five years," Dave says, "and before that I lived in the back of my truck. Been coming here for fifteen years. But I don't rough it like this anymore. I've got a new camper parked right over in the field."

The bus has graffiti rubbed into the paint by the door, things like "Dave you cheap bastard," and "Dave is a . . ." with something he didn't appreciate rubbed out. The folding door is wide open. We step up inside where the floor is covered in yellow shag and the cabinets are flaking off their veneer. Dave reaches behind the driver's seat and hands me a funnel. I'm amazed he can put his hands on something so small in the midst of what looks like wreckage. He picks up a painting that's propped on the driver's seat.

"Take a look at this." It's a woodland scene, not a paint-by-numbers. I wonder if this is his ironic way of revealing that he painted it. Maybe he wants me know there's more to him than a guy in a speeding golf cart.

Yeah, I say, that's nice.

"You want it?"

"Sure," I say, "but maybe you should hang onto it."

"Yeah, this is oil, for sure. Unsigned. Who knows, might be worth something. Yeah, I think I'll hang onto this." He sets it back on the driver's seat, facing out the open door.

"Decoration," he laughs. "Decorate the place."

He drops me at my truck and tells me to throw the funnel in the door of the bus when I'm done with it. Then he tears off across the lawn.

It's too late to cook now. I fill the bottle, take the funnel back to the bus, and sit down at the picnic table to tie three emergers. Above the bridge, the same fish are rising in the same places to the same hatch, only now the sputtering hatch of the afternoon has blossomed into a flurry of duns coming off and spinners returning. They coast down, perfectly poised until their first attempt at flight. Some lift off and disappear into the evening sky where the swallows are feasting on the wing, while others skitter across the surface like ungainly kites. Sometimes their progress ends in a swirl of jaws and the crescent of an adipose fin. I try the clipped dun from the morning. It meets refusal after refusal. The trout want those angelic silhouettes, and I've sabotaged my only dun and tied three ugly-duckling emergers. I try one anyway, and then five other flies in succession, finally resorting to a grasshopper as long as my index finger. The fish rise all around me, oblivious of my efforts.

Near dark, I decide to heed the advice of the woman in the store. I cross under the bridge and fish my way down the run with my clipped dun. Bats are whirling across the water, and I can hear their wings, invisible but close. I refuse to go back fishless with so many trout rising around me, and I cast and cast as true night falls. Finally an eight-inch brown sacrifices itself to send me home. It comes to hand like a ghost, and I release it gently into the dark water.

Following my flashlight beam back to the campsite, I feel lonely all of a sudden. Rock music and laughter echo through the trees. Families have gathered around their campfires with marshmallows on sticks. I feel like a solitary bear rambling in the dark and witnessing all this revelry from the fringes. I fire up the cookstove and boil capellini to eat with a dollop of cold tomato sauce and artichokes from the jar. It tastes pretty good after all the peanut butter.

It's after eleven, and most of the campfires have burned down to embers when I finish, but it's three hours earlier in California, so I can call Nicola from a pay phone outside the store. There's no booth, just the phone and a yellow light with moths and gnats fluttering and buzzing in circles.

She picks up. My mind is suffused with images of home at the sound of her voice: there is the kitchen where there must be peaches and tomatoes now in the wooden bowl by the sink, and there is the table with today's newspaper and roses in the green vase we got as a wedding present, and there are the books she's reading, poetry books, fertility books, in my absence.

"Have you thought about what we should do?"

"I can't talk about that right now."

It turns out she's next door, about to eat a lovely dinner with our neighbors. Don't tell me what you're having, I tell her. I rub my scalp and wish I was there, just for the night, so I could wake up here and keep fishing. But I can't, and dinner there is on the table. I say *bon appetit* and good night and hang up, climbing into my tent with the candle lantern dangling precariously from the nylon roof. The tent glows like an orb of light in the darkness.

The clouds return under cover of darkness and settle in for a siege. I awaken to steady rain thrumming the walls of the tent and water trickling in under my sleeping bag. The bottom of the tent is soaked, and so are the folds of the bag resting against it. But I've slept soundly through the night. I get up and find my raincoat and break camp in the rain, tossing the wet tent in with the dirty dishes. Everything in the back is a jumble of clean clothes and wet socks and empty food wrappers and fishing gear, but it's too wet to sort anything out.

I drive along the river to the one-street downtown of Downsville for breakfast. I'll drive anywhere, just so I don't have to sit in the cab and eat while the rain streaks the windshield. I dash inside a diner and plant myself on one of the stools at the counter so I can sit with the single men and stare at the pies in the glass case and the downpour reflected in the mirrors. Everyone else seems to be smoking cigarettes in discouragement and poking at their breakfast meat. I pull back my hood to reveal my hair, wild and shaggy at the ends, plastered flat with rain in the middle, and look myself over, taking note of the way my eyes have sunk into dark circles. A mug shot. I try to look friendly as I leaf through the listings in a real estate brochure and imagine myself a local here, living in one of the fixer-uppers around town. I eat everything on my plate, the white-bread toast with Concord grape jelly scraped from little white plastic cups, the home fries, the omelet; even the garnish tastes good.

It's still raining hard outside, but I can't bring myself to just give up. Shinhopple is on my way back to the highway, and I stop in at the fly shop. I catch a glimpse of Al in the back, the news flickering in front of him. He isn't watching the river today, but having slept by this river, eaten dinner by it, seen it ice over and thaw countless times, he doesn't need to see it to feel its presence right outside the door. The woman says it's supposed to pour all day. We stand in the doorway and watch the mist roll upstream. Raindrops stipple the surface like the rises of small fish. I don't want to look like I lack conviction, so I pull my waders up over my raincoat and go back to the run below the bridge. I fish down it one last time, catching nothing, even when I reach despair and tie on a nymph.

The defroster blows over my red fingers as I drive along the lower reaches of the East Branch. So many miles of river sketched in the condensation on the side window, vanishing behind. A journey like this one cannot proceed without regrets.

Beetlemania

I drive back along the West Branch of the Delaware, turn south into Pennsylvania past the fast-food corridor of Scranton and the other old steel towns with their smokestacks and vales of recovered greenery. Outside of Harrisburg, the sun vaporizes the morning rain, and I roll down both windows to cool down and turn the radio up loud to drown out the big rigs and the wind. I don't realize how loud it is until I slow down for a red light and suddenly the radio is blaring an advertisement for pimple-zapping cream.

Crossing the broad back of the Susquehanna in Harrisburg, I wait for the sight of Three Mile Island's nuclear reactors to appear while remembering the appalling silence that fell between my dad and me as we heard about the accident on the radio news while driving home from soccer practice. I expect to find a curse visited on the place, but somehow as I roll across the vast river I am struck by the elegance of the sculpted steel holding me aloft, as if the power of industrial imagination met the power of the river here and offered a tribute of beauty in return for passage. I've never crossed a bridge without at least a glimmer of amazement and gratitude, for the view as much as the way over. If I do pass the nuke, I don't recognize it, and I realize that they wouldn't exactly advertise its presence with a commemorative billboard, although perhaps they should.

The thunderclouds have trailed me the whole way, and the horizon to the east is heavy with their progress. In Boiling Springs I see farm fields growing vinyl-sided colonials instead of corn, and bulldozers at the ready beside piles of torn-up topsoil. In the center of town is a pond where the icy water bubbles up from underground caves. I have no time to fish, however. I've got Click and Clack on the radio jabbering about sticky brakes when the Emergency Broadcasting System cuts them off with that pinging, squiggly emergency-operating-system noise. A bad storm is currently stalled over Camp Hill, with severe lightning and rising flood waters expected in unexpected places. Do not attempt to drive through rising water. Drivers should seek shelter on higher ground.

I find myself turning into a Wal-Mart to escape the storm. From the looks of the sky, Camp Hill can't be far, because the clouds have risen up over the city like an impending tsunami. The cusp of the wave is spilling down on the parking lot as I sprint inside. The alcove inside is full of ragged-breathing parents bent over, catching their breath after the race, kids fingering the chrome slots of the gum-ball machines. I've never looked up to consider the roofing of such a place, but now I gaze along with everyone else at what looks like an inadequate layer of tin. We can hear the staccato popping of hail, and feel the boom of nearby strikes. The fluorescent lights are quivering up there. I'm glad to be inside.

Gas stations, supermarkets, shopping malls—this wasn't what I dreamed about, interludes of fishing between long stretches of tarmac and fast food. There's nothing to do but embrace the banality. I thought I wanted to get closer to the elements, closer to water in particular. In fact, it's fair to say that I have been obsessed with the pursuit of the natural in all its organic, eco-friendly guises. I am the guy who plants native species in the yard, who listens to acoustic music, who has undyed cotton sheets on his bed. But what makes me think that going deeper into the natural world will help me resolve the quandaries of artificial reproduction, when the barriers between nature and myself feel like a refuge now? I have all kinds of forebears on this journey, of course, with Thoreau's trumpeting the idea that living simply in nature clarifies the mind. I see him, plumbing the depths of Walden Pond, or better, paddling his canoe down the Merrimack River and declaring his solidarity with the fishes beset by the artifices of dam and hook. Tales like these have led me here, when perhaps I should be traveling in hyperspace with the French philosopher Baudrillard, who famously declared after his own tour of the amusement parks, shopping malls, and casinos of the country that America was "more real than real." I might come to conclusions after a month in that heart of simulated reality, Las Vegas, prowling the ever-glittering facsimiles of the strip. All you can eat and a handful of tokens sound pretty good to me now.

It's nearly seven, and I haven't even looked for a place to sleep. I decide there is no way I'm spending another night steaming in the back of the truck; I'm headed for the luxury of a cheap motel. While the storm continues to roar, I indulge a sudden craving for plastic boxes with lids, hoping that maybe I can stuff all the chaos of my day into clear plastic, slap on the lids, and keep it contained.

At the motel, I drag everything into the room, drape the tent over the blasting air conditioner, spread the ground cloth between a chair and the table, drain the cooler into the sink, hang up the sleeping bag, pile the dirty dishes on the counter. The rain has stopped, but the clouds linger, as if regrouping for another assault. I shut the door and close the curtains; I don't want anything to do with the outdoors. I want all the artifices of cool air, television, flush toilets, and lamps I don't need a match to light. I take a cold shower, then a hot one at full blast, and sprawl naked on the bed with the television remote in one hand and a peanut-butter sandwich in the other. The Weather Channel reports mudslides and flooding throughout western and central Pennsylvania. I flick around until I find Dirty Harry limping through a darkened stadium out in San Francisco. That's better, I think, and fall asleep.

I wake up to find that at some point the subconscious portion of my brain managed to get the television turned off, but not the bedside light. I've been wasting nuclear-generated electricity all night. I click on the television to numb away all thought. With CNN's *Headline News* blaring, I take another shower and shave again, just for good measure, and then open the drapes on a sunny morning. It's after ten and muggy already when I finish arranging my goods in their plastic boxes.

I've always loved the name Yellow Breeches. Too frequently rivers are named after some historic figure; think of all the waters Lewis and Clark pinioned with their fame, the Lewis River, the Clark Fork of the Columbia, the Clark Fork of the Snake, to name just a few. I like the Yellow Breeches better than the Yellowstone because it's humorous, and human. Stories are enfolded in that name. Is it a metaphor for the way the river wears its garments in shades of saffron, or shorthand for some dandy who waded there, only to emerge with his trousers stained?

The water is indeed a tawny yellow, stained slightly chocolate by the rains. I can't say the river seduces with its purity, the way a mountain stream might. The Yellow Breeches has a corporeal feel to it, a body of water whose color suggests the products of the liver and kidneys, the liquids of jaundice and fever. It's a body one might grow to love, but not at first sight.

The woods, thick with brambles and vines, are suffused with an almost tropical scent of rot. I recognize the green lobes of unripe paw-paws up in the trees and realize I've crossed into a southern climate of gum trees and copperheads where I've never imagined trout fishing. Yet I feel like I've been here before, not on this creek, but on a river like this where the summer jungle presses its humid canopy down to the brink of the water. Normally my first volley would be a deer-hair caddis, my old standby, but now with my fly box open I remember the August before my senior year of high school when the afternoons ended in a monsoon bath and the neighbors were out with their lawnmowers daily. Nights full of katydids, caterpillars browsing in the bushes, profusions of ants on the wing, roses disappearing under Japanese beetle congregations, everywhere the sound of mandibles chewing and wings rasping, trills, buzzes, and drones. Beetlemania. The terrestrials ruled until the rains battered them down into the brooks where the trout devoured them as the sun went down. For two weeks I fished nothing but what fell from the trees, and then one morning the dew looked like frost, and the tomatoes began to wither, and the bugs were gone.

The flies of that era are still in my box, where I haven't noticed them for years. I find a black beetle with trash-bag wings that has lost some polish but still looks like it could crawl away. There are flying ants, and cinnamon ants, and small beetles with cork abdomens disguised in black dubbing. I have more terrestrials than just about everything else, which, since I tend to lose flies fast if I use them at all, suggests that in the West I had no confidence in them.

I tie on the biggest beetle as a good fish rises behind a flood-downed alder whose branches sweep the surface. The beetle slaps down, and I let it drift behind the alder and down into a small pocket. The bigger fish lets it pass, but just as I begin to bounce the fly back to me over the surface, a tail slaps the water and a twelve-inch brown is suddenly on the line. Just as suddenly it wriggles free. I take a few steps and cast again to the next pocket; another fish follows the beetle and strikes as I pull it across. I'm breathing shallow and fast and grinning, all symptoms of Beetlemania.

Where Boiling Spring Run flows in from the pond, the current is clear and frigid, like tap water rinsing a saucer of lukewarm coffee. Trout scatter around my feet, and a nice brown takes up position in the wake below my legs. They refuse to leave the colder water. Downstream, the creek flows through long, murky runs without blending away this colder strand. I watch a big fish rise below another alder snag. I plop my beetle upstream and work it along the log, and the fish responds by ending its meal; whatever it's taking, it isn't falling from the trees.

I switch to the clipped blue-winged olive and wonder why I lay there watching Dirty Harry destroy vehicles when I could have been filling my fly box. Two fish are sipping regularly in front of a downed trunk, while behind it two big shadows surface occasionally like bobbing logs. I fish the water in front first, even though I know the fish are small, so I can gather information before I make the jump to the big leagues. I manage to catch the two in front, a brown and a rainbow, with the clipped dun. They total twelve inches between them.

The cast over the tree is tricky. The fly lands in the bright water, rests for a second, and then the current tugs it away like a water-skier. I pause. A big shadow drifts into the light and rises again. I wade a little closer. The move doesn't help the drift, but it changes the angle just enough that my fly catches the underside of the tree. I'm caught. I jerk the rod to try to break the line, but I'm afraid I'll lose the rod tip again if I pull too hard.

You got the bull by the horns, I see. Montana Slim, lasso champion, has returned.

I wade out to the tree. I still want to see these trout, even if it's just the sight of them fleeing. Two twenty-inch fish, one brown and one rainbow, dodge under the log along with a horde of small suckers. I'm intent on watching them as I put my hand down to steady myself in the current. Something moves. Spread like a hairier version of my hand on top of the log is the biggest spider I've ever seen, a fish catcher just like me. Big enough to have a personality. A misanthrope, by the looks of it.

Slim panics. *Kill him! Get him before he gets you!*

He won't get the satisfaction of crunching chitin from me. I use a stick to dislodge my fly. The other fishermen have gathered in the slow pool above an old mill, crouching to make short casts under the trees, staring intently along their unmoving line. They look like trico fishermen. Although they don't appear to be catching anything, the sight of them makes me uneasy. I'm feeling less and less like the competent fisherman I'd like to be. I've always thought there were two types of angler, epitomized for me by the authors I read as a child, Ernest Schwiebert and Nick Lyons. Schwiebert's ethos was intellectual. He was always obsessed with the details, offering a list of twenty different midge patterns distinguished only by a slight change in abdominal ribbing. I imagined him casting precisely, matching the hatch perfectly, contemplating the rise as a set of quadratic problems to be solved. Lyons, on the other hand, was regularly incompetent and frequently fishless, but often discovered some delicate emotional truth in the experience of rivers. I saw him as the Woody Allen of angling. I've always wanted to be more like

Schwiebert, but I've always found myself more of a Lyons figure, more alert to the rise of epiphanies than trout.

Below the one-lane bridge built of stone slabs by the Amish and now traversed by rumbling dump trucks bound for subdivisions, the creek has scooped away the bottom to create a deep chocolate pool. A Styrofoam worm cup sits impaled on a floodwater stick, but otherwise I'm far enough above the cold infusion of Boiling Springs to feel I'm discovering a secret. I simmer with an iconoclast's delight—I'll show those guys something about fishing! The current rushes under the knobs of undercut trees and then swirls around, defying gravity. Where the eddies merge in a line of foam, I drop the beetle and let it sit there, trapped in the jumble of flotsam and food. It lingers without signs of aggression for a long time, and then I feel a strong downward surge, and the line peels out of my hand for the bottom.

Big one! Exultant, I keep the line carefully taut and work the fish away from the roots. I've fooled a big one where there aren't supposed to be any! This isn't Schwiebert searching for a world-record brook trout in New Zealand, but it's big time for me. It seems like it must be a brown to stay down and make runs like this, but the way it throbs against the rod feels suspicious. I pray for it to be a brown.

When it begins to tire, I catch sight of a round silhouette. Finally a scaly bronze tail paddles the surface.

Well, well, says Slim. *Now that there is a real trophy. Put that sucker on the wall and let him sing to ya all day.*

You should be happy, I tell myself. This is a really good-sized smallmouth, a few pounds at least. An excellent panfish. Lots of people would be happy to catch a bass like this, and you should be too.

The exhausted fish floats to my hand with a frown. Most trout gape like innocents at the moment of capture, but the bass rotates its bulging eyes to follow my fingers, like a mistrustful patient about to go under the knife. Bass devotees may find such expressions endearing, but to me the fish looks like a goblin. I slip the beetle from its jaw, and the fish sinks with all my glory. I can see the others, still casting elegantly, upstream.

Green Rage

Back at the truck, I strip off my waders and console myself with the knowledge that I've got a lot of water left to fish. I'll find those foolish lunkers somewhere. I'm thinking I should hit the Letort, since it must be nearby, but I feel a bit like a prize fighter who wakes up on the canvas—I want an easier bout, not a match with the world champ. I ask for directions in the fly shop, and I also ask about reports in *Trout Streams of Pennsylvania* that the Letort is no longer what it was thanks to sprawl.

"No place is what it was," the proprietor says. "Truth is, the Letort is still one of the best in the country. The difference is that on the Yellow Breeches, you go out and catch twelve fish. On the Letort, you catch one or two and you're a good fisherman."

Immediately I'm preoccupied with wondering where I rate on this scale; how does one good-sized panfish figure into this measure of angling skill? Do six-inchers count?

It turns out I've been up and down Bonny Brook Road twice before in my search for the Yellow Breeches. The Letort here is a channel of golden gravel sparkling among beds of watercress. No signs of tannic acid here. Elodea, cressbugs, water that fizzes like champagne from underground springs—I've reached the scene of my boyhood dreams.

I open the door and am instantly assaulted by the sound of grinding, mashing machine teeth, so loud I can't hear my own dismay. Beneath the sign for a nature trail someone has tacked a notice: "Letort Under Threat!" Home Depot plans to build a new store on the banks of the creek downstream, complete with acres of tar for parking. The city council has approved the plans.

The deafening machinery grinds on as I read and get angry. "What the hell is going on here?" I head down the nature trail toward the noise, which intensifies from drone to bellow as I cross the creek. I feel as if I should be wearing earplugs. The trail ends in a giant gravel pit where conveyor belts jitter loads of rock into the crusher and a stream of pulverized limestone pours down through clouds of white dust into waiting truck beds. The row of trees along the stream has been dusted white.

"Nature trail?" I howl above the din on the way back to the truck. I can barely hear my own rage. "Nature trail?"

The notice asks concerned fishermen to write a letter to the city council. I take down the address and vow to write immediately. I can't fish here. I get back in the truck and compose a letter as I drive.

"I was discouraged . . . disheartened, no, *appalled* to learn of your plans."

I shake a finger and imagine I am not just writing a letter but addressing the council with an impassioned speech.

"The Letort is a resource of national significance, a national shrine."

"The Letort deserves better."

"You can build a Home Depot anywhere, but there is only one Letort."

"I find your plans leave me no alternative but to discourage fellow anglers from visiting the area. So reconsider, you corporate lackeys!"

"I urge you to reconsider. Strongly."

Unfortunately, I can't drive and write, or I'd have pages of dignified protest and crossed-out fury. That's the quandary of this rush across the country—I can't get involved. The transience is both welcome and unbearable.

Off the Wagon

Penns Creek, Poe Paddy Campground, Pennsylvania

On the way out into the hills I begin to have truck problems. Every time I accelerate, and before I shift up to a higher gear, the battery light flickers red, the color of danger. When I shift, it fades away. I get a dart of adrenaline each time. I know cars are supposed to be an expression of manhood, but I'm not one of those guys. I'm not mechanically inclined. You won't find me out in the driveway on a Saturday morning polishing the wheel wells.

Out on the road, the distinction between the mechanical and the biological begins to blur. The truck now feels like an extension of myself, as if I'm a turtle and the truck is my shell, my shield against the harsh realities of the world. I know no more about the systems under the hood than I do about the state of the digestion and combustion systems inside my own abdomen, but if the truck is having problems, I am too. The light is like a low-grade fever. I try to rationalize it away by telling myself that it's normal, just the engine telling me the revolutions are too high. I know better. It's a cryptic warning—but of what? Don't go? Turn back now or face the consequences? Make a bad decision and you will regret it for the rest of your life? What is the issue?

A flashing light in the middle of nowhere: it may be that the truck intends to teach me a lesson in self-reliance. Every adventure is a measured kind of vulnerability. The attraction of unanticipated adversity is the chance to cope, to get to the edge and successfully return. Of course, the edge for someone like me is not exactly Everest. I've wrestled a flat off a Forest Service truck in the Crazy Mountains, forty miles from the nearest town, twenty-five miles from a paved road. I liked the feeling in my hands after I drove away from that one, although it's always a retrospective satisfaction.

First lesson in vehicle maintenance: never forget that your auto has an appetite. I had parked along the East Fork of the Blackfoot River and spent the evening wet to the waist, casting and casting. The stream had been kind, and had offered up a legion of large and surprisingly gullible brown trout, summer refugees from the warm meanders of the big river below.

It was one of those northern-latitude nights when darkness struggles to evict the sun, and the sky stays luminous well past bedtime. Walking back to the car, I was busy visualizing the can of beef stew that was sitting on the kitchen shelf at home. As soon as I got back I'd crank off the lid and dump that jellied brown tube into a pan. I was going ladle it into my mouth while it was still too hot, which would be painful but worth it. The last gravy I would wipe away with a slice of buttered bread, and I would follow this last greasy sop with most of a package of economy cookies.

I slid behind the wheel and went through the ritual motions of departure. My hand rose to the gear-shift, ready to pull it down into reverse. My foot prodded the gas pedal twice.

Unusually languorous seconds elapsed. I glanced at the control panels. Certain sounds and silences were beginning to intrude. Where there should be the noise of pistons and belts, there was none. Where there should be no audible voice, the starter was keening, a hysterical falsetto.

I let my hand fall back from the key, a deviation from the script. It occurred to me for the first time in quite a while that I was sitting in a machine with gears and gizmos and fluids under the hood. There was an entire automotive system beyond the dashboard, and I was oblivious to it, had taken it for granted like my colon, my thalamus, and all the other limbic organs that I expected to just keep churning and secreting without a thought.

Now I needed to concentrate. I had the silence to do it, an unwelcome silence. The gelatinous tube of stew slipped back into its can, and the can leaped back onto the shelf. Bread slices shuffled back into their bag and twisted their twist-tie shut. Economy cremes breathed a sigh of relief, safe in their cellophane.

"Come on now, baby," I said, sending earnest vibrations in the engine's direction. I turned the key. A hoarse sputter ensued, the hack of a cat struggling in vain to expectorate a hairball. The starter wanted to get things going, if only to end the ordeal, but some other part was refusing to comply. "Breathe! Breathe!" I hissed over the steering wheel. I sat there with the mute interior, with a view of swallows and purple clouds, stumped.

Despite the dent along its flank that looked like the unhealed scar of a shark attack, Moby, as I called it, the Great White Whale of a car, was generally reliable. As a companion it neither demanded much nor complained. It did, however, have one dysfunctional quirk, a passive-aggressive bid for attention. When parked face-down on a hill, it had a habit of misplacing its fuel. The gasoline was in the tank, but the car would pretend it was empty. It wouldn't start unless I rolled it to flat ground, where it would roar to life with sudden appreciation. The gas needle would rise mysteriously, not to the mark of plenty, but to adequate. Maybe it just got nervous, the way a dog does when its owner leaves the house.

I was stuck. The front wheels were propped against a railroad tie. Of course I tried heaving myself against the grill in a bid to push the car uphill. I even jumped on the trunk and bounced up and down, hoping I might splash some fuel up into the intake. I could hear it sloshing around in there, but by the time I leapt into the cab and turned the key, it had drained away.

Those northern nights take hold slowly, but when the sun finally fades they come on cold. Stars spread like crystals of frost across the eastern sky, while my wet clothes wicked the heat from my body and whisked it away into space. I popped the trunk, hoping for dry clothes and nourishment. I found candy wrappers, half a bottle of motor oil, a cardboard box, and a crowbar. No clothes, no blanket, and no food, but a clanking of glass revealed four forgotten bottles of beer behind the box. I remembered buying them for a Fourth of July party last year. They had been fermenting in the trunk ever since, and had probably reached a yeasty zenith of flavor about now.

I considered my options. I could drown my sorrows. Beer had calories, didn't it? Carbohydrates? I could curl up in a wet, hungry and drunken ball on the back seat and wait for daylight to start walking. Or I could start walking now. Ovando was eight miles away. I could hitch-hike, although traffic was light and the prospects for lone men trudging along an empty stretch of road were slim. Eight miles would take me about two hours. I'd get there at one in the morning. I tried to remember if there was an all-night gas station, or a bar with a phone. I couldn't remember seeing either.

It occurred to me that nobody knew where I was. I hadn't left a note at the Forest Service bunkhouse where I lived, primarily because we didn't tell each other our whereabouts. I imagined my coworkers standing around the kitchen, speculating, even worrying. *Have you seen Jim? Nope. Me neither. You think he's okay? It's getting awfully late. Yeah, it's not like him to be out this late. Hasn't he been fishing the East Branch lately? Maybe we should take a drive down there, just to check.* I deluded myself with this fantasy for about a minute. Those bastards were scratching themselves in bed, oblivious to my plight. They wouldn't even think about where I was until morning, when I failed to show up for work. I could be out here all night, and nobody would even miss me.

I'm on a lonely stretch of highway again. No signs of human dwellings, not even a trailer. The truck is still rolling. I decide to roll with it. I turn down a dirt road at the crest of a forest-clad mountain. A sign announces that I'm entering state forest. For fourteen miles I rattle my way along a steep ridge with the geometries of corn and cattle laid out below me. The truck bed has always made a squeak when it hits a bump or a pothole, but before it was only a note of protest at the moment of impact. After ten miles of ruts, however, the truck changes its tune. It sounds like I'm hauling a load of rodents that whimper with even the tiniest jiggle and break into a chorus of squeals when we bounce.

I pull in at Poe Valley State Park and squeak to a halt. There is nobody in the office at the gate, and a phone is ringing out into the trees, loud as a car alarm. All day I've been pursued by incessant mechanical sounds—isn't that the first sign of madness? I suppose this question of sanity comes up when you haven't talked to anyone in a while except yourself and the fish. It's a surrealist provocation. Who can be your sounding board when the only voices come from the radio? This is my human contact for the day. I feel like I'm driving through a David Lynch film, the rural version of Mulholland Drive. The phone keeps ringing into the trees like an audible delusion, with no one but the sighing trees to reply.

There are times when you are desperate for human contact, and the face that appears isn't the one you hoped for. I set out for Ovando that night. After a few hundred yards I topped the crest of a hill and burst into a caper of gratitude, arms waving as if I'd been marooned on a desert island for years. Salvation! Among the desolate buttes were signs of human habitation, a medley of junked automobiles, tractors, piles of tires. A trio of gaunt horses grazed, watching me. Two brindled and husky dogs watched me too, without barking, although I could see the hair bristling along their spines and the flash of white spikes between their lips. They were roaming free inside the six-strand barbed-wire fence with its single electric line humming across the top, and there appeared to be plenty of canine-sized gaps.

In the midst of this jumble of artifacts and menacing faces, it took some time to locate the residence, a single trailer, sided in white aluminum and parked on cinder blocks like the other immobilized vehicles. A homesteader's shanty had collapsed in a pile of weathered boards behind it, half of one wall still standing around the empty socket of a windowsill. The light over the trailer door was on, although the windows were dark.

Nobody home. I followed the length of the power cables down from the pole to where they disappeared into the wall. There it was, my lifeline, out of reach. If I could just call the bunkhouse . . . Was there any point in knocking? The dogs were acting funny. I followed their eyes to the opened hood of a pickup, where a pair of legs in blue jeans was visible.

He didn't seem to know I was there.

"Hello there!" I called to him, causing the dogs to yelp and snarl. He looked up at me across his grease-smeared shoulder, keeping his hands embedded in the engine. He was younger than I imagined, hair cropped short, a day's worth of stubble shadowing his chin. He didn't smile, and it occurred to me that he'd seen me already and decided to let me pass. I was approaching what looked like a gate across the driveway, a gate I hadn't been invited to enter. Maybe he mistrusted my motives, a stranger on a lonely stretch of highway at night. What was I doing outside his fence? I would have to lift my voice to explain.

"I was wondering if you might be able to help me out. I'm parked over at the access, and my car won't start. I was hoping I might be able to use your phone to call a friend to come pick me up. It's a local call and everything."

I tried to sound harmless, which isn't easy to project across a distance. The dogs growled. The man gripped and twisted something I couldn't see. He wasn't looking at me anymore.

"Don't have a phone."

My first instinct was to plead. *But wait a minute. You don't understand. I'm wet and hungry and stranded here. I need help.* My next was to accuse. *What do you mean you don't have a phone? Everybody has a phone. Don't try and tell me your place is too remote. The federal government guaranteed availability to everybody, nationwide, way back in the fifties. Besides, I can see the cables going right into your house. You've got a phone and you just won't let me use it? Why? Why not?*

"Oh. Okay," I said. I stopped in front of the gate. There was a large sign hanging there, hand-painted in neat red letters. "Government Workers and Others," it read. "Beware! $10,000 Fine for Trespassing on This Property! You Will Be Prosecuted to the Full Extent of the Law!" Another sign was tacked to a young tree nearby: "This property protected by a .44 Magnum!"

The picture of a loaded pistol was all I needed to feel like a target. What if he found out I worked for the feds? Would he sprint to the trailer and get his gun while the dogs clamored for blood? Was I on the verge of entering a *Deliverance* episode? *It's night. Nobody knows where I am.*

He couldn't know I was a government employee. I had a soccer ball on my T-shirt. I looked like a regular guy who went fishing and ran out of gas. I decided to risk one more exchange.

"Actually, the situation is that I'm out of gas. I mean, I have gas in the tank, a quarter tank actually, but I'm parked downhill and it can't reach the intake. Do you think you might spare a little gas, like, a cupful or something, just so I can get it started and back up? All I need is a cupful."

I thought the automotive details might appeal to him; a bond might form over problems under the hood. He didn't look up.

"Just got enough to get to town."

But you've got twenty vehicles sitting out here. You mean to tell me that you can't spare a cupful of fuel from one of them? They're all empty?

This time I couldn't stop myself, despite the danger. "What about all these other cars? Isn't there a little gas in any of them you could spare? I literally need a cupful."

"Nope. Got just enough to get to town."

You can't do this to me! I'm going to get my law enforcement friends to raid this junk pile as soon as I make it home! That's right, buster, you've just ignited the fury of a federal worker!

"Well, thanks anyway," I said, and started walking.

"Try the neighbor's place," he said, without looking up. "They might have a phone you can use. Quarter mile that way."

A gesture of humanity, however minimal. He continued his tinkering. I marched on. *You just saved yourself some big trouble, pal. Big-time trouble.*

I knew the next place would be futile long before the dog started barking. Another savage canine, another trailer, another gate. A long driveway to trespass along before reaching the door. A knock in the dark, a commotion inside, a taciturn and suspicious gaze, the dark eye of a loaded rifle. No thanks.

Ovando began to seem very far away. I could hear the sound of my footfalls on the tarmac. How many of those would there be? I walked for a mile into the darkness, checking the glowing face of my watch only once. Nearly eleven, and seven miles to go. There must be a way to get at the gas. Could I siphon it somehow? Could I open the fuel line like I'd seen a mechanic do once? Could I level the ground somehow? Could I lift the car somehow? Let's see. Could I lift the front somehow?

Salvation. I found myself running past the junkyard rancho, certain I had it now. I glared at the dogs. *I don't need your gas, fellas. Intellect has triumphed!*

I got the jack out of the trunk and found the arm under the hood. I'd never used it. The nose of the car rose slowly, until the front tire dangled in the air like a paw. The manual warned me never to attempt to enter a suspended vehicle. I cranked the jack up to the final precarious notch and climbed inside the cab.

The moment of truth: the same routine, but every gesture now heavy with significance. Foot priming gas pedal twice. Hand on key, the now-familiar whine of the starter, and the muffled roar whose every nuance I could feel in the pounding of my chest. It started.

I leapt down from the cab and jabbed the jack mechanism into reverse, pumping it furiously with my foot. Slowly, too slowly, it descended. In my mind, the gas was draining away from the intake with every tedious inch of descent. Finally I worked the pedestal free and reversed to level ground. I let the car idle while I walked, leisurely now, across the lot to pick up the jack.

I passed the trailer within minutes, covering the same ground. The guy had gone inside and turned off his porch light. The television glowed inside. The whole scene was going by so fast now. I didn't feel angry anymore; the pleasure of self-reliance was too strong. I gave the guy one long toot on the horn. Then I turned the heater up to full blast and got back to imagining my can of beef stew.

Poe Paddy Campground sits in dense forest right on the bank of Penns Creek. There are other human faces around! I announce my arrival with a chorus of squeaks, and everybody looks up from their hot dogs and easy-chair snoozes to see what all the fuss is about. I nod apologetically at the senior couple sitting at a picnic table in the site next to me. They're about to get chomping on some ears of corn. Normal folks, thank goodness. I ask them where I pay for the night; usually there are envelopes and a metal tube at the entrance, but I didn't see them when I came through.

"That's because they're back at Poe Valley," the old gentlemen says, pointing back up the road with his corncob. "Four miles that way."

"You've got to be kidding me," I blurt out. It's another surrealist provocation, and my internal censor has fallen asleep. "I mean, I just came from there. If I'd known I would have paid."

He says everybody complains about the same problem. I say I'll pay on the way out. He nods. But I know already that I'm heading out the other way along the creek, and there is no way I'm driving eight squeaking miles back and forth for the privilege of pitching my tent here. I don't want to hear that phone again. I'm not paying.

Evening is falling under a cloudy sky, and already the shadows are gathering under the trees. I suit up without setting up camp; I'm ready to get lost for a while in the meditation of moving water.

I follow the path to the rocky bed of a surprisingly freestone stream. No signs of champagne springs here. Despite the rains, the creek looks low, as if the summer has concentrated its essences into the color one might get by rinsing a blue watercolor brush in skim milk. Dried crayfish skeletons litter the rocks, and the living are on the prowl in the shallows. They rocket backward as I approach, claws splayed.

The water feels cool to the hand, but as I wade, the chill I hope to feel against my ankle never materializes. At Mohawk Rod and Gun Club I pause. Their lawn ends at the streambed. The windows of the white cabin are shuttered, and clearly nobody is there. I picture a bunch of golf buddies grilling steaks and smoking cigars, trading farts and tall stories on the porch. They probably wouldn't appreciate my passage, but they aren't there. I scramble across the rocks, figuring I'm below the high-water mark, and stop where a small creek trickles out of the pines. Rusty mats of bacteria have turned the stones into lumps of bread pudding; sprigs of watercress wobble like garnish beside them. I feel the cold come through my waders. Here, if anywhere, there should be fish.

Where the cold water mingles with the creek I see a small fish rise. I cast, and a ten-inch brown somersaults right over the fly. Just downstream, I give the caddis a little bounce and a seven-inch brookie can't resist the twitch.

An invisible hatch is on, some kind of sporadic egg-laying activity that has the small fry leaping to intercept ghosts. Dragonflies are chasing my fly through the air; they're hungry and stumped too. I tell myself I should just walk away; why waste my time on these runts? I loop a lackadaisical cast into the current, figuring I'll just torment a couple to justify the trudge down. That one cast is all it takes to imprison me there, one pointed refusal from a puny snout. I can accept a snub from big, wise fish. But not from little fish like these—it's too humiliating.

Casting a fly has a natural rhythm to it. When I can't catch anything, I begin to notice the cast itself, the flexion of my forearm, the graceful figure eights of line over my head, the way my fingers seem to know just when to release more line and when to clamp down on the back cast. When this fluid motion aligns with the pulse of the river and the beat of a rising fish, the result is a harmonic convergence of nature and artifice that is the soul of fishing. One of the first rules of juggling, however, is never to think about it, just feel it. Paying attention transforms the magic of the natural act into a debacle of self-awareness. Inevitably, I watch my line sag and flop as my hands miss their cues.

Nicola and I tried the rhythm method for almost three years. The temperature of a woman's body rises and falls cyclically, with a tiny spike announcing the release of an egg. With a thermometer, a journal, and a meticulous, persistent mind, you can chart the movement of degrees and plan ahead for a certain evening of maximum fertility. Of course, because you are counting on this particular span of time, things will inevitably get in the way. You come home exhausted from a long day at work and want to flop down on the couch and never move. Too bad. Or you come home with your pockets full of enticements and recall that you have guests staying for the weekend. The walls are thin. Too bad. Say good-bye to spontaneity too, because on the other days around the peak, you have to conserve your own resources for the big moment. If you do manage to pull it off, the odds are still against you. Twenty-five percent is the best you'll do.

In the midst of this perplexing time, you begin to hear stories. Couples who gave up on the notion of having kids, who tried the rhythm method, IVF, ICSI, and everything else and decided to just give up. They got pregnant. Naturally.

Like a gambler on a losing streak, I'm convinced my luck will turn around on the next cast. I place bets on everything I've got—tiny mayflies, beetles, grasshoppers, emergers. Every one of them proves a loser. Dusk falls as I realize that a litany of curses has been pouring from my mouth for some time.

You stuck up little shits! Come on, help me out here. You can't do this to me! You little bastards, you're too young to be this picky!

I'm wiped out; there's nothing left to try. I hike back along the road to the lights and smoke of the campground, telling myself that I like not catching fish, that not catching fish is what keeps me coming back for more. I'm building character here.

Back in camp I set about erecting my tent and then consider my options for dinner. Most of the other campers are brushing their teeth. I'm not hungry enough to light the stove and wash the pans. I make a peanut-butter-and-jelly sandwich, pick the black ooze from the remains of my salad leaves, and gobble a plum, washing it all down with swigs of warm orange juice straight from the carton. It's somehow nearly midnight and the moon must be racing past me behind the clouds. They say gamblers on a binge have a way of losing track of time.

The End of the East

🐟 Spring Creek, Bellefonte, Pennsylvania

I wake up to sunny skies and chipmunks stealing crumbs off my picnic table. I'm hoping vaguely for a trico hatch, or a blue-winged olive hatch, or any kind of hatch that is actually visible by light of day. A few tiny spinners dance in mating swarms over the water, but nothing is rising. Even now, the creek looks like it's waiting for autumn, like it can't bear the thought of another sultry afternoon. I should stay and fish. I should amble back down to the club and show those six-inchers who's boss. But I've been reading about Spring Creek, and now I've got those visions of sparkling water and verdant clumps of watercress again.

I hold a parley with myself. The luxury of the trip is that I can move; if the fishing is no good or I'm overtaken by whimsy or I like the name of another stream I can be on my way in a flash. I don't have to stay. But I know it's always farther than it looks on the map and that I'll certainly get lost and miss the morning rise. I'm here for the morning rise, and I should fish here.

There's no point in reasoning with me. I take off, and, as predicted, lose my way on the back roads. The red light keeps flickering, but nothing terrible happens. Afternoon is approaching when I plunge down a steep dirt road that the rains have scoured with waterfalls. The shocks squeal like feverish piglets all the way down into the valley. There is the creek, my beautiful spring-fed dream. The road clings to every meander, interrupted only occasionally by an old cottage. I can look right down into the crystalline water and see long beds of swaying medusa hair and channels of glittering gravel. I don't see trout, but sometimes the current tears loose a ball of weed and it unravels downstream, stems pulsing like the arms of an octopus.

At the fishing access, only one other car remains, and the driver is sitting on the bumper and pulling his feet out of his waders. The noon sun makes me squint as I get out of the truck and ask if he had any luck. He says the tricos were falling earlier, but the trout were too picky. He switched to a size-16 nymph and did okay until it started to get a little warm. Since the parking lot is steaming like a clearing in the Amazon, I assume his "okay" really means that he hauled in a school of trout. I tell him I just came from the Yellow Breeches, and he tells me that if I was that far south I should have hit Falling Springs Run down by Chambersburg.

"Falling Springs, now that's a trico hatch. Tens of thousands on the water and every fish in there just tipping up." He weaves his hand up and down in the air with the thumb pinching the forefinger in time. "Sip, sip, sip."

I had thought about driving the thirty miles south to Chambersburg, and I even had it marked on the map. I tell him I wish I had known the hatch was happening down there; Penns Creek was a bust. He's never fished Penns. The fishing has always been too good right here.

"I used to be able to come here and fish the edges with a crow-wing beetle and catch four or five twenty-inch fish. Not anymore. They just don't go for it anymore."

He tells me the story of the creek. He's been coming for years, even after the creek was devastated by a chemical spill in the headwaters near State College, and the state made the whole stream catch and release for health reasons. The poisons killed almost all the fish, and the hatches disappeared, and for years nobody really fished the creek. Slowly the stream healed, and the trout returned unannounced, so that for a few years he could fish here alone. Now the word has gotten out.

"We're standing in Paradise. That's what they call this stretch. I think the state secretly wants to keep it catch and release. That spill was years ago but they still haven't released any health data saying the fish are okay to eat."

I tell him a bit about my trip. He's full of suggestions about Colorado and Montana. I tell him I lived in Montana for several years, and we swap stories about the Beaverhead and the Madison. He says I should try Slate Run, a freestone stream near the Ohio border, and then reconsiders; if Penns was bad, Slate might be even worse. He says if he were me, he would floor it for the Montana border. One night's driving and you're there.

"I'm bound for Michigan first," I say. "And Minnesota. Some nice spring creeks down in the south there. But I'll get to Montana again, believe me."

Montana is a long way off. Right now I'm spellbound by the waters of this spring creek, at hand and back from the dead. My old Nikes haven't been dry in nearly a week now, and they're beginning to smell like it. I grab the clammy tongue and pull on the right sneaker, and my big toe pokes out through a new hole. They're decomposing, and the algae soup bubbling along the shore won't help matters.

Once I'm in the water, I don't notice them anymore. Sunflowers and purple coneflowers vie for sunlight with the willows, and the honeybees ramble from bloom to bloom. I make a radical choice and leave the tan caddis in the box, picking instead the battered old beetle. In the pocket water at the tail of a shallow run, I twitch it into a cave of elodea. A nice fish splashes at the fly. On the next cast I watch the same trout slant across the current to follow my retrieve, intrigued but not convinced. I'm surprised to find a fish here, because really I'm just working my way to the real water, where the flow gathers itself and slides into a rapids.

Here I let the beetle disappear into the white water. The line straightens into the froth and the rod pulses in my fist. I'm tied to a big fish! On a beetle, not a nymph! Vindication! I do have skills!

I want to kick up my algae-covered heels, but I've got to fight the fish first, and already I'm losing the battle. I don't know how to cope with weeds. I catch a glimpse of an eighteen-inch figure slashing across the current and plowing into a mat of green, then bolting forth with a shroud of torn-free stems hung up on the leader like laundry on the line. It dashes to the weeds on the other side, then back into the fastest water to stretch the leader. It feels like I've hooked a flounder down there. Slowly I have to accept the fact that I'm not fighting a fish anymore, that it's just dead weight now. I reel in a giant vegetation ball with my beetle caught somewhere inside. This is spring creek fishing.

I search for more swift water, but it proves to be unusual; long, shallow runs are the norm here, where the trout spend their siesta in the shadows under the weeds. I fish the edges with my beetle, under the trees, and just as the guy in the parking lot predicted, I don't fool any fish. The longer I fish, the larger his tally grows; I imagine him catching a dozen, then twenty, then forty fish, until finally I figure they're all nursing a sore jaw from his nymph and giving the finny finger to my efforts.

Eastern fish! a disgusted voice exclaims. It's Montana Slim. *Quit wasting time on these ingrates. Let's get on the road. I can see the Big Sky country, my friend. It's waiting for us.*

You must be getting dehydrated, I tell myself, and turn back for the truck. I find my water bottle boiling on the front seat, hot enough to make a mug of tea. I rinse a nectarine, and steam rises off the skin.

In Bellefonte, a pair of percolating air conditioners lures me into a pizza parlor. Two ice-cream salesmen go over receipts in the booth next to me. Business is good. I drink an iced tea and suck on the ice cubes, waiting for the meatball sub I've ordered. Just down the street, Bald Eagle Creek is roaring in a murky flood under the bridge. Dreams die hard, but I decide I've had enough humiliation—any more failures and champagne will become a permanent nightmare for me. These eastern fish are just too unfriendly, too closed-minded, too cynical and cosmopolitan for me. No more spring creeks. I'm finished with the East.

Good deal, says Montana Slim.

The Puzzle of an Eccentric Friend

I cross the last Allegheny ranges where Bald Eagle Creek has blown out a bridge, and the detour takes a crooked, barely paved track over an ancient and defiant mountain, its slopes surrounded by an ocean of green corn far below. Soon I am roaring around the snake bends and leaving the last of Pennsylvania behind. The truck plunges into the corn. The fields conjure their own heavy atmosphere, and I can taste pollen and raw unfurling leaves through the open window. On the turnpike, I join a convoy of massive trucks, and we rumble over the plains with the setting sun as our guide.

Without the benefit of a book on tape, a CB radio, or even one of those little televisions that plug into the lighter socket, I'm forced to think out loud. Sometimes the radio catches a station out of Cleveland, but mostly I am alone with the road and my thoughts for company. I wonder what Nicola is doing, and what my friends are doing, and what the fishing is like in Montana. I'm wondering about my friend Doug, whom I haven't seen in a couple of years. "I've got to try and figure this guy out," I say to the fields and the truck wheels.

He's still driving a forklift in the cardboard factory where his dad worked, and he still lives at home. *Now why the hell would someone with a college degree in biology want to work nights in a factory and live at home in South Bend, Indiana, when there is so much going on everywhere else?* The voice is my grandfather's. I try to picture myself working shifts, and the only way I can relate to it is to imagine my grandfather screwing transistors into televisions at General Electric, or my grandmother getting up for the late shift at the tomato-sauce cannery, both of them always miserly with themselves so their sons could escape to college. For me to work in a cardboard plant would mean squandering their sacrifices and defeating their hopes, a downward spiral.

I have a hard time with my own censors, those voices that whisper it would be okay if he wanted to work with his hands in certain ways, as an organic farmer, or a furniture craftsman, or some kind of artist.

But waste his life in a factory? The factory floor is off limits. That's what gets to me finally, those nasty little whispers.

"Whew!" I blow out the window, and stick my face out there to shake them loose. I'm such a prude. Here's a guy who's kicked aside the corporate ladder and stepped off the treadmill of car payments and mortgages, and here I am shaking my head in disapproval while I'm off on some kind of crazy trout quest that I'm bashful about explaining to people. I'm afraid they might think I myself have fallen off the ladder to success.

I'm thinking about how he refuses to cut his hair when I realize this whole troubling array of insecurities has got me weaving in and out of the lanes where truck wheels are spinning like turbines. The battery light is flashing, and I'm way over the speed limit. I ease up on the gas and slide into a gap in the slow lane. Now I can consider how he adorns his head.

It's clean-shaven except in the middle, where a strip of long hair rides like the pelt of a blond Persian cat. When we were at college he didn't look like anyone else, but now that the cultural zeitgeist has come around he looks like one of those Internet millionaires whose nonconformity has become marketable recently. Or they look like him. I thought for a while that Silicon Valley might be where he would wind up and be redeemed. But he refuses to participate in the technological revolution. He won't buy a computer; he still writes long and densely scripted letters. They're just about the only ones I still get, mixed in with all the junk mail and bills.

Pondering hairstyles when I should have been looking at a map, I wind up trapped with the commuters in the rush-hour mess of Cleveland. Another storm rises up off Lake Erie and pelts us with rain, and everyone sits with their headlights glaring at each other as the ambulances wail past us. Night has fallen when I reach the Indiana Toll Road, and I still have hours to drive, and now that I've crossed a time zone, it just got earlier on me. I stop for a bag of corn chips and two artificial fruit pies at a truck stop; I can't bring myself to eat the withered hot dogs revolving under the heat lamps.

My hands know the way instinctively. His house is on a cul-de-sac off what was once a rural highway and is now a glittering strip of gas stations and video stores. I turn down the street, and the surprising darkness of a cricket-and-star-filled night engulfs the truck. When I park under the canopy of gigantic elms, Doug's father flicks on the front porch light and stands behind the screen.

When Doug came back from Montana with some debts to pay off, his dad, who had just retired from the same plant, put in the word and got him a job at the factory. They make for an odd pair of housemates: the parent, reared during the Great Depression, wears the worn beige workingman's trousers I recognize from my grandfather's wardrobe, while the son favors the flamboyant, the dapper, the debonair. The father hoards cardboard boxes of odds and ends that might come in handy some day; the son collects piles of useless, intriguing items.

The phone is ringing. Doug's dad checks the clock on the dining room wall. "That Doug! His break is just about over. What's that boy doing?" He hands me the phone.

"Jim! You made it! Make yourself at home!" Doug says. He tells me there is cantaloupe in the fridge from a nearby farm. The industrial gears are whirring in the background.

"I can't talk long; I've been waiting for the phone." I can hear the beeps of forklifts in reverse. A bell rings. "There goes the bell. I got to get back to work. Don't wait up."

"That's Doug," says his dad as we sit down in front of the television, "always cutting it to the last minute."

There's nothing on the tube. We talk a little bit about the weather and my plans. After a while I get up and pronounce I'm beat, and he shows me the bed. "I thought he cleared this out for you," he says, scooping up an armload of shirts and jackets draped over the bed. "He's taking over the whole house!"

The room feels like the attic of a museum, full of things an eccentric might collect in rummage sales for next to nothing, knowing that the tides will turn and suddenly what was out of style will be all the rage. There's an MC Hammer "Please Don't Hurt 'Em" commemorative wall plaque of the sort you might win for shooting ducks at the fair, and goofy, ornate 1950s lamps, stacks of Fiestaware that just might be radioactive, paint-by-number portraits of Jesus on the walls, woolen fedoras, gabardine mercerized shirts with a variety of collars, and bags of smoked chili peppers dangling from the ceiling. He's filled three rooms of the house and most of the basement like this!

I plan to wake up when he gets back from work, but when I open my eyes it's morning. His father is watching the wake-up news shows on another television in the pantry behind the kitchen. It occurs to me that he may not have gone to bed. Doug is already up. He claims to need only two hours of sleep a night. I hear him rummaging around in his bedroom, although I can't see him. He's packed the space with shelving, and here he keeps his record collection, archaic books, ties draped over hangers like a collection of strange tongues, vintage Kangol caps, and suede Adidas sneakers, along with some timbers from a demolished barn.

"Doug?" I say, unsure if there's even room for a bed back there.

"Jim! Just tidying up a bit in here!" He emerges and sets down a stack of magazines, and we shake hands and slap each other on the back.

"What's new in here?" I ask him.

He picks up a commemorative New Kids on the Block pin and folds it out into a triptych of faces. "Remember these guys? Before there were Backstreet Boys, there were New Kids on the Block."

I want to groan; I hate all boy bands. I suppose that must be the thrill of collecting, to know what is valuable when people like me dismiss it. There are different ways for the imagination to roam, to reconcile the need to explore with the fidelity to home. Instead of going off on a journey, he is gathering everything here. The room is exploding with the fruits of a fertile mind. Someday, New Kids nostalgia will be all the rage.

"What about clothes?" I used to chuckle at the way he wore elegant suits to the dining hall when we were in college and everyone else slouched around in T-shirts. When skinny ties were in style, he tied broad swaths of silk around his neck and tipped the brim of his fedora to friends. Secretly, I wished I had the guts to have my own style, and I even went so far as to poke around in a few thrift stores, only to discover that men were much smaller in the old days. Most old suits I squeezed into left my wrists bare and my ankles sticking out like Frankenstein's monster.

Someday Doug will tell me he found this amazing suit that's way too big for him but would fit me just about perfectly. It hasn't happened yet. He says his sources have pretty much dried up since The Gap started pushing swing dancing in their commercials and the whole lounge thing caught fire.

"Haven't seen any good stuff on the racks in a long time. Too much competition. I'm getting some fine material from the late eighties now, though." He picks up the Kangol cap and tilts it onto his head. I find I'm shaking my head in dismay. I'm ready to look like a Gap commercial, but LL Cool J? No way.

"Check out what I've got in the car," Doug says, and we head out to his weather-beaten Subaru hatchback. Its predecessor sits under piles of maple and birch logs Doug has set out to cure for stick-furniture construction. The back of the car is filled with hundreds of framed paint-by-numbers.

"I've got a friend in Kalamazoo who collects these too. I keep meaning to head up there and give her these as a present, but I haven't gotten around to it."

I want to ask about romantic possibilities here, but I stop myself. Dating to me is now just a prelude to the question of parenthood. Next I'll be asking him what he thinks about having kids, and he'll be looking at me like I'm shouting across the mouth of a canyon. When you begin to contemplate having children, a gulf opens up between you and your single friends. It's wider than the parting of ways brought on by marriage. The barfly, the athlete, the angler, the thrift-store junkie—that guy disappears, and somebody more sober takes his place.

From behind the seat Doug pulls out a framed black-and-white photo, faintly colorized. "Mesa Verde. Probably from the 1940s." I hold it while he pulls out another of a Colorado mining town, and then two more western scenes.

"I bought these at auction. Guess how much I paid?"

I know it can't be much. He's in his element now. "Fifty bucks?"

"Now Jim, that seems a little low. These are genuine articles of history, and I had to outbid somebody interested in just the frames."

"Okay, a hundred bucks."

"Five bucks."

"Each?"

"Nope. For the whole lot."

We sit down for a big breakfast. Doug came to be something of an epicure after a stint as a cook in a Mexican place in Juneau. How Alaskan versions of South-of-the-Border cuisine inspired him I don't know, but he came back with a passion for sharp knives and hot peppers, the latter of which he reignites with periodic jaunts out to Santa Fe when the pasillas are roasted in the fall. He knows all the old Italian and Scandinavian bakeries in South Bend, and we spread kugele and sugar-powdered ricotta turnovers on the table along with peaberry coffee from a place that roasts it in Chicago. He has decadently ripe melons from the farm stands and glowing peaches from the Lake Michigan orchards.

I stuff myself with delicacies and confess that my own pleasures in food have been stifled by my travels; I've been surviving on peanut butter, jabbing dirty knives into the jar, and wiping the blade clean with the corner of my shirt. Fast food has been my treat.

His dad is still out in the pantry watching television. I'm struck by a sudden, vivid memory of his father and mother watching an afternoon soap opera together out there among the same coat racks and boxes. It was the first time I'd visited, they were cheerful and friendly, and I thought it was strange that the whole spacious house was dark and silent while they chuckled together in the very back corner. I ask if his dad has eaten already, and Doug says he doesn't like this kind of food. Organic, whole-meal, gourmet—no thanks. He tries to make meals for his dad because otherwise he just won't eat right; he'll eat a baloney sandwich on spongy white bread, with mustard as the vegetable.

"How's he doing?" I ask, which is my way of broaching a delicate subject. Doug's mother passed away last year after several years of illness, and the furniture is the same, the paint on the walls the same, but she's not there. Grief lingers in the shade of unopened curtains.

"Not so well."

It dawns on me that his abrupt departure from Missoula was probably more complicated than I thought. He left his graduate degree at the university unfinished, completing the semester and never coming back after the summer break. We had a room for him in the house I shared; I rented it to someone else and finished up my own degree while he started work in the factory and my puzzlement began. I called him up and tried to entice and cajole and reason with him to come back out, and failed. He said he had to work off his debts, and he didn't like the city that much, or the program. I didn't find out his mother was ill until I left Missoula with Nicola and came east with all my belongings, on my way to England to get married. We stopped in South Bend—his mother was in a wheelchair. At the time I was too glib and blinded by my own fortunes to do more than flinch at the prospect of suffering.

Now his father watches television alone, just like my grandmother, and the pantry doesn't feel the same. I try to restrain all my own anxieties about my grandmother, my guilt at not being there when she tripped and fractured her wrist just last week, and listen to Doug explain why he hasn't gone down to New Orleans to drum in a jump blues band, or moved to L.A. to design furniture, or traveled to Maryland to start a cultural studies program.

"I try to get him interested in other things," Doug says, "but the fact is he never really had any hobbies. That's why I can't leave."

I've been so intent on conception that the sense of what comes next has begun to escape me. I've thought of a son as a legacy, but I've never thought of myself becoming his dependent. Having a child must be like planting the seed of your own ultimate mortality; perhaps it's only with your offspring around that you recall your place in a generation with a limited life span. I can imagine myself with an infant in the car seat, barely. But of course we would both be adults one day. We'll have to negotiate the strange territory of the child growing up and the parent growing old, the reversal of responsibility. Whole societies are built around the premise that the child takes care of the parent, and yet it seems as alien to me as the image of myself as an old man. I think of my own family, scattered across the continent, convening for holidays, growing older without witnessing the changes, so that each visit is a small shock. Doug and his father certainly defy the contemporary logic of interstate mobility, but I'm not sure they're happy about it. There are certain places where fathers and sons team up and spend time together—the work place, for example, may be a scene of intergenerational conflict, but the family business is nevertheless the place where we expect father figures to trade advice and barbs with their progeny. The domestic scene, on the other hand, feels more like a place for the son to visit: the home is the father's castle, not the son's. Doug's father must be wondering when on earth his son will get married. When will he move to a house of his own? When will he have kids of his own?

I always regress when I go home. On one of my last visits, I was chasing my brother around the house with one of those giant, pump-action soaking machines. My dad had jazz playing on the stereo until I fired, raking the wall with water as my brother ducked. Stan Getz went suddenly silent. Somewhere inside that black box of receiver, the fuses were shorting out and beginning to boil, like the anger in my dad's face. Hadn't he told us not to shoot in the house? Where would this go— back to the confrontations of my teenage years? Fortunately, we both thought better of that, and the sound of the saxophone eventually came back to rescue us.

Biology and the rebellion against it make for a strange mixture in fathers and sons. My father didn't teach me to fly-fish. He took me along on a couple of his early-morning walleye jaunts on Oneida Lake, where he and a buddy sat puffing cigars while I stared at the puddles of oil and water in the bottom of the aluminum boat, ready to explode from the tedium of it all. I doubt I would have taken to fishing at all had it not been for a backwoods friend, Myron, who let me cast an old rod in the yard, let me fumble with feathers and dubbing at his fly-tying table, and took me out on my first forays to the Deerfield. Myron had dogs for hunting rabbits and grouse, a taste for venison and bourbon, a shelf of books by people like Schwiebert and Lyons, and a subscription to *Fly Fisherman*. He and his wife were facing the same situation Nicola and I face now—there was a problem with scar tissue in the fallopian tubes. This was before the first "test-tube" baby, however, so they didn't have the options we have now. Only recently have I begun to realize that for a while at least I was a kind of surrogate son for them, a relationship uncomplicated by biology. There's hope in that.

Doug and I pull on our sneakers and pump up the basketball. The prospect of getting outside and running around is a relief. We have a tradition of one-on-one basketball that began with a match in Townsend, Montana, when Doug passed through on his way back to South Bend. I won that one, but the score stands at three all, with Doug winning three contests in South Bend and me taking one in Kalamazoo and another in Wendell.

He has always piqued my pride by asserting that I've gone downhill since I left Missoula. I've offered the defense that my legs are always jet-lagged when we meet, but the truth is that he is in far better shape than he was then. Whether it's lifting pallet loads of boxes at work or taking hundred-mile bike trips out along Lake Michigan on the weekends, his life here has made him strong, lean, and tireless. I haven't played ball in over a month, and I'm a little dubious about my jump shot.

"You sure you want to play this time?"

He says sure, we'll shorten the games to eleven and play best of five. He cans a jump shot from outside the three-point arc.

"You know, Jim, I think the last time I played at all was that time in Kalamazoo." It looks like it, I say, and miss badly. The rim is welded to the aluminum backboards to ensure longevity and remove any chance of a favorable bounce. Doug swishes; my shots carom out into the parking lot.

Only when we start do I realize that the voyage has toughened me up instead of tiring me out. I have a terrible habit of relying on my height to cover up my laziness and fatigue, but now I'm reveling in the release from the confines of truck cab and sadness. I bounce and leap when I would have squatted and waved. Doug can't shoot over me, and he can't keep me off the boards. I post him up and score, and since we play winners, he can't get the ball back until I miss. I reach eleven before he breaks three.

This is the point when my valor normally sags, and instead of playing defense I stand still and shout gibberish as Doug shoots. I also like to avoid expending energy by taking three-point shots, and Doug usually dares me to make them. He hangs back near the basket this time, taunting me with the void between us. I can't resist the temptation.

"Go on, Barilla. I'm giving it to you," he says as I launch a three. It zips through the net and shocks us both. He hands me the ball and backs away again, giving me the same shot from the top of the key.

"Go ahead, take it, I'll give you that all day long."

I do, and with the same result. Now he has to come out and guard me.

"All right, Barilla," he says, and drops the ball in front of me. When I look up his palm is inches from my nose. Nevertheless, I win game two as quickly as the first, and although game three is closer, I pull away with another flurry of jump shots. I never once shout "YabbaDabba-Doo" or "Lookeythere!" or "Wallabingbong" instead of playing defense.

"You've gotten some game," he says. "You must have been playing a lot out there in California."

"I'm just wound up," I say. "It feels good to run around."

I take a shower and get the truck packed up and then follow Doug's car to New Buffalo, a tourist town on the lake, for lunch before he has to leave for work. But he's already cutting it close; he has to take his food on the run in a paper bag. He buys a whole meal to take home to his dad and pays for my food before I can protest.

"Take care of yourself, Jim," he says, and "say hello to Nicola for me." You take care too, I say, and then he dashes out the door. I'm on my own again. I munch my way through a couple more slices of pizza, then box the rest. I'm thinking about that blue-collar rebel on the wing with me across Ohio, who seems a phantom of diesel fumes now. Someone more complicated, sad, and real is on his way to work.

Troutarama

Pere Marquette River, Baldwin, Michigan

I drive north along the finger of land that is Michigan, glad to be moving, and the nose of the truck cuts through the aqueous haze like a speedboat prow jittering over chop. I can't see the lake, but it owns the horizon, and I can feel the swells off to my left, coughing up clouds that taste of Chicago and Gary, too heavy to budge. For an hour the waves tug at us with crosswinds, sucking at the wheel wells, until the dark mass of the front towers over us. Rain drops spiral down, then pellets of hail. We tunnel through, wipers flailing, and surface into clear and glittering light. A cold Canadian breeze flutters through the leaves and twists their white bellies. I breathe in deep and let the sharp air clear my head.

"Troutarama!" the banners proclaim in Baldwin as I pass through downtown. I've missed the trout extravaganza by several weeks, although a giant rainbow still swims across plastic sheeting on the roof of the local tavern. I stop at the Pere Marquette River Lodge and Fly Shop, my last hope as the downtown disappears. They've just finished a float, and the guide, still in his waders, is offering his report to another guy behind the counter. He says they did pretty well on big streamers, banging them along the banks. "Anything rising?" I ask, betraying my naiveté.

"Not unless you want to catch smolts," he says disdainfully. I don't tell him that most of what I catch probably qualifies as smolts.

"No, no, big browns, big browns is what I want."

The guide doesn't look too impressed. He finishes signing some forms and heads back outside. The owner, on the other hand, takes a shine to me when I tell him I'm on a trout quest across the country.

"I used to be a trout bum myself," he says, as I finish filling out the nonresident fishing license form. He means it as a compliment. He's a little older than I am, with a well-groomed beard and the kind of tasteful, high-performance outerwear—the shirt with the patented sheen that keeps the rain off, the pants bristling with zippers and secret pockets—that I have never been able to afford. Until this moment I hadn't really thought of myself as a hobo, or at least it hadn't occurred to me that anyone else would identify me as such. I sneak a look down at my soiled and rumpled shirt, at my pants with their own dubious sheen accumulating above the knees.

"Used to save up twelve hundred bucks and fish around Montana all summer," he's telling me. "Be headed back on fumes, believe me, but I had some phenomenal fishing."

I'm poor enough and cheap enough and dirty enough to qualify as some kind of tramp, but am I a trout bum? I don't think so. I'd like to be. I'd like to wake up with nothing but water on my mind, go to sleep with the river washing everything else away. I'd like to be that devoted to angling, but the wistfulness in the other guy's voice suggests that this is an ephemeral state of mind. I'm wondering what Nicola is doing. I'm wishing we could catch dinner and a movie. I'm thinking about what it would be like to have my child asleep in the crook of my arm.

I imagine this entrepreneur as a *confrere* of mud, fish slime, cheese powder, and sundry other smells. While I'm busy transforming him into a bum, he's reeling off river names, encampments, and hatches, like so many false casts. It dawns on me that I'm missing valuable insider information, but when I come back to catch what he's saying, he's just about done.

"All that was way back in 1986," he says, "before fly-fishing really took off. Back then nobody had ever heard of whirling disease on the Madison." He pauses, reflecting. He's got some eddy in mind, with fish rising, mayflies swarming, sun sinking into a pink haze. He's made a cast and the fly is drifting and the fish is rising and . . . he blinks. He pulls himself out of it; after all, he's selling gear in Michigan now.

"Of course, Montana is unbelievable," he tells me, reopening the conversation, and to share the moment I nod and gaze off toward the wall as if locating my own Big Sky reverie. "But I came back and opened this shop because the fishing here can be fantastic too. World class."

He shakes his head apologetically. Right now, he tells me, the fishing's real tough. "Two hundred and forty-one thousand anglers come through here every year. Guess when they come?"

I shake my head.

"All at once for the steelhead run. In about two months this place will be rocking, but right now, there's hardly a soul out there. You've got the place pretty much to yourself."

"That could make me look like a real genius. Or a complete idiot." I'm not reassured by the fact that I've wandered off the beaten track.

"Well, there's no reason for it," he says, to reassure me. "The trout are there. The original stocking of brown trout in the U.S.A. was right here on the Pere Marquette." He pulls out a Chamber of Commerce map that shows every bend and pool of the river. "Plenty of trophy browns, all through here. I recommend you fish Clay Banks, right here. This is a good spot for a trout bum. You can pull up and pitch a tent for free out there, and the fishing is real good. Just slap something big down and strip it really hard and keep moving. Let me show you what to use."

I follow him to the fly cases. He picks out a strange black beetle with a white tail, four white rubber legs, and a deer-hair wing. It looks like a killer popper for sunfish, or an experiment in hybridization I myself might try, an attempt to splice my long-standing faith in the deer-hair caddis to my newfound addiction to beetles.

"Now this we call a skunk. You can have this."

I take the free fly sheepishly, feeling a bit like a panhandler with a welcome dollar bestowed upon me. All this advice, and I won't be buying any of the expensive raincoats on display all around me. He tells me to come back tomorrow and let him know how I did.

I follow the map past a series of aluminum-sided cottages that ends with the pavement at the railroad tracks, only a few blocks from the main drag. Past the tracks lies the realm of backwoods trailers and barking dogs, where the road loops down to the river. Clay Banks. There are fire rings and beer-bottle tops, but the place is deserted. It feels like the kind of spot I might find after a long journey into the woods, but I can still hear the traffic rolling down Main Street. The sound of the passing cars makes the place feel all the more desolate and eerie, a spot for true bums to gather on the outskirts of town. I promised Nicola I wouldn't camp alone in places that made me uneasy, and this is the kind of desolation I had in mind.

The river winds without riffles past downed trees, spilling sand from the banks, slow and amber, full of shadows. Sand traps bolster the opposite bank where the current would otherwise bite deep and gorge itself on sand. Someone has spent a lot of time making them, cutting alder stems to length and nailing them to planks to form what looks like a series of fallen ladders. The results are obvious. Where the traps protect the bank, the current narrows and rushes underneath, creating a perfect shelter for fish. Where the banks are exposed, the sand piles up and covers everything. To avoid some leaning alders I step on what looks like a beach and sink to my thighs, recalling as the methane erupts around me the fly-shop owner's lament.

"Erosion. That's our main problem. This used to be virgin white pine forest. When they cut those huge trees, the river started eating away the banks. We're still fighting to stabilize the channel."

I fish the skunk as instructed, twitching those white grasshopper legs across the surface. I am besieged by smolts. One rockets up and strikes at the head of the sand trap, then another attacks in the center of the run, then another takes a bite as I finally pull the fly back to me and begin to raise the tip for another cast. None of them are big enough to get their jaws around the fly. Beneath the alders and along the downed trees it's the same story. Smolts, smolts, smolts.

My internal critic recounts the guide's dismissal for me.

"Not unless you want to catch smolts . . . heh, heh." Hey, smolt fisherman! Over there, by the bank—I see a little guy rising!

My fly can't drift two feet unmolested. It gets tugged down and spit out like the phony and worthless meal it is, while the big browns watch with invisible grins. Darkness is rising into the treetops. My watch says 9:30, and I don't know where I'm staying. I have to get back. The imperative comes as a relief; I can reel in without conceding defeat.

The map says that Gleason's Landing, several miles downstream, is the main put-in spot for the kayak crowd. I hope that means there will be more people around. It turns out I'm not alone in heading for the campground. My headlights catch the red glow of eyes in the road, and I stop before a bewildered opossum that twitches its nostrils at the rumbling engine, sighs with fatigue, and steps slowly aside. I pass another sequence of eyes, this time a whole family of raccoons turning to watch me as they waddle along a shortcut through the woods. The strong perfume of skunk rides with me in the air.

I reach our destination before they do, the parking lot where the dumpster is overflowing with trash. The bags piled up beside it have been torn open and the riches inside strewn across the lot and dragged into the trees. The fires of other campers twinkle along the river bank. I'm grateful that at least I won't be alone.

I find a site by flashlight, passing two baby raccoons clinging to tree trunks along the way. They look puzzled, as if they're wondering whether this impossible stab of light could actually be revealing them. As I set up the tent, squeals erupt from the brush, twigs snap, and the bushes shake. There is no moon; the night is coal black among the trees, and my flashlight is dimming.

To conserve the batteries, I decide to sit in the truck and read the fishing guide. As soon as I close the door, it becomes clear that what I think of as a place to park is something else entirely in the minds of my fellow creatures. The parking lot has become a battlefield, and I've settled into the no-man's-land of garbage pickers. I hear snarls, and a scuffle erupts right under the truck. Coyote chatter rises into a crescendo from the direction of the river.

They get me thinking about the etiquette of interspecies encounters. Wildness, I'd like to think, is often just a misunderstanding, not knowing how to behave toward each other. The lonelier I get, the more important the notion of an ecological community becomes. I'd like to think that I belong with the other riparian creatures, all of us helping each other along through rituals of behavior. Angling is an elaborate invocation of the predator and prey relationship, but we lack such rituals for dealing with our competitors on the food chain, as well as those who clean up after us. Are we all in ruthless competition with one another, or are there other lines of communication?

Instinct tells me that the others would prefer to be left alone. I'm normally a libertarian misanthrope when it comes to fishing. I don't like sharing a pool, and the more rules there are, the less I like the fishing. Rules mean scarce resources, an intrusion of the human community onto the plenitude and freedom of the water. Nevertheless, I know how to behave on a crowded stream. Social rules, often strict, govern the movement of fishermen around each other, from the shoulder-to-shoulder scrum of a lakeshore Opening Day to the beats of a Scottish salmon river. They keep us from flailing each other with expensive rods, from garroting our rivals with lengths of monofilament, and, in many cases, from piercing earlobes with airborne streamer hooks.

The anarchy of solitude is safer for different species. Things are pleasant enough on the river until we fellow anarchists meet. Encountering one another on the bank, we have no protocols to guarantee the best spot on the pool. We have to negotiate. Sometimes might makes right. Sometimes he who hisses loudest keeps the pool. Sometimes it takes awhile, a bluff, a bit of guile, to keep hold of a prized position.

I'm fishing a stretch of Wolf Creek, in an unscenic and therefore deserted area of Yellowstone National Park, where the big '88 fires sizzled through the lodgepole stands. The dead trees have toppled over the stream like an endless jungle gym. I scramble over and under them, straddle some, hang like a chimp from others, until I arrive at a bend where the water deepens. Fireweed waves over a bank of fresh silt, proof that this pool was once almost a pond. I've had enough experience with small streams to expect a school of brook trout here, finning in formation down at the bottom. I tie on a hefty nymph, clamp on a split shot, and tilt the rod back for a cast, aiming for the dark middle of the pool.

The split shot pings off the ferrule and revolves around and around the guides. I leave it there, snarled with the fly. A face has emerged in the center of the pool, right where I intended to drop my fly. Imagine looking out through the glaze of an apartment window and into the murky depths of the night beyond. Suddenly a face appears on the other side of the glass. Would it matter if the expression was hostile or the face was cute? Heart thumping, I stumble backwards and bump into a log. Two limpid brown eyes ogle me from under a glistening slope of brow, while terrified trout dart every which way in search of cover. A slice of ripe cantaloupe appears to be hanging in a crescent from the beast's mouth.

I know how to communicate deference to a grizzly. Don't make eye contact. Back away slowly. Mumble soothing phrases. But there's no shaggy brown hump, no giant snarling maw to make me fall to the ground in a fetal position. This isn't a bear. I realize what my own startled face must look like, the slack tunnel of my mouth, the eyebrows crinkling my forehead. This thing scared me into a loss of dignity! Before I can protest, the beast dives. I watch its body undulate through the brown water, long tail swaying like a rudder, melon-bellied brook trout still clamped in its jaws. It's an otter, a fisherman like me.

It pulls itself up on the bank, and I notice for the first time the slick chute that winds into the bushes, evidence that for the otter this isn't just a casual afternoon jaunt in search of fish; this is home, and I'm standing in the kitchen, uninvited. Nevertheless, I'm in no hurry to leave. I've bushwhacked for an hour just to find this spot. Up ahead are more dead trees, and then the beginnings of a marsh. With an air of regal, anthropocentric hubris, I declare this my spot. I've worked for it, and now I'm claiming it—at least for a few casts.

Not so fast, says the otter, as I ready another cast. Before I can release my line it slides off the bank, where it's been gnashing raw flesh with relish, and glides to the center of pool. Right where I intend to land my fly, it bobs and stares at me, nostrils flaring. Some believe the origin of mermaids lies in this gaze, in the doe-eyed spells that sea otters cast over forlorn sailors. I don't see it. I would have to spend a long, long time at sea, and be suffering the delusions of scurvy, before I mistook this bristled snout for a beautiful woman.

"Get out of the way, pal," I mutter. At first I'm slightly amused. I've never seen an otter like this before, ten feet away and holding steady for me to get a good look. But after a couple minutes it gets old. I've seen his whiskers twitch. I've discovered the little hollows that must be his ears. I want him to listen to me now. "Okay, I've seen you," I say, "Go on, now, go about your business somewhere else." I scowl at him. I wave my rod suggestively, a dismissal. He doesn't budge.

"I don't think you want me to catch you with this hook, my friend," I say, twiddling the nymph so the hook catches the light. The otter stares at me. There's no expression there that I can read like the glare of an angry dog. It's an impassive, nonviolent gaze. I've got a protest on my hands.

It occurs to me that despite my threat, I wouldn't want him on the end of my line either. He's not exactly small, and, judging from the way he dispatched the fish, his teeth aren't small either. I decide on subterfuge. I turn my back, duck under a tree, and pretend I'm conceding. I clamber over a few more trunks and stop, listening. I don't hear him splashing, and I can't see him. I give him a minute, just to be sure, and then I hurry back.

He's gone when I arrive. I chuckle at the triumph of my superior human cunning and ready the line for my first cast. I reach back and . . . his face emerges from behind a log, whiskers twitching. Before I can sweep the line forward he has dipped into the pool. One sweep of his rear feet sends him right to the middle, bubbles erupting from his nostrils, trout streaking away again.

I cast anyway. Too late to stop, I tell myself. This isn't about catching fish anymore. I swerve to avoid hitting him, and the nymph lands in the silty backwash near shore. A short stripe of line floats to a halt on the surface, only a few feet from his head. I've upped the ante. I've violated his airspace. I await his response.

He dives. An instant of panic grips me, and once again I almost turn to run. What if he's coming for me? How can I beat down a marauding otter when I left my pepper spray at home? I stay put because of a platitude about barking dogs: don't let them see your fear. At a speed that might seem reckless were it not so graceful, the otter does a full circuit of the pool, stirring up clouds of mud and darting through them like circus rings. When he comes up, he has another belly dangling from his lips. He returns to the center of the pool, where the fish spasms while he treads water, watching me, in no apparent hurry to feast or leave. If this display of prowess is meant as a commentary on my own crude attempts to catch fish, it hits home. I've been outclassed. I draw in my line. It's clear who owns this pool.

I'm thinking about the otter as the animals rummage around in the garbage outside the truck, making meals out of what people have thrown away. Good for them, I'm thinking. I'm willing to consider some more complicated, mutually beneficial version of the ecological community than "might makes right," until I turn out the truck light and open the door to get out. I hear a low growl, like a dog warning of its intent to attack, emanating from the complete darkness under the truck. It's growling at me. Cheeky bastard. I sit for a moment, letting this challenge to my human supremacy sink in. The beast inside me begins to assert itself. I can't see whatever is lurking down there; it could be a raccoon, or a skunk, or it could be a bear, for all I know. I'm not about to stick my ankle out there just to find out.

I pause for a second to consider my technological options. Is there room for negotiation? I once reached an acceptable resolution with a striped skunk I met on the bank of the Wise River. The river was rampaging down to the Big Hole at the height of spring run-off, and I was picking my way carefully along the rocks to avoid getting swept away. So, it turns out, was the skunk. We met each other at an unfortunate turn in the path, where the chain-link fence of a nearby yard left only a narrow path between brambles and rapids. I had forced my way, crouching to avoid the prickly canes, for quite a distance. I didn't want to back up and do it again. The skunk, who had come the other way, didn't want to back up either.

Thus we found ourselves within a few feet of each other, with no way out but backward, forced to develop ways to speak each other's language. There wasn't much in the way of diplomacy. First I tried to pull rank by stomping my foot and threatening to pounce. The skunk called my bluff. Black eyes blazing, it stomped its feet and lunged at mine. I backed off and scratched my head, looking for an out. Those teeth looked sharp, but so were the blackberry thorns. The skunk looked around for an escape route too, surveying the whitewater and the wire. No place to go.

I picked up a small stone and showed it to the skunk, who snarled in reply. Then I chucked it at him, not to hit him, but to show that the opposable thumb was a weapon of superior force. He'd better back up. The stone skittered over the rocks and bounced into the river, close enough that the skunk winced. I bent to pick up another stone.

The skunk began to dance. Shifting from paw to paw, it wriggled and swayed in time to some angry music, eyes fixed on me the whole time. Head and body made for a strangely mesmerizing contrast, the face full of rage, the body gyrating to some hidden disco beat. The significance of this movement immediately took hold. Skunks have a number of communications that precede their spraying. Spotted skunks, I've been told, even stand on their heads, like clowns, before they fire. The striped skunk patters its forepaws in a little jig before it raises its tail and shoots. I was on the verge of a chemical attack, and I needed to make some quick conciliatory gestures to escape it.

"Okay, okay, I'm backing up," I said, dropping the stone and fumbling backward with my hands outstretched. A cane grabbed my collar and ripped along it with the sound of a zipper. This one missed snagging flesh, but there were more, a lot more, behind me.

For every step I took, the skunk advanced, dancing. A stream of gibberish dribbled from my lips, things like, "You're a nice guy, really, you don't want to spray me," and "You're the man," and "You got it your way, have it your way, your way or the highway, that's it, take 'er easy, nice and easy, yes, no hassles here." I backed along until the brambles had embedded into my shoulders and were doing what cats do to the arms of sofas: sharpening themselves at my expense. One was slithering across my scalp, just waiting for the slightest twitch to hook me there permanently. I couldn't retreat anymore.

"I'm begging you not to do this," I said, pleading my case. "I'm caught. I can't go back any farther. Nice skunk. Nice skunky."

Did the skunk somehow recognize my plight? War is politics by other means. My adversary ducked through a hole in the fence and disappeared, and nobody got stoned or sprayed.

Might makes right . . . The flashlight beam feels too feeble to ward off whatever is lurking down there. But there's one way of asserting human dominance over this mob: the roadkill machine. I fish out my keys and crank up the noise. The starter alone sounds like the hack of a sleeping dragon, but when the engine catches it erupts in a full orchestra of menace.

Growl at me? Listen to this engine growl!

I click on the headlights, throwing the garbage scene into stark and lurid light, and jerk backwards to expose what must now be cowering in terror underneath. Nothing is there, just gravel and sand. I circle the lot like a gladiator in a chariot, just to be sure. Where the lot ends, red eyes glare at me. I fall asleep to their yelps and cackling, and the tread of paws outside the tent.

Dawn finds me awake and cold, the woods now silent, even the trills of birdsong few and distant. My sleeping bag is too thin; it's supposed to be good down to 35 degrees, but that guarantees survival, not comfort. I can see my breath. Steam also rises from the river, where nothing is hatching. Occasionally a smolt snaps at a bit of bark or a leaf.

The animals are gone for the day, but it looks like there is plenty more trash to paw over. Flies are warming themselves in patches of sunshine, getting ready for their turn, beginning to roam. Packing up, I realize I don't even know what day of the week it is, let alone the date.

Baptism of the Smolt Fisherman

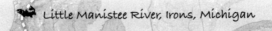

Little Manistee River, Irons, Michigan

I drive north out of Baldwin to where the Little Manistee crosses the highway. There's a Forest Service campground here, with a campground host to keep the raccoon riffraff at bay. But the river here reminds me too much of my failure on the Pere Marquette; it's a sinuous ribbon of shadows just visible between alder thickets, without a riffle in sight. This ubiquity of sand confuses me; absent the stones that signal the head of one run and the tail of another, I don't know where to begin or end. I grope around behind the seat for my Michigan guide, to check what I remember reading in the truck last night. I'm sure they said the Little Manistee had more water that I could understand, more riffles and fast water than the Pere Marquette. I get the page open on my knee.

"The upper stretch, above Highway 50, is a small stream with a narrow channel and difficult fishing."

So it is.

They suggest the stretch below the town of Irons, which I find without incident, and follow the line of dulled neon bars, trailers, and cabins to the edge of town. The river disappears into the woods, and I follow it through a maze of dirt roads without the benefit of landmarks.

Finally, and unexpectedly, I emerge onto a paved road, somewhere in the back corner of the county, and I can see a bridge and a Forest Service sign just ahead. It's a fishing access, and there is the river—larger, faster, and whirling between stones—water I can read. I rejoice at the prospect of actually drifting a fly through its familiar course, until I look down over the bridge and startle a twenty-pound chinook. It bolts into the shadows under the bridge, and then several more follow, flashing the silver of their sides. They're fresh from the lake, and I'm thrown into confusion again.

Salmon may serve as a metaphor for my journey, but I don't like to fish for them. Part of it is privacy; I don't want to get involved in their sex lives. But it's also something to do with the limitations of my imagination. I can understand what drives a fish to feed, and I like the sensation of proximity to the food chain. What I can't grasp is the desire of a fish that isn't hungry, that has stopped eating altogether, to bite some outlandish facsimile of food, like one of those purple-and-hot-pink egg-sucking leeches, for example. There's something tragic in the gesture, something of a dying wish that gives me no pleasure.

They make it hard to fish a dainty dry, since my arrival at a pool sends them thumping for cover under the logs. Their presence threatens to render the whole enterprise absurd because the only fish foolish enough to respond in the midst of this torpedo assault are the tiniest, the smolts. The rampage of a terrified giant doesn't put these little guys off their feed; they attack my fly with the same gusto as before. I pull in a four-inch baby rainbow, and while I bend to release it, fish as long and thick as my thigh burst through my gaping reflection.

Size does matter. In desperation, I decide to go after the salmon with the biggest fly I've got, an olive marabou leech I found hanging in a tree back in California. I do my best to be annoying. I skitter the leech across their snouts; I jig it up from the bottom and parade it in front of them like a street clown who refuses to go away. I can see their gills working, and the slight shift in reflected sunlight as their eyes turn from the fly to each other and back to me. Occasionally they shift and snap at each other's fins. I get more and more annoyed myself. The salmon, obsessed with sex, confronting death, have a lot more to worry about than a drab bit of marabou. Only the smolts are seduced; they peck the wavering strands of feather until I give up in frustration.

I need ice and a break, so I drive into the coastal city of Manistee, crossing the broad bends of the Manistee River where it washes into Lake Michigan, then set up camp in the woods at Bearpaw. The strain and disappointment of the fishing is making me tired. I crawl into the tent, zip up the flap to shut out the view of the woods and the river, and take a nap with the sunbeams streaking the nylon and a single moth fluttering against the ceiling.

I wake up at six. The sky is still a bright blue, but the sun has lost its heat, and already a chill is beginning to spread out from the shadows. I've made a decision. No more dries. Bad fishing demands desperate measures. It's time to tie up some weighted nymphs and figure out how to fish them. I'm winding the lead onto the shank of a size-14 hook when a woman hurtles down the road on a mountain bike, her black helmet and wraparound sunglasses making her look like a riot-control officer about to pounce on a looter. She sees me and skids to a halt. I notice a patch of sheepskin on her chest; she's wearing a fishing vest over her Lycra biking shorts.

"What are you tying?" she asks, and sets down the bike. Now that she's stopped, she looks less martial and more motherly. She points to an RV across the road, where a bearded man in a shapeless hat and two skinny teenage boys are snapping branches and crumpling up paper by the fire ring.

"We're camped right over there. I've been fishing for three nights now, and I'm still trying to figure out what to use."

I tell her I'm tying a fur-coated sinker, and I confess that I've tried everything and I can't catch anything but smolts, that I've fished the Pere Marquette and now the Little Manistee without any success whatsoever. I haven't even seen a brown. She says she saw one, but it wasn't rising to her fly. It was taking off.

"Might have been a salmon," I say. "I've seen plenty of those."

"I might try a mouse tonight," she says. I nod and try not to betray my disbelief. A mouse! Fishing a mammal imitation strikes me as the mark of true desperation.

"You never know," I say. "It's worth a try."

We wish each other luck, and she joins the family by the smoking fire ring. I can smell their hot dogs. I feel better. At least I'm not alone in feeling desperate. I finish wrapping brown muskrat fur over lead wire and drop the two nymphs into my palm to test their weight. A dry fly would float over the skin; these bounce like split shot.

I wade into the current above the campground, and a salmon immediately rockets away downstream and burrows under an overhanging alder. I might have fished that spot, but now I head upstream, fishing the nymph dead drift down the current with my rod tip high and a vague eye on the line. The fly is too heavy to cast with any semblance of grace. Flopping forward, it splashes down and disappears. I let it find its way back to me with the patience of the despairing; I don't expect to catch anything.

I'm fishing a deep pocket below a stump, my mind on the verge of a daydream, when the line stops. It tightens, and in doing so appears to be defying gravity and slithering upstream. Startled by the strangeness of this motion, I jerk the rod tip and feel a jerk in reply as a smolt struggles for a moment and shakes free. Of course I've heard about this phenomenon of the line pausing or even pulling downward with a strike, but I've heretofore regarded it with the same skepticism I reserve for the yeti, tarot cards, and other probable fallacies and supernatural phenomena. The notion that an invisible trout could bite my invisible fly and somehow I would know about it has always struck me as a leap of faith, one I've never quite been able to allow myself. I've always twitched the line and given the nymph an artificial hop, just to keep our connection palpable, a method akin to groping for a light switch in the dark.

This is a moment of conversion. I cast again and watch closely. The line coils loose, flabby, and hopeless, and the point arrives when I have to suppress the urge to twitch, just to make sure the fly is still there. Then the line straightens. I pull upward again and feel the brief, quivering connection to another smolt. I'm a little late in my response, but it doesn't matter, because I've found the faith. I believe I will see the line move, and sure enough it does and I do. I hook smolt after smolt, and let each one serve as reinforcement, even though I still can't find any sign of the browns. It seems that, at least in Michigan, I am a smolt fisherman.

At sundown I quit near a bridge where a dog warns me against trying to go any farther. I drive out of the forest to a one-stop gas station, grocery store, and pizza parlor, where the smell of charred flour and melting cheese pours out a vent on the side. There's a phone stuck on a post in the parking lot, and I call Nicola as a pair of locals rev their dueling monster-truck engines in my other ear. I tell her about visiting Doug, but it's impossible to be more than perfunctory: I spent the night there; we played basketball. I saw his dad. He seemed okay.

"Have you been thinking about the IVF at all?" I ask.

"Sometimes I think we should do it. Other times I think we should wait and try a few cycles with the IUI."

Intrauterine insemination seems like the midpoint on the road away from natural birth. You use the rhythm method, and then on the day of ovulation, you hurry over to the doctor's office. You go to the little room with the provocative magazines, and the doctor loads a needleless syringe with your sample and deposits it much closer to the egg. You can combine the insemination with a course of fertility drugs, hormones that stimulate the ovaries to ripen more eggs. The insurance companies will pay for this procedure, presumably not because it's more natural, but because it costs a lot less than IVF.

"Yeah. I don't know about the IUI." After three years of attunement to biological rhythms, I've lost faith. My gut feeling is that IUI won't work. Of course, I have the luxury of gut feelings. I won't have to be sedated while the doctor pierces my abdomen with a needle and "harvests" a clutch of eggs from my ovaries.

"I've been thinking about the IVF. I've been seeing kids and wondering what it would be like, you know," I say.

"Me too."

Nicola has always been good with kids. She would baby-sit for friends just for the pleasure of spending time with their little girl, putting her to bed, fixing her a snack, reading her favorite stories, again and again. My history with children is more mixed. I can recall only one babysitting episode: I took charge of my infant brother while my father and stepmother went for dinner with some friends. I was just home for Christmas break from college; I was about as far in spirit from infant care as I am ever likely to be again. Things were fine for about an hour; my brother napped and I watched television. Then he woke up. There I was, a fumbling stranger looming over his crib. He screamed. The burst of sound, the crimson of his face, terrified me. I made a frantic call. Pick him up, they told me. Walk around with him. Talk to him.

"I did all that," I said. I had him in my arms, wriggling and choking on tears. "Come home now! Right now!" That was a bonding experience I was loath to repeat. I haven't been in charge of a baby since.

"I heard some kids in a tent. They sounded like me and my sister."

There is a river of emotion flowing through my voice that I cannot convey into the receiver. It's hard to talk to someone you miss badly while standing in a parking lot thousands of miles away.

"Do you miss me?"

"Yes! I wish I was there right now!"

"What?"

"I said I wish I was there right now."

What always amazed me about the chronicles of Neal Cassidy and company was that they seemed to be able to leave without anguish. "Off we rushed into the night . . ." They were always rushing off into the night, promising their wives they would come back exactly two hours later, at three fourteen, and breaking those promises without any appearance of guilt. *On the Road* seems like an expurgated version of their journey now, with all the pained pay-phone calls edited out.

Nicola says the train from Oakland stops in Chemult, Oregon, and that we could meet there for a couple days before she starts teaching. It might mean cutting a day or two in Montana, and I don't even want to think about which river I might have to drop from the trip. But I'll be there.

I hang up, and my mouth fills with a watery lust for pizza. I swab my tongue around like a dog, fighting the urge, knowing that pizza isn't really what I'm looking for, and then I say what the hell and go inside to order. I'm all set for a real greasy pie—can even see the orange fat pooling into little puddles around the discs of pepperoni—but the lady behind the counter lifts her harassed face and with powdered hands still punishing a dough ball tells me I can order now, but it'll be an hour's wait; she's got four to make and a store to run. "I . . . ," I say. My tongue rebels; it's willing to wait, but I can't wait an hour in the parking lot for a pizza. It's crazy. I've got to find the campground while it's still light. Thanks anyway, I say, and drag my wretched mouth away.

I fire up the stove while the last light fades from the camp and slice the lid off a can of baked beans, eating quickly, without thinking, even tasting. Loons are calling from the river, and when their fluttering wails subside, whippoorwills whistle from the bottomlands. I listen to them for a while and drift away into sleep.

Smolt Killer

East Branch Ontonagon River, Kenton, Michigan

The Upper Peninsula is a lot farther away than I thought. It's three hours before I reach the bridge at Mackinaw, and I hoped I might traverse the same space in an hour. Where Huron and Superior join, the waters are as blue and wide as an ocean, turquoise in the shallows and shades of cobalt in the distance, flecked with white-fringed waves. The bridge itself reminds me of a pale and elegant relative of the Golden Gate; there is the same magnificent span of water, the mysterious contours of island and headland, the funneling of wind, and the same incongruously frenetic arc of heavy traffic. I sit and listen to the flag-snapping breeze thrum the hood, prodding the clutch to roll a few feet farther until the brake lights flash in front of me again.

It's slow going along the flat, forested length of Route 28 as well. Traffic gathers at the stoplights in little towns and then plods along behind precariously piled logging trucks. When the road straightens, I poke my nose out into the other lane, only to confront the looming face of another logging truck. I duck back into line, and it chugs past, clanking its chains, huffing like the engine of a train with a line of other cars in tow.

This is storied terrain, although there's little drama to be found in the relentless and somber expanse of trees. The Big Two-Hearted River winds through these tamarack and alder swamps, and so does the Fox, where Hemingway actually fished. John Voelker, who chronicled his swamp-slogging days and whiskey-bingeing nights under the pen name

Robert Traver, found trout magic and madness along the Escanaba River, to a degree far too vivid and unseemly for a circuit judge.

I plan to pay my respects with a visit to Voelker's stomping grounds along the Middle Branch of the Escanaba, figuring I might capture a little of the magic myself, but the stream is so small where I cross it that were it not for a sign announcing its presence under the culvert, I would have dismissed it as a ditch. I stare down at the sluggish brown water meandering out from a scrubland of dying pines, trying to picture anyone working themselves into an ecstasy on its shore. It's impossible; he must have fished this river far downstream. I try to get there by following the nearest dirt road into the sloughs, past shotgun-blasted "No Trespassing" signs and a junked washing machine, until I finally dead-end in a mound of torn-up dirt. There's something emphatic about this piling of dirt—something that tells me the house I can see doesn't take kindly to visitors, let alone trespassers. I imagine someone observing me right now through the crosshairs of a scope, waiting to see if I dare to cross the line. It's not worth it. Traver's river will have to wait for another trip.

I check the map and find the Ontonagon River farther on; each of the branches crosses the road, and they all sound good in the book. It's nearly evening when I reach the bar, post office, and general store that mark the crossroads town of Kenton. Rather than waste an hour driving around the backwoods dirt roads again, I go inside the store for directions.

There's a big plywood ice-cream cone by the door, and although the chocolate paint has faded to mocha, the appeal works on me. It's strategic, I tell myself. I figure there's something festive about buying an ice cream, more so than dropping a bill on the counter for a Slim Jim and a package of Ring Dings or whatever other garbage I might gather instead. It takes longer to scoop, and with all the conversation about flavors, cone or dish, one scoop or two, it offers more chance for interaction. After all, it worked back in New York, I tell myself as the screen flaps shut behind me.

Perched behind the counter with the oldies station bantering softly behind her, the proprietress greets me with a noncommittal nod of her nearly grown-out permanent. The air smells of a recently extinguished cigarette. I smile at her, and she pinches her lips in prim courtesy. Her eyes, flickering behind those lenses that darken with the light, aren't smiling. That's what people mean by a flinty gaze, I think, and look quickly away to the flavor board." Let's see," I say, reading Rocky Road and Butter Pecan and taking stock of the situation. Why is she suspicious of me? She acts as if I've stepped into her living room without knocking. *Come on, lady,* I want to say, *I'm buying an ice cream—wayfaring brigands don't order double-scooped chocolate cones.* I'm getting indignant, until I follow her glance to the grunge of my unfurled sleeve. There's evidence of last night's baked beans there, along with dirt-encrusted pine sap and accumulated grime. I have to remember that, having slept in a tent for the last two nights, I probably don't look as upstanding and honorable as I feel.

"That your grandson?" I ask her after she's knuckled out the ice cream and handed me the cone. There's a Polaroid of a grinning cherub taped to the register, struggling to hold aloft a large brown trout. Below, someone has written in crabbed pen, "16 1/2 inches" and "4 1/2 years." This is a slightly disingenuous opening from me; what caught my eye was the youngster's glassy-eyed and slack-jawed companion. But it occurs to me, as the woman smiles tentatively and pushes her glasses farther up her nose to get a better look, that interest in her offspring might lead to better information too.

"That's him," she says. "We couldn't believe it when he caught that thing. Look at him smile."

"Yes, yes, quite a smile," I say, trying to sound casual. The kid is doing better than me. "Quite a catch, too. Where did he catch it?"

She tells me he caught it right at the bridge. I don't know where that is. "Right outside the door, right over there in the yard." She points out through the screen. It seems I've crossed the river without noticing. "He caught it right in our backyard."

I thought I might do a little fishing myself, I say, and ask her the way to Sparrow Rapids. After all the slow and serious waters I've been fishing, I like the sound of rapids. She gives me good directions, generous with details. She's a grandmother now, and I'm clearly a sportsman with an ice cream oozing over my hand. I thank her, lick my cone, and leave, glad we've cleared things up.

Her directions lead me past the goldenrod and saplings of an abandoned farm. Deer bound across the road, trailing terrified fawns. I slow down. The road ends in a deserted Forest Service campground. Even the host has given up and left. I'm off the beaten track again.

When I get out of the truck, a few blue jays swoop down into a nearby pine to investigate my arrival. One lands on a picnic table and cocks its head at me while the rest scream in disappointment; I don't appear to be planning a picnic anytime soon. I can hear the exhilarating music of the rapids rising from just beyond the truck, and I hurry into my waders and scramble down the side of a steep ravine. The river has carved down through sediment here, pushed aside the stones, and arrived finally at the bedrock backbone of the hills. The water rolls over bare ledge, breaking into riffs of whitewater where one glistening slab joins another. I follow the trail to the edge of a foam-flecked pool where the water pauses before rounding a bend.

My hands are wobbly with excitement, and I'm trying to calm myself enough to get the line through the guides, when something big shifts its weight in a maple across the river. I look up and regard what appears to be a white-crowned bear, or a giant skunk, crouched in a low branch over the pool. It's big enough, and close enough, to give me a shock. I look around for an escape route in case the creature decides to leap down and attack, but instead it lowers a shoulder, revealing a single pale and unfriendly eye. It glares at me, keeping its shoulder drawn across its features like the fringe of Bela Lugosi's cape in the old black-and-white *Dracula.*

"What the hell is that?" I blurt out, and my voice carries over the roaring of the water, not loud, but the creature hears me. The shoulder lowers some more, so that both eyes can peer down at the intruder. I catch a glimpse of a powerful beak, and suddenly the shape makes sense.

"Bald eagle!" I exclaim, mostly with relief. As if offended at the vulgar proclamation of its name, the bird lowers its wing. It's a face that graces too many stamps, express-mail envelopes, and coins to be surprising, and yet the animate bird, with its disheveled and slightly soiled crown of white feathers, is somehow so much more—cold and powerful as a bad winter, graceful and malevolent as a thunderstorm.

It disdains to look at me again. Turning away on the branch, it drops off into flight. A few beats of its wings carry it around the bend. I'm left feeling almost abandoned. Now that I know who my companion was, I would have liked for it to stick around for awhile.

Fish are rising in the pool. The surface is pocked with rings, mostly small, but a few have the heft of worthy quarry. Some small grayish caddis are fluttering over the margins, and an occasional blue-winged olive vaults from the surface and rises into the sunlight. I'm happy to find familiar structures, to know where to expect the trout to hold. I start with the fast water at the top, and on my first cast a ten-inch brown slashes through the bubbles to intercept the bouncing caddis. I'm unprepared and twitch too late; there's the flashing resistance of a missed jaw, and my line piles up in loops around me. I drift the caddis along the same path, hoping the fish won't sulk. But as I expected, it's gone into hiding somewhere. It's exactly what I would do under the circumstances.

I've often wondered how long I would wait before consuming caddis again if my last attempt at a meal ended with the taste of sharp steel. How hungry would I have to get before appetite triumphed over caution? There are certain foods I cannot face, years after an unhappy episode. The very aroma of cashew butter inspires a visceral heave, twenty years after I got sick on a sandwich. I imagine a similar reaction underway in the shadows beneath the standing wave. The first encounter with a hook must be something akin to the terror of an acute illness, a narrow escape from appendectomy. But it's different with veterans. I've seen trout—especially brown trout, and especially when the water is clear and the regulations favor catch and release—rise to inspect my fly not just from below, where the curve of the hook is concealed against the abdomen, but from the side, where its telltale shape is revealed. More often than not they descend again, unconvinced, maybe even horrified, leaving me to wonder when the next great advance in fishing, the transparent hook, will come to market. When I do fool these fish, they betray the limp and half-hearted resistance of the familiar prisoner. They come right to hand with minimal fuss, and wait without thrashing for me to unpluck my needle from their face. Their jaws are scarred with what looks like acne, the many half-healed wounds of previous encounters.

I leave this fish to ponder today's strange lesson and send the fly along the cusp of another promising lie, giving it what I hope is an enticing jiggle across the tops of the waves. Nothing happens. I cast again and dance the fly some more. Again, blank water flowing where I expect a fish is watching, where I hope for a breach. Only when I leave the fly to almost drown along the same line does another ten-inch trout rush to the surface, startling me again. I'm too late to set the hook; again my slack line falls around me.

Having missed the only two legitimate strikes I've had in the state of Michigan, I'm in no condition for an encounter with the horde of smolts rising in the body of the pool. I can't allow another lapse, and my wrist twitches with every flash of fish activity, regardless of whether my fly is in the vicinity. The smolts are busy grabbing every bit of flotsam that passes by, and the approach of my fly ignites a frenzy of competition among them. They race each other to the surface, smacking the fly in succession, and I flinch with the barely suppressed urge to set the hook, like I'm having a bad reaction to psychotropic medication.

I should just look out at the scenery for a few minutes, because when I'm this wound up, a flying fish is inevitable. I can feel the crisis rising in my arm, and when an unfortunate youth makes a splashy cartwheel over the fly, it happens. Before I can stop myself, my arm is ripping the line from the water and the somersaulting smolt is airborne again, this time stilled by sheer force into a quivering missile.

It flies toward me, following the trajectory of the line, and lands with a fleshy whack on top of a floating log. I gather the line to find him, hoping he'll still be struggling, but he slides to my feet like a skydiver whose parachute got tangled in the lines and never opened. He's five inches long, trembling ever so slightly in the fins, and convulsed with infrequent spasms in the gills. There's no outward sign of blood, and at first I hope he's just stunned. But I notice the speckled gold dust of the iris is stained red, and the expression in the eye is flat, as if he's staring inward at the world beyond. I clasp my palm around the body and push it back and forth through the water, hoping to flush oxygen through the gills and bring about a resurrection. When I open my hand the body revolves slowly until the white stripe of its belly bobs on the surface.

I'm haunted by the question of cruelty. The skunk and I got away from each other unscathed, but that kind of intimate encounter seems rare. I could watch birds. I could observe. But to communicate, to participate, seems to entail causing pain.

There's a voice that always tolls at moments like these, with just enough bite to make me lose my way. It's not Montana Slim. He likes the taste of trout, and he likes to show off a trophy. It's the voice of a housemate who knew just how to get to me: "Heading out to torture some poor little fish again, huh? Ripping some lips?"

I left dirty dishes in the sink; he made snide comments about my propensity for blood sports. One remark would be enough to set the hook: as I felt the sharp cold of the Clark Fork rush around my calves, the question of cruelty, and my participation in it, would sting for the rest of the evening.

The moment of what should have been exaltation hit me like a needle in the jaw. I winced as I set the hook and the deluded trout tumbled against its fate. Would the hook prick the rim of cartilage and be easy to remove? Or would it be lodged deep in the throat, snagged among gills, trickling blood? Often I played my quarry quickly to hand, pinched the shank of the barbless hook, and slipped it backwards without removing more than jaws from the water. The fish would drift down and disappear, none the worse, I hoped, and maybe even wiser than before.

It sometimes happened, however, that when the mouth came to the surface there was nothing to be done but cut the line or perform surgery, and these were the moments that I tried in vain to push from my mind. "Why am I doing this?" I would ask myself, reaching inward with my forceps during a moment of calm between the thrashings of an animal desperate to be free.

I marshaled an array of facts in my defense. Trout don't have many nerves in their jaw. Their lips aren't sensitive like ours. I knew that the mortality rate for barbless hooks was low. I knew the average cutthroat prowling the smooth eddies below Yellowstone Lake was caught over three times a summer. I remembered the browns below the dam on the Swift River, how they rose to inspect my fly from every angle, searching for the telltale curve of metal, and how, if fooled, they accepted their plight with a minimum of fuss—they knew better than to waste energy in a struggle. They were irritated by the inconvenience, but they didn't panic; they came right over and practically presented themselves for a quick removal.

Not only didn't the hook hurt much, most of the time, but the very act of fishing was the salvation for most of these fish. Think of all the license fees anglers pay, think of all the efforts we make toward habitat restoration. Think of the fights we wage to protect free-flowing rivers and trout habitat. Think of the Johnny Appleseed of salmonids, spreading the gospel of trout from continent to continent, coast to coast.

All of these arguments made sense until I encountered Old One-Eye. In the long, still pool between Mount Sentinel and Mount Jumbo lived a trout of unremarkable size and wisdom, a rainbow in most respects save for the cutthroat slashes beneath its gills. What made this fish different was its luck and tenacity, for unlike the other twelve-inchers that hung around a series of half-submerged boulders, Old One-Eye had lost half his face. An ugly crater of scar tissue had formed where eye and cheek should have been, the mark, most likely, of an osprey's claw. I imagined this fish dangling from the talon of a sky-bound raptor, the bird's grip just awkward enough that the trout freed itself with a desperate twist, dropped through the air, and landed with a splash back in the river but terribly wounded.

I came to know Old One-Eye because I caught him more than once. He and I liked the same stretch of water, and I could recognize the shape of his rise, a disc occasioned by his sideward approach as he lifted his one good eye to appraise a floating object. He was a survivor, but the wound took its toll. While the others were sleek and plump at the end of summer, he was slender, with gaunt pockets between the adipose fins. He was hungry, and easy to fool. When the other fish refused my fly, Old One-Eye would grab it. Sometimes I knew it was him and could stop myself from striking. Often, however, I realized too late, and would gingerly draw him to my hand, hoping the slack line would release him first.

I never had to disengage a deeply embedded hook from his mouth, fortunately, but his disfigured face became familiar, and with that familiarity came a loss of conviction. To identify with the quarry is to lose the capacity for sport. "Why don't you at least eat what you catch?" Nicola once demanded. I thought about my answer for a long time. I imagined slaughtering Old One-Eye, the survivor of an aerial attack, reduced to a battered fillet in a sizzling pan. I didn't kill him because I didn't need to; if I was hungry and living on the fruits of my hunting skills when Old One-Eye happened along, I'd make sashimi of him, no doubt, with no regrets. But I didn't need to be a predator. I could just as easily simmer tofu as trout.

I haven't arrived at an answer to the question of cruelty. And I keep on fishing. An ambivalent predator, I need to enter into the life of rivers, into life cycles that are predatory by nature. There are other delusions at work, the spell that keeps us separate from the whirl of nutrients that were once trout and human beings, even as we wade across rocks that will be there long after we are gone. I haven't reconciled myself to my own mortality. I try not to think about it as I wade out into the stream.

I've killed the smolt, and it's too small for me to eat. There's nothing to do. I leave it floating along the shore, a slip of white lapping against the sand, figuring the bald eagle might find it. Somebody will find it—

a raccoon, crayfish, some insect scavengers of the stream bottom. But knowing that it will reenter the food chain doesn't make me feel much better about being the cause of its demise. I wade downstream, still casting, more to escape the evidence than to enjoy the possibility of killing more fish. I'm hoping the body might be gone when I get back.

In the next run I capture my first Michigan brown, by accident, since I don't set the hook at the tiny splash of its attack. In fact, I'm trailing my fly in the current while attending to the location of a serious rise downstream when I notice that something very small has fastened itself to my fly. It's two inches long, and how it got its jaws around the hook and managed to embed the point I don't know. Only a tiny filament of flesh keeps the hook attached—not a mortal wound, fortunately. I slip out the hook and gently proffer freedom; the trout is instantly gone.

The larger fish is rising to pick off the emerging duns. In the current by my knee, I watch a mayfly pop from the husk of its nymph-hood, suddenly graceful as a tiny swan. But it's struggling to get its new wings under control, and the current is taking it down into the run. It had better launch its maiden flight pretty quickly, I think; it's set to drift right into the Devil's Triangle, where all struggling mayflies meet distress. This one takes too long; wings and all disappear in the whirlpool of a mouth. I shake the flies around in the compartments of my fly box, hoping to find a misplaced size-16 blue-winged olive just hiding under a grasshopper. I know I've lost them all back in Shinhopple, all except the one I left in an alder on the Little Manistee. I decide to try a small cream variant, rubbed against algae to darken the body.

It lures this trout like a spoonful of cashew butter would entice me to the dinner table: it immediately stops rising. Now the mayflies wobble downstream with plenty of time to get their wings in order. I cast and cast again, just to be sure, but only the smolts are willing to reply.

It's time to test my new faith. I tie on a small but heavy nymph, a green apple-hued bead eye I found tangled with a split shot after the spring flood had receded on the Yuba. I want to know what's swimming under those barren surfaces. I hook more smolts, but I also locate a nine-inch leaping-and-tail-dancing young steelhead where the current chafes the banks.

My pulse picks up at the head of another deep pool, where all the tidbits that have fallen from the shore and cut loose from the bottom get funneled into one headlong rush of sticks, gravel, needles, and food. I fish the way I did on the Little Manistee, trusting the signs of the line, letting the fly find its own way downstream. It finds its way into the funnel, where the waiting trout have to make a snap decision: snap it up or let it go by. I don't know, because I can't see down there, but I imagine that the trout in this position samples most of what passes. After all, if the morsel winds up tasting like a pine needle or a clot of algae, the fish can always spit it out. It makes the fish vulnerable to a concealed hook, since the fly, although it may taste like mothballs and musty feathers, isn't so easy to cough out.

I watch the line for subtle clues. It's slack at the start where I'm hoping the fly will sink, then it's slack where the waters come together, and then, where I would be if I had fins, it stops. I set the hook. There is a brief struggle between us, during which I see the flash of a polished brass flank. The hook pulls out, but it's good enough. I've found the browns.

"I've been fishing all my life," my fly-fishing mentor, Myron, once said to me, "except when I was about eighteen. I had other things on my mind for a year or two." He winked at me. I was nine years old, in love with wild trout, fast water, and evening rises. I had no idea what he was talking about. How could anything else get in the way?

I fell madly in love with Nicola when I was eighteen, and during long evening strolls, holding hands, during indolent afternoons on the beach, gazing into each other's eyes while reciting significant passages from an anthology of love poems, I found out what Myron meant. Rivers flowed out of my mind. They went dry in their beds, and willows grew tall and shaggy in the arroyos. My fly rod sat in the closet with last year's caddis clipped to a guide, suddenly unloved, like an old pair of favorite jeans kicked off into the corner.

It was a month before I confessed to Nicola that I liked to fish. A lot. She nodded and smiled, but I felt the watery recesses of my soul had yet to be laid bare, even when I resorted to making casting motions with my arm. I could be talking about any old hobby, a passion for golf or an addiction to video games, when I really wanted her to know what it was like to wade out into a river at dusk and lose track of yourself, how I would disappear for a while as the trees dissolved under an opalescent sky.

There came a point in the relationship when the rains came again, when I felt brave enough to introduce one love to another. I suggested a walk along a small stream I'd never seen before, and I mentioned, casually, that in addition to the bottle of inexpensive but impressively labeled chardonnay, the one wine glass and pint of strawberries that I intended to pack, I might bring my rod along too. She said that would be fine, and we set off into the Maine woods on a borrowed moped.

I had a vision of this excursion. We would spread a blanket in the sunshine and goldenrod of a meadow, under the mottled arms of an old apple tree. We would sip the chilled wine I had managed to obtain in clandestine underage fashion, and bite strawberries from each other's fingertips. While she lounged and observed, I would amble over to the stream and cast my poetic loops over the murmuring waters. When my line caught the light, she would see how graceful it all was, see the artistry of it and be spellbound, enthralled. She would see what fly-fishing was all about.

A passionate romance and a passionate desire for rivers—different ways of losing the self in another, paradoxes of conquest and dissolution, narratives saturated with illusion. The dream that love never ends, and the fantasy that through fishing we can enter the life of lively water without causing harm, both come true frequently enough to remain poignant, and yet in each there remains the threat of endings, of some revelation in which cruelty and mortality figure prominently.

While it has often been said that blood sports are the proving grounds for male mastery, in fact, the contemporary ethos of catch-and-release fishing is more complex. To catch a fish, and let it go, demonstrates competency, but more important, it represents an attempt to get caught up in lusty, deadly rites while releasing ourselves from the obligation of these sacrifices: the recognition of our own mortality. By releasing our quarry, we sustain the spell of our separation from the whirl of nutrients that once were trout and bears and human beings. We seek to retain a sense of immersion, of selflessness, while concealing the fact that the narrative of release, despite our intentions, may end in death.

I doubt this evasion of mortality is prominent in many anglers' minds. Myron taught me to release the fish I caught, not as a way to walk an ethical tightrope, but as a pragmatic form of streamside rationing. Trout were not plentiful in the warm and heavily fished waters of Massachusetts, except when the hatchery truck dumped its load in the spring. When I hooked a fish, played it to the point of fatigue, and then reached down, gently, to disengage the barbless hook, part of my satisfaction lay in knowing that I had fulfilled a debt to the fishing community, that I had not depleted the commons, but had in fact enriched it. That fish would not be so foolish the next time around, and some other angler would be grateful for the challenge of stalking wiser prey.

When I imagined fishing with Nicola, the soggy corpse of some unfortunate trophy never entered my mind. I might offer her a glimpse of the radiant stars along a brook trout's side, but I would keep it in the water where it belonged. My triumph would be bloodless, exemplifying my concern for the welfare of others, both fish and fishermen.

The first sign that my bloodless triumph was not going to appear as planned was the stream itself. With the moped tires churning up a long plume of dust, Nicola and I bounced over a culvert and barely noticed our destination, a trickle of amber water glistening between moss-bearded stones. The brook we were seeking flowed, barely, past some slash piles and disappeared into the somber claustrophobia of a dense stand of evergreens.

"Look," I said, unable to relinquish the image of chardonnay and strawberries and poetic loops of line, despite a glance at the uprooted stump that blocked our path. "I know this isn't great for walking. Maybe we could just go a little ways along the stream. I could show you how I fish."

Nicola swished a deerfly from her face and said okay, if I was sure this was the place. I nodded vigorously. A manic and desperate cheerfulness had overtaken me, marked by the need to whistle. With "We're Off to See the Wizard" burbling from my lips, I pulled out my vest, jointed the rod, and coaxed Nicola, who was wearing sandals, down the blackberry-tangled embankment to some flat rocks. We stooped under the tunnel of trees, our eyes adjusting to the dimness, our skin tingling with the chill. The stream I had imagined was bright and buoyant, almost giddy with light, with pools like fountains of overflowing champagne; this water smelled like freshly dug roots, the lees of a dark, astringent potion.

"I don't like it in here," she said. I said she was right, it was kind of dreary right here, but there was a patch of sunlight upstream, and maybe even a pool where I could cast. We could make our way up there, and if it didn't open up, we could quit and find somewhere else. She looked at her feet, then at the moss-covered rocks, and nodded an assent.

Mosquitoes discovered and pestered us. We passed nothing worth a cast until we reached the brink of a long, shallow run. In the spring, it might have been a lively stretch of froth and undulating current; now it was nearly still, mirroring the needled boughs above. The rotten crag of an ancient sugar maple stood near some fragments of a stone wall at the head of the pool, its branches long whittled away until only the trunk, festooned with the warts of various fungi, held sway over a small patch of sky.

With the rest of my vision in tatters, it seemed imperative to justify this excursion with a capture. There would be no golden pasture, no calligraphy of line swirling artfully through the air, but at least there would be a point, a victory she could observe, however small. I would conjure a wild beast from these waters, show it off, and then I would let it go.

"Stand back," I said.

I flicked a bow-and-arrow cast out to where there was a tremble of current. The bow and arrow is not the most elegant maneuver in the fisherman's repertoire; with the rod bent into a curve over my shoulder and the fly pinched between by fingers, I felt like I was aiming a spitball. The caddis dropped into still water. Slowly, as the leader straightened, it found a path between the rocks and swung out from the bank. I glanced at Nicola to see if she was watching its progress. Our eyes met; she was watching me, not the fly. I tried to smile, as if to say, "Watch this!" but found the sides of my mouth already taut, clenched in a grimace of nervous expectation. She looked puzzled, almost bewildered, and in that look I knew that whatever vision of grace and beauty I had in mind was not only rendered invisible but negated by the fierce-eyed primate crouched before her.

The fly was riding the folds of the main stream; it was too late to relax, to do more than watch with involuntary fascination as the caddis hovered, spun round, and quivered with the current. I felt those movements as little shocks in the already rigid muscles of my arms.

I don't recall the impetus to yank. I do remember the sharp hiss of line and water parting, and the clumsiness of a small and sudden weight, the weight of a fingerling flying through the air. I watched the spell of its sailing, helpless, horrified, as it skittered across some gravel and came to rest with a fleshy snap against a stone. I glanced at Nicola. Slapping at her legs, she looked dazed and harassed, but no more than before. She didn't seem to realize that this wasn't part of the normal routine.

"Was that a fish?"

I nodded.

"It was tiny."

"I know," I said. It was still on my line. I could see it, a black sliver gleaming between contours of dry stone, motionless. I didn't bother trying to keep my feet dry as I sloshed downstream to where it landed. This was clearly an emergency: a fish out of water, making no effort to get back to where it could breathe, while the woman I loved, already dubious, watched the proceedings from nearby.

"Is that supposed to happen?"

I dunked my hand and scooped the skinny slip of charcoal and sunset off the rock. The baby brook trout made no attempt to evade my grasp or struggle its slippery self free of my fingers. It regarded me, unfortunately, with the deadpan gaze and slack jaw of a dead fish. I cradled its body in the water, and petals of blood bloomed and dissolved around the gills, gills that didn't move unless I pushed water back and forth across them. I shook its head. I rolled the body right way up and swam it between two stones.

"What are you doing?"

Praying, imploring, ordering this baby to stay with us, I wanted to say.

"He seems a little dazed. I'm reviving him."

I heard some ferns rustle and snap. Nicola was coming over for a better look.

"He's fine," I said, urging some glibness into my voice. "Just hit his head a little." As if in reply, a spasm rippled through the little cadaver, jerking its head. "There, you see, he's coming around."

"He looks dead to me." She was getting close enough to lean over my shoulder, close enough to see my bloody mistake up close. One more stone and she would get the wrong idea, think I was into killing small things for sport and pleasure. What kind of sick beast would I seem to her then?

I opened my hand to the current. The fish rolled, white belly and scarlet fins streaking the surface, dead eyes just visible under the yawning lower jaw. It drifted away, gaining a bit of momentum, nudging around a stone, and slipping into the riffle below. I felt her hand reach my shoulder, steadying herself on the last rock.

"That poor fish was dead, wasn't it?"

I didn't want to face her. I pretended that to keep her balance I needed to stay as I was, watching that belly for signs of life. "Well, it could revive itself . . ." The belly had paused against a branch. It hung there like a candy-bar wrapper. Somehow this lack of motion made things final. "But it doesn't look good. Yeah, I think it's probably kicked the bucket, unfortunately."

"You're just going to let it float away? You're not going to eat it or something?"

I wished I had never taken Nicola fishing, had never found this place, never insisted on fishing unless the locale was perfect, as I'd envisioned it.

"It's too small to eat."

I turned to look at her. She kept her balance, her hair brushing my shoulder. I could smell the fish slime on my hands, and the coconut of her sunscreen. She looked mortified by what I'd done, by what I'd revealed about myself.

"I mean, I know it's a waste, but something will eat it. It doesn't normally happen like this."

She didn't say anything.

"That's why I like fly-fishing, because you don't kill the fish. You let them all go."

"It's horrible," she said, and backed away into the ferns.

The body of the dead smolt is still floating along the bank when I return. I've forgotten about it. I rub the back of my neck and climb the trail until it's out of sight, hoping that someone else will come when it gets dark and make a meal of it. I hope it will be gone by morning.

The Road Warrior

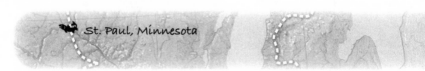

St. Paul, Minnesota

Back in Kenton I stop at a pay phone to call my friend John. It's after seven, and I'm beginning to realize I've got a lot of ground to cover. In fact, I had been thinking I would be in St. Paul around seven. The U.P. is huge. I tell him I won't make dinner—I won't be in until late, I don't know how late, but late, unfortunately. I ask if it might be better if I camped somewhere in northern Minnesota and showed up tomorrow morning. He and his wife have a five-month-old baby, and I don't want to wake her up. Sleep, I imagine, is probably in short supply in that house. But he says don't worry about it, she's sleeping through the night now, a heavy sleeper. They'll leave the key under the pot on the stairs outside the porch. I can come in and find my way upstairs to the bedroom, and they'll see me in the morning.

It gets dark, and I'm still in Michigan, outside the Porcupine Mountains. It's nearly ten when I hit Superior, Wisconsin, and pull over for gas. The deep-sea darkness of the lake makes the white lights over the pumps seem lonely, stars in the void. Mayflies have gathered around the lights, leaving the shucks of their dun stage glued to the once gleaming, now sparrow-turd-spattered, cobweb-coated, moth-wing-dusted metal posts. They're plump and brown, possibly the remnants of the Hex hatch that sweeps over some of these towns like a lake-effect blizzard. It's a scenario out of Hitchcock, with the roads slick with crushed bodies and the locals sweeping mounds of dead bugs off their cars in the morning with the brushy end of an ice scraper. After the tiny blue-winged olives I've encountered, these look like birds. One can only imagine the danger if these mayflies had mouths that bit or an appetite to feed.

I reach the sprinkled lights of Duluth around midnight. It's the edge of the lake and the start of the fast-lane highway. I can barely keep my eyes open. I set the speed at seventy-five and roll down the window for the air and the noise. It's not enough; I'm drifting with my eyeballs wide open and staring. White-line fever. I've got to sing. I doubt a more plaintive and hoarse version of Neil Young's "Out on the Freeway" has ever been voiced. I sing snatches of whatever I can remember, churning them up from my junior-high unconscious, even songs I hated, like this Journey number whose title I can't recall. "He took the midnight train going anywhere . . . Nah, nah, naah, nananana . . . Some are gonna sing the blues . . ." Lyrics like these keep me appalled and awake.

At 2 AM I arrive on the deserted streets of St. Paul. The storefronts are all dark, reflecting the urban glow of the streetlights, and I catch glimpses of my own passage there, flowing across them like a specter. I park the truck outside John and Andi's house on a quiet, leafy street.

The porch light is on, and the crickets are singing in the yard; a faint breeze jingles a wind chime. My very pores are jubilant, so coddled, so nurtured by the balm of a suburban night that I find myself sighing, my heart slowing down, all my limbs slackening with relief as I sit there. I can smell the perfume of cottage roses lingering by the front steps, and freshly mown, rain-infused grass. Only my fatigued brain is uneasy with the juxtaposition of where I am and where I've been. I feel like a stray dog out on the curb, and I have to force myself to intrude upon the scene with the pinging light of the open truck door. I stuff all my valuables into a bag and lift the geranium pot for the key.

Inside, the unavoidable ruckus of my steps brings me to a halt. Gunshots, ship masts splintering in a gale, great pines toppling under the saw: the floor boards make a drama of my every footfall. I've got to get across the living room to the stairs, and I'm certain I'm going to wake the baby before I get there. What a way to greet your old friends, I think. Like a burglar caught in the living room. While I stand still, the hush of the sleeping house, the sleeping neighborhood, the slumbering city, descends in a cloud of silence. But I'm going to make noise; I don't have a choice. I creep as quietly as I can up to the guest room, past the nursery where Astrid lies sleeping. The door is ajar, probably so her parents can hear her. As I pass, on tiptoe, the sound of her stirring, a kicked coverlet, a gurgle, escapes the door. I hold my breath and listen.

In the guest room, a whirring fan blows the calm of the night through the window screen. I'm as tense now as a treed cat. I consider the renewed drama of locating the bathroom for a tooth brushing, reject the idea, and instead take a glug from my water bottle, swish it around, and call it good. Tartar control will have to wait until morning. They've pulled out the futon for me. I find myself reading the spines of the books shelved along the wall. They're mostly titles I don't recognize, but I have no inclination to lift my arm out from under the sheet and pull one down. My body dissolves, a warm weight luxuriating in the clasp of pillow and comforter. It takes longer to lull my mind.

The bookshelf and the futon are relics of the days when John and I shared a converted attic after we graduated from college in St. Paul. We both worked as waiters in a nearby restaurant, and many nights I would get home, kick off my black shoes, and throw myself on my bed, still dressed in my stale-bread-crumbed, *au jus*–smeared, black-and-white false tuxedo. I would disgorge my bundle of tip dollars from my pocket and begin counting, while John lounged on this same futon across the room, both of us trying to figure out where to go and what to do with our lives while the late-night jazz show murmured on the radio. I often felt like I do now, dead in the body, wired of mind, and I would confess the agonies of my long-distance romance with Nicola, curse the manager who refused to cut me when my section emptied out, make a raunchy joke, shoot a rubber band across the room.

It became a bachelor routine, until one night he said he and Andi were thinking of getting married. What did I think? We were both just about asleep; the lights were off, a night like this one had settled over us. Don't do it, I said. You're too young. You got plenty of wild living to do. Don't rush into anything you might regret. I couldn't see his response, but I could sense the resistance, righteous resistance to this whole notion of sowing wild oats, and I was too tired to rephrase. Our last words lingered in the ambiguous truce that finally blurs into an agreement to sleep.

I think I might have said something different if I'd been thinking about it more clearly—something more sensitive, that had less to do with my own terror at the future. In fact, I recall waking up the next day feeling vaguely regretful, a feeling I chose to disregard. I went to work and hoped to forget about it, and a couple weeks after our talk, they announced their engagement. John told me when they got back from a weekend away. It was early in the evening, just after we had scrounged a meal from our separate shelves in the fridge. I had a bowl of cornflakes splashed with the last of my milk. He had something more elaborate, a salad of boiled potatoes and cherry tomatoes that involved actual culinary preparation. We each retired to our beds again, since we had no room for a couch, or even a stuffed chair. "That's great! Congratulations!" I said, trying too hard. He said thank you. I went back to slurping my cereal. A few months later, we both left St. Paul, and those postgraduation days were over.

He's gone when I wake up, meeting friends for coffee down on Grand Avenue. I try to sleep some more, but it's too late; I can't force myself unconscious. I feel jetlagged, like I've flown across the Atlantic. I take a shower. I shave. I put on clean clothes. I brush my crusty teeth, vigorously. While I'm dressing I hear the porch door open. I tromp downstairs, realizing it's been more than five years since I've seen either of them.

They look good. I recognize them. I get scared when I meet people after a long time that they'll be unrecognizable, ballooned or bald or grizzled, a reflection of my own anxiety at the subtle marks of deterioration in the mirror. They look healthy and rested, cheerful, content. Astrid is stuffing her wet fingers into a smile. I lean down and wave my fingers hello.

"Welcome back!" John says, and we embrace all around and pull chairs out from the dining room table to talk. I ask if they heard me last night. They say they slept soundly. Andi bounces Astrid on her shoulder, and then passes her to John. He taps her back.

"Burping," he says. She can't keep her eyes off my strange face. It makes me smile.

Time has passed since those days in our garret. I feel it most clearly in the way we talk, the way we hit the big themes instead of the details. I wouldn't ask John how work went yesterday, or what he was doing next weekend. The crummy and confusing but nonetheless intimate details of daily life—that's gone, and we're both happier now. I ask if he likes his job. "Not really," he says. He works in public relations, and there isn't much to say, except that it pays better than journalism. He's hoping to cut down to four days a week, spend more time with Astrid, maybe do some freelance writing projects.

What I really want to ask about is having a baby. I haven't told them about the IVF. We haven't told our friends. The news has had a discombobulating effect on our parents. The difficulty in conceiving has set us apart from the legions of couples who go through the normal rituals. They are speaking one language—the language of development and diet and stroller—and we are speaking another, the language of the childless, the secret lingo of IVF. I feel it most when I meet a friend's child for the first time: this is us, they seem to say to me, this the ultimate expression of who we are now.

John wipes some white curds and saliva from Astrid's chin. I feel a little squeamish. "See what you're missing, Jimbo," he says. Astrid keeps smiling at me. Definitely a mixed bag.

"Yes, and diapers too," I say, thinking about how I'd handle it all. "Oh boy."

I ask them what it's like to be, you know, parents. Andi laughs. It sounds weird, using that word, *parents,* with people you knew best in college, a time when you *had* parents, potentially embarrassing parents, but with any luck you wouldn't *be* parents for a long time.

"The first couple months were hard," John says. "Everyone tells you that, and it's all true. You just survive. Getting up every hour. Never getting enough sleep. Worrying about everything. It's all new. But we've got it down now."

"That's good," I say, "You know, getting into a routine. I thought for sure I'd wake her up last night."

"We're lucky. She's a really good baby. She doesn't cry and fuss."

"Yeah, she's really sweet," I say. It's nice when a baby smiles; adoration is impossible to refuse. Maybe I could deal with a baby like Astrid. But what if I spawned the other, bawling kind? I've had babies, including my own brother, burst into fearful tears at the towering sight of me. Astrid smiles. I smile back. This is much better.

"Have you and Nicola thought about it?" Andi asks.

"Well," I say, and sit back with a startled and jolly harumph. I knew this was coming. Why is it that in moments of fear and indecision, I wind up in St. Paul? I don't want to pin myself down. I'm not making any promises. I'm undecided.

"Yes, we've thought about it. We're considering it, for some time soon. But I'm not sure when. I mean, I'm sure we will but not right now. But soon. Relatively."

They nod, that astute journalistic move. I'm dealing with two adept interviewers here. I feel compelled to fill the pause. "That biological clock keeps on ticking, keeps on getting louder, getting faster. Got to make a move soon. But, but, need to get our lives in a more stable situation, if you know what I mean. Like what you've got here . . . A stable situation . . . responsibility . . . comfort level." I sound like a politician starting to sweat. I've got to escape this talk. "Yeah," I say, "so, we're definitely considering it, or planning on it, in the future. But what about today? Did you guys have plans for today?"

We spend the day walking around town. The city is much more prosperous and cosmopolitan than I recall, bursting with sidewalk cafes and art galleries and couples dashing around with boutique shopping bags. I find myself wondering where these people go, how this public effervescence survives, during those winter months when even the buildings seem to shudder. I remember trudging up these streets to work in the morning past rows of cars that would not start, their hoods up like opened tombs. I stepped through the plumes of exhaust from idling tow trucks, heard the squelch of their tires as they rolled over snow as dry as sand to the next vehicle. Eighty below, wind-chill; thirty below, actual temperature; and my eyelashes were sticky with frozen tears, the scarf over my mouth a chunk of frost. That's probably why everybody is so elated, I tell myself. *Winter is gone! Summer is here! Get outside, run around! Wear little clothing! Exult!* We don't get that emotional thaw in California.

As we walk, the newspaper-bin headlines catch my eye. Were it something colorful about the ex-wrestler, now governor, I would have ignored it. If it were the latest developments in the Middle East peace talks, or some local tragedy, I would have glanced and passed on, unfazed. I'm not in the habit of reading the front page of newspapers through Plexiglas as the "Don't Walk" light flashes. But the bold captions sink in and start working. I read a bit as we wait for the walk signal at a corner, then read some more when we pass another set of bins at the next corner. Finally I stop and crouch down. The more I read, the worse it gets.

"Wildfires Scorch Western States." "Worst Fires in 100 Years, Officials Predict." "Huge Blazes Burn Thousands of Acres across Montana, Idaho." "Governor Declares State of Emergency." It's not the first I've heard of the fires, but it's the first time I've paid them much attention. I lived in Montana long enough to learn that there are always fires burning somewhere in the summertime—fighting them provided a reasonably reliable income for several of my friends. Lightning struck, the blaze commenced in some backcountry grove, the helicopters swooped in along with the troops in yellow shirts, and nobody in Missoula knew any different.

This year's fires got minimal coverage back in Massachusetts. An occasional skinny news item, picked up off the wires, cropped, and buried among the ads on page three—that's what I'd seen back there. Thousands of acres were burning, the stories said, and I said, "So what? Thousands of acres always burn, don't they?" Nothing I read suggested anything out of the ordinary.

Now, on the verge of the long trip back across the Dakotas to Big Sky country, I start to get nervous. When we get home, while we wait for a delivery of Thai food, I get on the Internet and pull up the Web site for the *Missoulian*. Things don't look good in downtown Missoula, where the current weather conditions are "hot, dry, windy and blazing." It's 7:30 in the evening there, and it's eighty-eight degrees. Eighty-eight degrees, and nearly dark! If it had said that six inches of snow had fallen, I wouldn't have been a bit surprised—just raising a tomato to maturity is a tricky business there. But blazing nocturnal heat? I rub the dismay out of my neck and try to imagine an Arizona sunset scorching the hide of Mount Sentinel. The Bitterroot Valley has been evacuated. A big fire is burning near Salmon, Idaho. Another is spreading north of Helena, Montana. The hills near Townsend are ablaze. Smaller fires are burning across both states. I shut down the computer.

I had been planning to drive down the Bitterroot and fish the Salmon River near the town of Salmon. I've always wanted to hike down the Middle Fork into the River of No Return Wilderness, set up camp, and fish for a few days. It's a river of regrets, a river I should have gotten to know when I lived at the other end of the valley. I swam in the hot springs on the bluffs above the river, ate breakfast with the cowboys in a downtown diner, but I never got around to fishing, and before I knew it I was living thousands of miles away with that unrequited river on my mind. Now I've hauled my backpack halfway across the country, and it looks like I won't be using it.

"Maybe you should spend more time fishing in the Midwest," John says. We've been trying to remember this card game we used to play on dark January nights when we were bored. It involved turning over a card while shouting "Spit!" in unison, followed by a frenzied war of slapping cards down on different piles. We used to play with cards that had a different topless cowgirl on each one, a deck that John claimed Andi bought him as a joke in the Black Hills. Neither of us can remember how the game goes; all I can remember is that it was about who got there first, that and the friction of cards clenched between fingers and the sound of our fists pounding the table. We try it, but what seemed like vindictive fun then just seems pointless now.

"It seems like you're giving the Midwest short shrift," he says. He's dealing out hands for a game of hearts, another game I hardly recall. I know, I say, there's the Root River, and the Kinnickinnic, and the Rush River over in Wisconsin. I should fish them all.

"Don't forget the Whitewater River," John says, picking up his hand.

And the Whitewater, I say, all valid trout streams that deserve attention. I'm offering this as a qualification, not an endorsement, but when I reach the point where I say "but" and list my reasons for skipping these perfectly respectable waters, I stop myself. That fly-shop owner in Baldwin would get what I mean in a flash. But John doesn't fish. I don't want to impugn the pride of the upper Midwest.

"But what?" John says.

I pretend to be engrossed in my hand, sorting out a potential run of clubs while considering my options. How can I explain that I can't be logical about all this? How can I describe the pent-up, irrational longing for the glorious and fabled waters of the West? The Kinnickinnic is a fine stream, but it isn't the Blackfoot. I fish the Blackfoot in my dreams.

"You're right," I say, looking up from my hand. "I need to spend at least one day fishing here."

He gets up and lopes barefoot into the other room, slaps magazines around, hisses, "I see what you're doing, don't cheat!" from around the corner, while I take the last slurps of my beer. The inclination to look at his cards never crossed my mind; I realize only after he warns me that in another era I would have stacked the deck in his absence as a provocative matter of course.

He returns with the DeLorme map of Minnesota open to the southern quadrant, where the blue lines of the Whitewater and the Root curl through the white space of what must be cornfields.

"This might help you decide. I still think you're giving the Midwest the shaft. Why don't you spend three or four days down here?" He fingers an arc across the map.

I should; I know I should, I say. I want to fish down there. But I need to get along. I need to get out to Montana. I know I'm probably going to regret leaving Minnesota too soon, but I just have to keep going.

Regrets to the Midwest

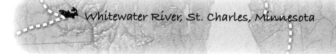

Whitewater River, St. Charles, Minnesota

I should spend more time here, I think, as I get out of the truck and step down into a patch of mint and sunflowers. Yellow warblers are cackling and chasing one another in the willows that line the bank. A common yellowthroat pops up on a branch, inspects me, and darts back into the foliage, singing "Whitchitee, whitchitee, whitchitee." I could spend a lazy afternoon in this glade, just watching the birds and listening to the music of water over stones and wind through leaves. It's cool, the kind of day where you put on shorts in the morning and your legs erupt in goose bumps when you get outside. Storm clouds are massing over the bluffs like a distant range of troubled mountains. The Whitewater shines like a mirror in their silver light. The light won't last; I know the signs from Shinhopple. Already a gust, the gasp of a thunderhead, blows down and tousles the willow leaves.

I said good-bye to John and Andi after a quick bowl of cereal in the kitchen. I said good-bye to Astrid. It's hard to leave with the old bonds of friendship unrestored, and the tensions of the past still lurking, stale but uncowed. But what could I do about it? It was time to go fishing. I jogged over to the grocery store for some ice, told them we had a converted attic where they could stay if they ever felt like traveling out west, and we'd be happy to have them. They said maybe, some day, when Astrid got old enough to travel on a plane. They waved as I drove away.

The river is reassuringly cold when I step into the shallows and splash across to the other bank for casting room. I passed several glittering spring creeks on the way down to St. Charles, consoling myself that those golden flats are often just havens for schools of black-nosed dace. The Whitewater looks nothing like them. The bluffs, sometimes an abrupt wall of bare rock, sometimes a tumbledown face of sandstone and precarious trees, have caged the river in a narrow bed. The water spouts forth around bends, swells over and consumes a bank, but ultimately surrenders to the path of least resistance downstream. It's a dark and fertile river, its pools choked with the tendrils of aquatic weeds. The water looks high, earning its name, canopies of meadow grass swaying in the current along the banks. I can just imagine the frisky hoppers and foolish crickets making ill-considered leaps for the verge and coming down with a splash instead. Could they kick themselves ashore? I don't think so—just as the great whites prowl the Farallon sea-lion colonies, waiting for a frantic swimmer, here too the jaws must be waiting.

I start with the skunk, plopping it along the edge of the trailing grass and jerking it back to me so the rubber legs twitch. Of course, even an insect brain knows better than to swim away from shore and across the stream, and the trout know better too. Whatever lurks below those grasses stays put. I try drifting a nymph through the same water and come up with great gobs of snail-encrusted weed.

The weeds fold around my thighs as I wade upstream, and my steps churn up blooms of pale mud. At the head of the pool the river bends close to the road, close enough to demand a bank of chicken-wire-fastened rocks. The current rips through the curve and breaks against the piled stones in a surprisingly smooth display of speed. It must be waist deep, I think, as I edge around the side, and then, when I'm waist deep and still looking for the bottom, chin deep. I'm certain there must be trout. I can almost feel myself the absolute rapture of being a trout along that bank. There are eddies and undulations all along the riprap, small whirlpools and pockets in which to hold without effort. I tie on another lead-bellied nymph, picturing its course along the chicken wire and its end in the mouth of a fish.

The nymph follows the path I envisioned, except that no mouth intercedes. A small fish rises, tight against the rocks, right where I imagined a big trout to be. Another rises downstream. Then another, tight against the grass along the bank. An intermittent, maddening rise has begun.

I catch sight of a mayfly launching itself into the air, a tiny blue-winged olive, as ethereal as a snowflake that lands in your palm. I've got one of those in my fly box! Not quite so delicate, this algae-stained cream variant, but at least it's the right color and shape. I fish it through the run, but it seems the rising fish are downstream now, in the flat that I've just slogged through to get here.

When you look down a long stretch of water, the sporadic rises of a few fish can seem like a feeding frenzy, or at least that's what I find when I head downstream and discover long, empty stretches of water between rising fish and long pauses between the rises. A trout rises behind me, out of reach, where I had waited in vain for it to rise, holding my fly at the ready until I couldn't stand it anymore and shuffled away down the bank to the spot where another fish seemed to be rising repeatedly. Now the fish in front of me has disappeared, and the other fish is rising again. Upstream, it looks as if a school of piranhas has discovered a carcass at the bend; the current seems to writhe with fins and tails.

It's an optical illusion, I tell myself, a mirage. Don't go back up there. I waffle for a bit, watching, then turn away and keep fishing downstream. Where the pool eddies out I drift my now sunken and somewhat despondent mayfly. There's another long flat downstream, but before the river slows, it bounces over a swath of gravel and small stones. It's the kind of shallow stretch that, from a trout's perspective, is both dangerous in its lack of cover and efficient in its funneling of food. The feeding lanes here will be empty on a sunny afternoon, but during a hatch, even a feeble hatch, who knows what might move up from the sluggish depths to feed?

I watch a shadow—neither the silhouette of a willow branch nor the shade of underwater stones—sway over the background. It crosses paths with the end of my tippet, and I raise the rod tip just at the moment when I sense, without observing any sign, that the mouth must have reached my fly.

I'm a bit late. I battle a ten-inch brown that flips head over tail when it feels the hook and then grinds itself free against the gravel. I worry that may be it; the others may have been scared off. But the next cast yields another shadow, and I set the hook more firmly this time. The brown sweeps downstream, searching for obstacles. There's nothing substantial to find, and after a futile attempt to reach the deeper water, it surrenders to my hand with a begrudging splash.

Its colors are dazzling. Flecks of fool's gold glitter along its flanks in unusual profusion, and the nubbin of a fin above the tail is bright crimson. I wonder if it's the vivid mark of a unique Whitewater population, or whether it's the sign of European ancestry. In most American waters, the physical traits that distinguished Scottish browns from their German cousins have been erased as the two subspecies mingled their genes over time. Yet these trout don't look anything like the browns I caught in Wendell, whose sides were a wash of silver speckled with carmine and black. Of course, the difference could just be the reflection of a midwestern menu, or the expression of different minerals dissolved in the water and incorporated into the pigments of the skin.

I don't know the cause of their coloration, but I do know they are wild fish. The river is stocked with ten- to twelve-inch rainbows, to provide frying-pan fodder for the campgrounds downstream. The browns sustain themselves, despite the rigorous Minnesota winters, which have a chilling effect on trout eggs. The water gets so frigid in these parts that eggs nestled in the bottom gravel of nearby rivers like the Root die of cold.

I hook two more browns before I reach the end of the riffle, both about ten inches long. Nothing is rising in the pool. I look at my watch and find I am, not surprisingly, behind schedule again. It's after one o'clock, and I've got a long day's drive to eastern Montana ahead of me. I'm torn; I'd like to stay and fish the evening rise here. I have the feeling that a larger, wary predator is lying motionless in a cavern of weeds downstream, awaiting my departure and the advent of darkness so it can emerge. Right about sundown it will cruise into these shallows, the smaller trout sliding downstream in deference, and begin to rise. I could be standing right here, ready, when it makes its move. I could fish the

Root, too. The tricos are reported to be abundant down there. I could stay in the campground, fish them both, and leave tomorrow afternoon. Wild fish, profuse hatches, uncrowded water—why would I leave this place?

It's the grumbling sky that decides for me. The thunder is distant, but it heralds an evening of lightning bolts and driving rain, followed by a night of poor sleep in the hothouse confines of the truck. Besides, Montana is beckoning, with all the wild trout in the world, all the riffles and runs and mayflies and stoneflies and cutthroats and browns, brook trout and bull trout, whitefish and grayling one could ask for. Why risk rain when I can be there tomorrow? The Root will have to wait for another trip. I get out of my waders, turn the truck around, and head back to the interstate.

Firestorm on the Horizon

Bighorn River, Fort Smith, Montana

An hour's worth of highway passes, and I check my progress on the atlas while picking the tomato and lettuce scraps of a cold-cut combo out of my lap. I rub the mayo into my jeans so it won't show and hold the map up to the wheel for a minute where I can get a good look at it. I'm forced to acknowledge another miscalculation. I'd been counting on the fact that the state is taller than it is broad, but I've apparently lost my sense of scale and distance again. This is the Midwest, not Rhode Island, and I don't appear to have made any progress at all; I'm still in the southeast corner of the state. It's clear that there will be miles and miles of corn to cross before I reach South Dakota.

There are other wayfaring strangers out on the highway, a veritable horde of them. The big motorcycle rally is underway in Sturgis, South Dakota, and various posses of long-haired, scar-faced, leather-clad hostiles are roaring across the plains to a rendezvous with Malcolm Forbes–style bankers taking a walk on the wild side in their own exquisite costumes. I make a point of breaking up the monotony of the crops with speculations about the meaning of their tattoos, easing my eye along their sunburnt arms as they pull alongside the truck, figuring my sunglasses will obscure the movement of my eyes.

A hazy and unpleasant memory comes back to me. When I worked in Yellowstone for the Park Service, the law enforcement ranger who showed me around was obsessed with the hidden significance of biker tattoos. "They've got a special tattoo language they use," he told me, as we cruised around Mammoth Hot Springs trying to break up an RV traffic jam that had formed around some grazing elk. Our efforts that afternoon had already involved a number of plaintive requests over the cruiser's PA system, something benign like, "Good afternoon. Park ranger. This is a federal highway. Please return to your vehicle," which the drivers ignored completely.

For an hour we sat watching the line grow longer as seniors abandoned their vehicles and scampered past us, fiddling with the zoom on their video cameras. The elk didn't seem to mind, but I did. I wanted to grab the mike and scream: "Freeze! You're all under arrest for harassing wildlife and creating a nuisance. Throw your cameras on the ground and get your hands behind your backs!" Another violent desire, carefully suppressed, was to get out of the car, pick up a nice round stone, and send the elk galloping into the hills with a well-aimed throw. It wasn't worth the risk; in my two weeks of employment I'd already learned that a pissed-off tourist was far worse than a pissed-off buffalo.

The tattoos were a welcome diversion. I forced myself to concentrate on these emblems of mayhem.

"They've got a special symbol," the ranger told me, "a skull with some lettering. That means they've killed a law enforcement officer. We got a special bulletin about this with Sturgis coming up, and I read all about it."

I had yet to see a biker come into the visitor center. In fact, I hadn't seen any bikers on the roads at all, but we were on the alert for their arrival.

"They've got all kinds of initiation rites, and there's marks for each of them. They've got handlebars rigged up with guns that fire from either end, ways to conceal knives and shooting stars that shoot out when you pull them over. You push a button and out pops the blade. You should see this report. Gets you thinking."

It got me thinking, even though I never did see a biker that summer.

Now is my chance. Most of what I observe is a blur of skin and calligraphy before some chopper leaves me in the dust, but I catch glimpses of the usual fare—a naked, red-maned lady, fanged serpents and fuming dragons, frilly hearts with names like Sheila scrolled inside, even elaborate, multicolored tableaux of gods and goddesses entwined around elbows and biceps. There are, as one might expect, plenty of skulls and grim reapers and bat-winged death masks.

I can't remember what the special cop-killer lettering was, but I catch sight of a dagger above one guy's wrist, which rings a bell; the ranger said something about a knife being a symbol of murder, with the number next to it indicating how many the tattoo-bearer had committed. I speed up to stay abreast and see if I can spy any numbers on the back of his hand.

He isn't too impressive, as bikers go; he's clad from head to toe in a red leather jumpsuit that accentuates the curves of his belly, making him look like a biker Santa Claus, and his steed isn't even a Harley—it's a BMW. His hand is free of numbers, and when I look again I find that what I thought was a dagger is in fact some kind of greenish stain, possibly some anti-freeze that a restroom faucet missed.

I'm relieved to find that I am not sharing this stretch of road with a homicidal rider, and I'm also instantly bored with his company. My attention wanders to another source of interest and speculation, the women who straddle these bikes, clinging to the cowhide backs of the riders like baby koalas in helmets. This guy's lady is clad in a matching red suit, and there's something in her prim, windblown grimace that suggests this wasn't her idea of a vacation. But there are other women out there too, some with long blond hair swirling under a helmet smaller than a yarmulke, black-leather thighs clenched around the buttocks of some bristle-mugged warthog. The men appear to be grinning as they pass me, but that might just be the force of the wind blowing their jowls back. I try to justify my speculations into the nature of these beauty-and-the-beast relationships by calling them a sociological inquiry, but of course I'm really wondering what the heck these women are doing with these guys. I have to admit I'm a little envious, plodding along in my suddenly dull, cluttered cubbyhole of a truck while they're out there getting whipped by the romantic west winds.

There's obviously some virile force of attraction here between barbarian, babe, and steed, between centaur and maiden, that is as old as the Black Hills themselves. It's easy enough to envision these figures clad in buckskin, nosing a pinto over the same range. But the women who surprise me into staring are the ones who ride alone. Why adorn some rider's back when you can thunder past on your own muscle machine? My favorites roar past astride their own length of chrome and power, sending uneasy reverberations through the car door and up my spine as I gawk at buzz-cut hair and tinted goggles and frayed sweatshirts with the sleeves chopped off at the shoulder to reveal an array of insignia. No signs of make-up, no peering over somebody's protective shoulder, not a glance in my superfluous direction. These women ignore me completely.

I hit Sioux Falls, South Dakota, at dusk amidst a phalanx of Harley choppers, and we descend on the strip of red lights and fast-food joints like Marlon Brando and his bunch in *The Wild Ones,* only to find our thunder stolen. The streets are already clogged with rival gangs, and leather is the norm. In Burger King, I stand in line and listen to a young black man chat up what looks like a band of Viking pillagers—blond, belted around the waist with chains, and burning a short fuse over the wait for their burgers.

"You guys should be eating in Sturgis," the black guy says, although I haven't seen any sign that these guys are interested in idle, friendly chatter. "I go there myself." They nod and examine the value-meal options. Okay, don't push it, let it be, I want to tell him, that's enough; examine the "Supersize It!" possibilities or the linoleum floor pattern or the ghastly and inoffensive floral portrait, but the guy continues, goes even further and asks a question that demands a reply.

"This your first year?"

The response might be termed a grunt, an ambiguous rumble in the throat from someone in the group, but this doesn't stop the questioner; he keeps going to fill the space where their response should be, his voice rising with what might be his own hysteria or the reflection of my own.

"It's getting bigger, I hear. I'm from Nebraska, myself. Yeah, it's a good place, down near Lincoln. Lot like here. I like it out here." Will he ask where they are from? Force an actual word from them? He's singled out the one whose flowing gold mane and handlebar mustache make him look like Custer at Little Bighorn, a collector of scalps. His eyes are bloodshot, and he's working a wad of snuff between his cheek and gum. He doesn't say anything, but the way he leans back into the ketchup and mustard dispensers is more than noncommittal. It says get away from me.

"Yeah, you guys must like it out here. I like it out here too." There's an awkward pause as the black guy reconsiders this conversation. Then everybody looks up at the menu.

I thank God when the teenager in the headset hands out the food bags. I don't need any more suspense. I take my bag out to the truck, tear open the little ketchup packets, spread the fries out, and get back on the road, licking from my fingers before I have to shift gears. There are thousands of bikes on the highway, all the way to Sturgis and beyond. I pass their encampment, a swirling of wheels, campfires, and noise spread out beneath the hills like a medieval army out on the crusades.

At least I'm entering the mountain time zone, I tell myself, and gaining an hour on the night. But I'm still exhausted, catching myself on the nod. The radio's no help; I can't get anything more than a burble above the roar of static. I pull over in Wyoming, driving up into the sagebrush waste and stopping at a cattle gate. I turn off the truck and sit in the dark, listening to the rise and fall of distant vehicles, watching the glow of their beams grow and subside on the dashboard. It's spooky to sit on the side of the road, in the open, without a tree to hide you. I rest my eyes, but I can't fall asleep.

I reach the Montana border at two in the morning, mountain time, and head north into the dry mountain ranges that surround the Crow Reservation. The sky glitters with stars, and the road is empty, all the way to the square of street lights and cottonwoods that mark the entrance to the reservation. At three I reach the campground at Fort Smith, on a bluff beside the Yellowtail Dam. I can hear the river churning through the turbines and erupting below in a violent wash, the waves just visible under the fluorescent lights of the causeway. Electricity hums through the high-voltage wires overhead. I peer down through the chain-link fence, into a gauzy void of spume, my eye drawn to that point where the concrete dissolves into darkness.

As I wait for my eyes to adjust, the mist gathers on my cheeks and collects on my tongue. It tastes of the reservoir depths, of clams and soft brown muck. I wait for a minute or two, thinking about the grand artifice of it all. Generally speaking, I hate the thought of dams. I hate the idea of taming rivers, which seems to make me something of a hypocrite, because I sure appreciate what a bottom-release dam does to the fishing downstream. Without the dam there would be great catfish and sturgeon fishing here, perhaps, but no trout fishing, because it's this concrete wall that makes the water cold enough for trout to thrive, that collects nutrients at the base of the dam and then siphons them away to feed the underwater jungle downstream. The plants feed the insects, and the insects feed the trout, and the trout grow large and feed imaginations like mine.

In the windswept industrial park of a camping area, I get my first taste of the fires. The wind has shifted, and a sourness pervades the air, a charred bitterness that I inhale and immediately regret. These are the fumes of a cauldron that has boiled away whatever was green about summer and then simmered on, burning the metal. I look up at the sky, where the moon hangs like a rotting papaya, and watch as a poisonous wind rips through the cottonwoods along the levee, gathering grit and branches from the parking lot, headed my way without a drop of rain.

Before it gets to me I duck back inside the truck and decide it's too much trouble to make room in the back. It will be light soon. I push back the seat, lower it as far as it will go, and sleep as best I can through the gusts of wind that shake the truck.

Sleeping in the cab is like sleeping on a plane—it's great if you're short, but if you're tall, even an extra seat isn't enough to really slumber. I want to contort myself into a fetal position, and the cab wasn't designed to allow it. The seat-belt buckle is nudging my kidney. My foot is pressed to the corner for maximum leg extension, and that's creating skeletal problems farther up. First one hip, then the other, goes dead. Near dawn the wind subsides, and I remain in a state of diminished awareness until eight.

Once the sun clears the bluffs, there's no shade in the parking lot, and it starts to get hot in the cab. The smell of me seems to attract shiny green flies that come on in when I crack the window for some fresh air. They may have mistaken me for the deceased; I certainly feel like I've opened my eyes on the other side. I force myself to get up. Exhuming my stale remains, I push open the truck door and slip my sandals over my toes. Then I clip-clop to the back and fish a yogurt out of the melted ice water. As I eat, I swear off all smoked foods forever—no more applewood smoked ham, no mesquite-flavored potato chips, no smoked mozzarella, no smoked salmon. I feel like a kippered snack, like a bacon rind, like I've been turned slowly in a smokehouse all night long, and the smoke shows no signs of abating. It's as if someone has taken an eraser to the hills, rubbed them out, and left the cottonwoods sketched in pencil on a smudged white page. I can stare right at the sun without squinting, as if I were witnessing an eclipse. It could be that the fires are coming my way; the air feels hot enough on my face. But I'm too tired to be bewildered by such possibilities—I came to fish, and that's what I get ready to do.

At the fly shop in Fort Smith, a young woman leans an elbow against the counter, doling out advice with surprising patience to some desperate angler over the phone. I notice she's wearing a baseball cap with the logo of a shop I frequented in Missoula, the brim squeezed into a curve over her pretty, summer-tanned face. She has nice white teeth, which reminds me that, in my rush to get here, I haven't brushed mine in a while. I find myself wishing I had at least spit-combed my hair in the rearview mirror. Deprived of sleep, wrapped in rumpled clothes, and smelling like bacon, I'm not looking my best. I wonder if Nicola would even recognize the shambling mound of maleness I have become.

Christ almighty! You look like a pile of roadkill! It's Montana Slim, right on cue, offering up his best. It doesn't matter what I look like, I tell myself. *Smell like it too!*

When she's finished delivering the bad news to the other unfortunate fisherman, the woman asks where I plan to fish. I tell her I'm heading west to the Bighole, the Clark Fork, the Blackfoot, maybe the Yellowstone streams. I'm headed to Missoula, I say.

She gives me a slightly incredulous look, as if to say, "What rock did you crawl out from under?" I can feel my strutting cowboy self turning red, then beating a bandy-legged retreat. In fact, I can feel him looking for a rock to crawl under, leaving the unkempt rube to scratch his head and try to explain things.

"I'm from Missoula," she says. "Things are pretty bad down there. There's fires burning everywhere. The Clark Fork's bad. So's Rock Creek. The highway into the Bitterroot is closed, last I heard, and the river's unfishable. Maybe you should reconsider your plans."

Maybe you should reconsider your plans. It sounds like she's used this carefully constructed phrase a lot lately. It has that veneer of euphemistic calm about it, a gentle way of saying that all hell is breaking loose west of here and if you're smart you'll cut your losses, which is exactly what I don't want to hear. I'm as stubborn as an RV bound for Old Faithful: no road block, no threatening inferno, not even a row of flaming lodgepole tumbling onto the highway—nothing will make this dream die.

"Well, geez," I say, "I've come a long way to fish here. Are you sure it's really that bad?"

She crinkles an eyebrow and exhales, exasperated. Clearly I'm not getting it. "It's terrible. It's worse than you can believe," she says. "I'd stay out of there if I were you."

"Well, geez," I say again, still refusing to get it. I plead with her. "It can't be like this everywhere. There must be somewhere I can fish. Isn't there anywhere?"

"Again, you may want to reconsider your plans. The Bighole is closed to fishing, and they're talking about closing others. They may already be closed. I know they were talking about closing the Boulder just yesterday. I know the Jefferson was closed."

So matter of factly, so tactfully disabused. The rivers are closed. It sinks in.

"Okay", I say, and "Oh well," and even "Shoot, that sucks." What else can I say? I've traveled over a thousand miles, slept in the cab of my truck, foregone bathing and nourishment, and now I need to reconsider my plans. I try not to look pitiful as I fill out the fishing-license form, and I'm out the door before I realize that I haven't asked what they're hitting here on the Bighorn.

I don't want to go back inside—I just head down to the river and get out my gear. I'm not expecting much. On my last Bighorn trip I set out to fish a run downstream and never made it past the schools of fish rising in the transparent shallows right along the bank. How could I pass them by? The trout rose languorously along the path, massaging the current with their fins, pecking a tidbit from the surface, and descending to bask in the sunlight again. They ignored my profferings the way diners at a royal banquet might disregard the lowliest scullion—I did not exist.

"You're wasting your time with them," one guy said to me as he clomped past in his waders. "They don't make flies small enough to catch those guys." Yet somehow, even though I was the only one bothering to fish for them, I couldn't just reel in and walk away; everyone else waded out into the swift water, tied on San Juan worms, and hoped the current would disguise their efforts.

The river is lower now, and I'm on the opposite shore, watching boat after boat unload, pack up, and set off. Every outfitter in the state seems to be here, and given the conditions elsewhere, who can blame them? As soon as the guide pushes off, the clients begin casting. They're fishing split-shot-laden nymphs with what looks like a big, fluffy fluorescent bobber fastened halfway up the leader. It's a clumsy arrangement; the indicator swirls through the air like a pompom and then lands with a splat behind the splash of the split shot. But it works. I watch as a client's bobber disappears and he rips the line from the surface with the sound of tearing cloth. The rod tip bends and pumps.

"That's a nice one," says the guide.

They drift past, and the next boat approaches with one beefy, grinning client already fast to a fish on one side of the boat and the guide barking at a teenager on the other side to "Raise up! Raise up! Use your trigger finger!"

The trout seems to have control of that situation: the reel is bouncing around in the boy's hands like a hot potato, cranking out line. I wonder for a moment if the rod might just take flight over the side, but the fish breaks free instead. "Use your trigger finger. Like this, see," the guide tells him, wiggling a finger. He rakes an oar to bring the boat around, so the father can get a hold on the tired rainbow splashing beside the gunwale. The advice continues, growing fainter as the boat glides downstream.

The guides are polite enough not to drift too close, and I appreciate that. It's hard enough to bear their passage when I am straining on tiptoe, the water a wobbly inch away from trickling over the top of my waders, just to approach a rise they can reach with a single dip of a paddle. It's even harder when the clients are catching fish, and I am catching nothing.

There's no need for them to come close; the river is heavenly from shore to shore. The channel is broad and deceptively smooth, its bottom a green wilderness of weedy grottoes. Slicks at the surface belie the speed of the current below; my legs are locked in a battle just to stay put, a battle I sometimes fear I'm close to losing, and the water is too cold to risk a plunge. I can feel the burn of it through waders and jeans, a numbness spreading through me where the current has robbed my thighs of warmth.

Water this cold is perfect for trout. They're rising erratically all around me, but always just out of reach, as if they're tempting me to stretch just a little farther, wade just another step deeper. The cold eventually gets the better of me. I've burned through my breakfast, and I'm dizzy with hunger as I reel in and wade back into the warm, late-morning air. I undo the bungee cord around my waist and push down the chilly waders. My pants are soaked with condensed sweat, and my fingers are frosty stumps that can barely grip the truck keys. I chomp my way through a dozen economy-brand pecan sandies, glug hot water from the bottle that's been steeping on the passenger's seat all morning as if I planned it, and take the measure of my desperation. I need to know what the clients are using, and the best way to find out is to break down and buy some flies.

I haven't bought a fly since I got my fly-tying set for Christmas. That was 1979. It's a matter of economy, of course; I lose so many flies that I'd be broke in a week if I had to buy them. But it's also a question of pride. The same voice that wants to swagger around Montana like a native would never even consider stooping to the level of buying flies in order to catch fish—he'd rather have his favorite fly rod snapped into slivers.

"Shut the hell up," I tell Montana Slim, having missed enough sleep and spoken so little to real people recently that telling an imaginary character to put a lid on it seems the most natural thing in the world.

I drive back over to the outfitter's, taking a moment first to dig out my hairbrush and tug the least-stubborn cowlicks out of my hair. A part is out of the question. I splash my face with hot water from the bottle, dry it on my sleeve, and head inside, determined this time to be a little more respectable and a lot more communicative.

There's a new face behind the counter, a sprightly woman with the sinewy brown forearms of a rock climber, her smile radiating good cheer. Clearly, she hasn't heard about the ninny who shuffled in this morning. I tell her I'm having a bit of trouble figuring out which flies to use. Then those begrudging words come out of my mouth.

"I want to buy some flies."

We approach the plastic cases, where the flies are arranged in mounds of fluffy abundance. She says the fishing has been great in the afternoon on PMDs—pale morning duns—emerging right at two thirty. She points, and I pick out a size-18 dun with a scarlet abdomen and a primrose thorax and plop it into a plastic cup. I'm amazed by the detail—I would never bother wrapping thread around the thorax to simulate body segments, or splitting the tail into two strands to imitate a mayfly's forked tail.

"That looks promising," I tell the woman.

Eye candy for fishermen, not fish, a familiar voice grumbles in reply. Fortunately, my guide can't hear him. She says people have been doing well on the nymphs in the morning, and then on emergers and dries in the afternoon. In the evening, she says, the caddis have been coming off, and the fishing has been sporadic but good. Her finger taps two more cases; I pick out a peacock-green caddis larva and an emerger whose wing sparkles like a gemstone.

"Antron caddis," she says. I nod. Never heard of it. I've been cloistered for twenty-three years in my own fly-tying world.

"Good luck!" she says, after I've paid. "Be out there right at two thirty. They've been coming off like clockwork!"

Some of her enthusiasm has rubbed off on me—I find myself tempted to whistle, and there's an almost merry spring in my step. "Now that wasn't so painful, was it?" I ask myself, opening the truck door. Montana Slim offers an unpacified grunt. *Cost you nearly ten bucks.* My inner cowboy is also a cheapskate. I tell him it's an investment. I've purposefully bought only one of each fly so I can sit down and tie replicas of each one. I don't intend to use the originals unless it's an absolute emergency.

I park in the shade under a cottonwood and tie my home-style imitations, then crawl into the cab and take a nap as the flies stroll with impunity over everything but my face. The sleep is a tonic—not for my bones, which would sob if they could, but for my suddenly optimistic mind. I dream about catching big fish on this very stretch of river, and wake with a shudder to find the sun has shifted toward the western horizon. Hours have passed. My watch says 2:25. I have exactly five minutes to strap on my gear and get into the river before the hatch starts.

Pale mayflies are riding the currents downstream as I wade out. Several disappear into rings; the trout are coming up, sporadically. I feel my way out on the sandbar, so I can cast into the slicks, and put on a Bighorn strike indicator with a knot a few feet up the leader. It's a chartreuse number, just like I saw the clients use. Then I tie on my version of a PMD nymph, weighted with two split shot to send it down. I cast it as best I can, which is to say a completely ungraceful hurling of mass into the air. I can hear the split shot whizzing over my head, and the puffball follows like a tethered bird. They splash down in tandem, not far from my boots, and the drift begins.

The rig may be clumsy, but it works. I heave my second cast into the vicinity of a rise just downstream, and when the bobber gets close it takes a sudden plunge and I raise my rod tip into the weight of a strong fish. It makes a great leap when it feels the hook, vaulting skyward and beating the air to stay aloft as if its tail were a wing. I hang on, spell-bound, as it leaps again, and again. In the end it comes to my hand without resistance, a sixteen-inch rainbow with the burly shoulders of a young and healthy fish.

I pinch the fly to avoid touching the trout's body and cradle it in the wake of my waders, admiring the constellations of black speckles near the tail, the precision of the jaws working oxygen over the gills. I'm reviving it, of course, but I'm also loath to let it go. A Bighorn trout in my hand happens seldom enough to inspire a moment of reverence. Only when it flexes its tail for a push do I lift out the barb and let it sink down.

Swarms of pale mayflies are billowing over the river now with every shift in the breeze, like snow squalls. Legions of jaunty duns ride the current past me into the riffles, but the trout don't seem to care. The woman in the fly shop told me that nymphs were the preferred method even during the hatch, and it seems that everyone in the boats is heeding this advice. But they're not catching anything at the bottom. Soon my eye is drawn to the water downstream, where the river pours over gravel bars and divides into a series of shallow runs. It looks like the familiar water of a much smaller river: riffles and runs, shallow enough to prospect, easy to wade, difficult to float. As I watch, considering my options, a rise trembles in a pocket near the shore, and then another. The water there can't be more than a couple feet deep; I can see the bottom, the gravel burnished by the afternoon sunlight.

When I get close, standing on a gravel bar in inches of water, I can see the shadows, and I can hardly catch my breath. I feel as if I've stumbled into a fantasy. Is there any fable greater than that I find before me, the spectacle of enormous fish rising so close that I can see the white flesh of their palates gleaming as they cleave the surface for dries?

My nerves are so strained I hardly dare to cast; I follow one pale dun down into the waiting jaws, then another, before I even inspect my fly box. I tie on one of my pale morning duns, sight the path for a cast, and hesitate, caught by the vision of fish scattering everywhere as my fly strikes the surface. I don't dare take a back cast. I raise my rod tip slowly until I'm poised for motion like a skier at the top of a run. Everything will unfold from here; there's nothing to do but bring the tip down with the slightest twitch I can muster.

With a delicate flick of my wrist, the line curls through the air. My fly lands with a barely perceptible flip. I watch the current make sense of the coiled leader; it straightens and the fly begins its descent. I've stopped breathing.

There comes a point where I should see the shadow rise, where I'm watching with the electric gaze of a cat about to pounce on a bird, where if I had a tail it would be whisking the ground. My fly reaches that point, floats over it, and drags across to the shore. The fish gulps down another natural. I slump, exhale, and pull in the slack.

Before I can cast again, the fish rises twice, and another begins just below in the same pool. They've got me muttering questions and answers to myself, an internal debate about patterns and drifts.

Listen, skinny puppy, that fly's too big.

"No, it's all right. It's not that."

Now they're taking emergers.

"No they're not. Watch. There goes another dun right there."

Then you've got drag. You're dragging, boy!

Drag is the only thing that makes sense; the problem is trying to do anything about it. I can't get any closer without stepping on the fish, and I can't change the angle without wading in next to them. The only option seems to be extending my arm out over the current to reduce the length of line, and hoping my shadow doesn't spook the fish.

Again I hesitate, watching the currents, trying to learn which one might be causing the trouble. The riffle closest to me breaks around a small stone, and the mixture of turbulence and back eddy might be the source of the problem. It's nothing major, but if I can keep my line out of there, it might make the difference. I make another tremulous roll cast, and this time I lean out behind it. The fly drifts down with just the slightest suggestion of improvement, as if its tether now is gossamer instead of monofilament.

The shadow tilts and grows. The water parts, and the white-fleshed craw opens wide around my fly. I respond with a heroic backward slash of my outstretched arm and a cry of triumph.

The line snaps instantly.

I catch a glimpse of crimson spots and golden sides as the fish thrashes around the pool with shock and fury. It's a brown, at least twenty inches long. I watch it take off downstream. I'm shuddering with shock myself, and muttering again.

Goddamn it! I told you it was the drag! Don't go jerkin' his head off like you're lassoing a steer—use your trigger finger! Montana Slim, witness to all my western inadequacies.

"I'll give you the finger," I tell him, and search downstream for another chance. The next fish is still rising. All I have left is the PMD I bought, and I'm not ready to risk that—I know myself too well. I tie on a Light Cahill, trimming down the hackle and the tail until it at least resembles the hatch. The fish strikes it on the very first cast, and sure enough I can't resist a flamboyant swing of the arm that sends my tippet flying back in my face.

"Shitfire!" is all I can muster as I pull in the line. I'm disgusted with myself. Slim gets busy belaboring the obvious: *That's two! Damn it! Two!*

The good news is that I've managed to hook two large fish. The bad news is that the pool is now empty, and the next run looks even more complicated. Not only does the current tumble over a gravel bar in two distinct chutes, but it bends against the bank where a downed alder sticks out its weed-festooned limbs. Two fish are rising at the bend, one in a trough right before the tree, and the other nosing out from underneath the bank. I make a vow of restraint: I will not jerk. I will repeat this as a mantra during each and every drift.

It's a delicate maneuver, and I make several false attempts, flirting with disastrous twigs, cutting the cast too short, before I get the length just right and the fly lands with a plop above one many-fingered limb and glides beneath it. A white mouth opens like a water lily around my fly, and because I am busily chanting "Do not jerk! Do not jerk!" I manage to keep my arm frozen. The trout hooks itself, lashing the surface with its tail. Its side is a wash of metallic pink and green—a rainbow that looks to be eighteen inches long.

The rod bends into a precarious hoop and the knots in the leader grow suddenly prominent under the strain, like wet little beads that could pop and disappear at any time. We remain in a stalemate for some time, trading inches near the deadfall. Finally it changes strategy and bolts into open water, probably thinking it can put the forces of deep water to work against the line if it can just get down to the big pool where all the side channels join. But the big pool is far away, and in the open water I can put the reel to work.

At the head of the junction pool the fight ends. The fish rolls to the surface, spent, bloodstream clotted with carbon dioxide, gill covers spasming. Big fish will sometimes fight to the death on summer afternoons; poisoned by their own exertions, they can sink to the bottom and drown. This is a big fish for me, if not for the Bighorn, and I hold it in the water until I know it's safe.

Catching one big fish, after all the failures, has put me at ease. Where's that hangdog scoundrel of a cowboy now? I look around and breathe slowly, appraising the water as I whip my fly dry, feeling that mystical assurance that sometimes rises, that feeling that all the fish are vulnerable, that I will find them as surely as an osprey and cast to them with absolute precision.

The duns are still massing on the breeze, driven across the water like petals across an orchard in bloom. Just below a downed tree another white mouth opens, and I follow the sharp snout down. It's a long shadow, tapered like a shark and mottled with the halos and spots of a brown. It must be 22 inches long, yet the smolt fisherman is unfazed. I watch it rise again, calculating the angles I'll need with a matador's calm. The fish is fully exposed, holding in a small eddy, and the cast is easy. The fly drifts through the gap and under the branches, then rides the current down the two feet to the last branch. It skims the edge of the weeds and catches in the tiny whirlpool, and I'm watching it so intently I don't catch the movement of the trout until its mouth is opening around the fly, and suddenly there is the entire bronze length and gleaming eye, big as my daydreams.

I control myself too, control the primitive force that wants my arm to rear back as if the rod were a harpoon I needed to fling. Everything works out right, and I'm actually visualizing the battle to come as the fish descends—slowly. Two bubbles drift from its mouth. It should feel the hook, shake with dismay, and break into a run. I feel a quiver in the line, an instant of resistance that marks the scrape of fly across tooth before it loops back to me.

I feel as if the fates have betrayed me. That flash of friction, even if the hook never pierced flesh, should be enough of a warning for a fish this size. I don't move; one flinch, one movement of the rod, and I expect it to bolt, or at least to nonchalantly saunter out of my reach. I watch it hold in the current, watch the noncommittal undulations of its fins, wondering how long I would have to stand motionless before it might begin to believe that I'm a cottonwood stump. I'm thinking that could be days, but the fish answers the question in a matter of seconds. Before I can pull in my line I watch a mayfly tumble down under the branches, catch in the whirlpool of the last twig, and disappear in a swirl of bubbles. Another chance!

Three times the branches grab my fly, then relinquish their hold. Twice the fly rides a wave that carries it out of the branches and away from the fish. But the third time it drops and stays on the path. The trout anticipates its approach, moving to the cusp of the whirlpool, and I stiffen again, awaiting the rise.

This time the hook finds an anchoring, and a cascade of bubbles erupts as the trout opens its jaws wide in a failed cough. I'm fortunate; it turns away from the branches, line zipping from the reel, forcing me to stagger downstream. Feeding rainbows surge around my feet at the head of the junction pool. The brown collects a fat wad of weeds in its tour of the bottom, but there are no logs to wrap around, no jagged stones to saw the line asunder. Eventually its circles grow shallow, until just the leader reaches out past the rod tip.

The face that appears on the surface is not that of my customary small fish—plump, petulant, and childish—but that of an irascible adult, the face a cabbie might turn to you in some gritty urban zone. The gaudy touches of blue eye shadow and scarlet blush can't disguise a nose that has grown unmistakably hooked and bulbous with age.

I reach for the fly embedded beneath the nostril and draw back quickly. Blood spurts from pinpricks in my thumb. I've forgotten that a big trout's jaws are lined with crocodile fangs. I don't even carry needle-nose pliers—I've rarely needed them. Gingerly I pluck again at the fly, and the teeth scrape down my finger like sharpened Velcro. The scratches hurt, but not so badly that I wish them away. In fact, the scars might serve as proof when I'm telling this story at home. "See these?" I'll be able to say, pointing to the marks. "These are tooth marks. Trout tooth marks."

I pinch the blood out of my thumb and wipe it away. Upstream a fish rises—in the very same spot. Another brown, just an inch or two smaller, has moved into the vacant feeding lane below the hanging branch. A callous bastard, to move in so quickly on a recently evicted tenant. I figure to be the instrument of retribution, but the fish proves to be finicky as well as heartless. Can I read a trout's posture? I feel as if it has one eye on me as it rises; the crisp poise of the fins suggests it's aware of me and my wiles—not frightened, but mindful. Fortunately, I have one more trick to play—the store-bought PMD. I've been saving it for just this moment, the last play for the last fish.

The PMD finds its way around the last twig, and the fish comes up for an inspection, drifting sideways with the fly to get a look from all sides. Usually this close an inspection means failure. Trout seem to approach a dubious fly like a questionable wild mushroom—any doubts and they leave it alone. The fish hesitates, possessed by a lackluster compulsion to consume that won't let it sink and won't let it rise. Finally it pushes the tip of its curved nose through the surface and the fly glides under the teeth.

Surprise! I set the hook—this is definitely a bad mushroom. But the trout has a surprise for me too. It swats the surface with its tail, once, and then yanks the leader straight into the branches before I can shake off my complacency and put a stop to it. My store-bought fly is gone.

I look downstream into the distance for the first time in a long time. It makes me dizzy at first; I've been staring at this stretch of water for so long that the current swirls in lines across my retina. There are a couple of boats downstream. I can't tell if they ever knew what happened here. With the rise over, the revelation is gone without a trace; the riffles continue as if nothing happened, and in the runs the same silver sky shimmers over the blur of bankside trees. I find myself preparing to leave, not just for a few hours until the evening rise, but for good. Partly I'm just plain tired; I can't face an encore. It's also true that a big river has many secrets, and I feel like I've known one that I can take away, a richness that I'll remember if I leave, but that I might demean if I stay. I reel in my line, take apart the rod.

The question is, if I'm done here, where am I going? I decide to call my old fishing buddy in Missoula, something I should have done before I ever set out on this trip. It's been five years since we've spoken, and I was a little shy about explaining what I was planning to do. Not anymore. What seemed like it might have been awkward then feels compulsory now; hell, I'm desperate.

Mike is surprised to hear from me; I'm surprised he recognizes my voice. I explain what I'm doing and where I am, trying to be humble about my doings on the Bighorn. It sounds a little ludicrous to hear myself use words like "water" and "stream" when the air is so hot and dirty that it makes me hoarse.

"Well, it sounds like quite an adventure," Mike says, putting the best possible face on things, "but I'm not sure you've picked the best time to come through here. It's unbelievable; I've never seen anything like it. The Clark Fork looks like Rock Creek. There's no fishing, period."

I say that I remember the dry summer a few years before, how they closed the Big Hole and it dried up in stretches, how shopping carts and rusting car wrecks and all kinds of junk emerged from the Clark Fork, stranded in muck, and the trout kept on feeding and we kept on fishing. The fishing was pretty good that summer, too. Are you sure things are that bad?

"Things are worse than anyone can remember. That summer was nothing compared to this," he says. "Right now they're calling for a voluntary abstention from fishing, which I haven't heard of before. Most people are observing it—most of the guide shops here have canceled their floats, or they're sending them out to where you are. I haven't fished since the middle of May."

I deliver a list of names—Bitterroot, Blackfoot, Rock Creek, Madison, Gallatin, Yellowstone—and Mike replies with "Nope," "No way," "Dried up," and "Terrible," until I'm out of names.

"Well, that about spells it out," I say. It appears that I have a long drive ahead of me. Montana is a big state when all you can do is drive across it.

"You could try the Missouri below Holter Dam," Mike says.

Salvation! I try to stop myself from grinning like a fool; that might reveal just how close to despair I've come. I'm sure he can hear the sudden lilt in my voice.

"The Missouri! I thought about heading over that way." This is true; I did think about fishing the Missouri, until nostalgia got the best of me and I decided to stick to the places I'd known when I lived here. When I lived in Missoula, the Missouri was still a loosely kept secret; I knew it was good, but I couldn't justify driving two hours when the Clark Fork was five minutes away.

"I think it may still be fishable. You'd think if the Bighorn or anywhere else is still fishing, then it would be too. I haven't heard anything about closures."

"What's it like?" I ask him. I want to imagine the pools so I'll be able to wade into them when the drive over there gets long. He says the river is a lot like the Bighorn, only even bigger, a giant spring creek with long, slow runs and lots of weed beds and hatches. The fish are getting picky with the increased pressure, but they're not as wary as the Bighorn fish.

I'm ready to click my heels, jump in the truck, and speed north. I've forgotten about the fires, and how a wall of flames can derail even the best-laid plans.

"The fires might be a problem," Mike says." It depends on the winds. I know Helena was cut off for a while, and there was a big one burning down by Canyon Ferry Dam. If they close the highway to Wolf Creek, you may have to run the gauntlet to get there. In fact, I don't think you'll get there from where you are, period."

The idea of spending the night behind a roadblock, panting in the truck, puts a boot clamp on my eagerness to speed north without an update. I decide to look for a motel along the way, to get some news and some rest.

The highway to Billings is crowded with Harleys, all looking for a cheap place to sleep. I stop at a Super 8 outside of town; the lobby's packed with leather-clad bikers and families on vacation all crowding around the counter to ask for a room. Teenage boys are slumped next to sunburned biker chicks in the circle of stuffed chairs and fake plants that feels like an airport gate. The boys are frowning and thumbing their Gameboys, while their sisters sulk and watch CNN's *Headline News* on television. Their moms fret, and the lady bikers trade coarse language and save each other seats while they take turns heading out the door for a smoke.

The woman behind the counter looks like she's wondering how long she has to go until the end of her shift, and I can't blame her. She tells each hopeful guest that the price is fifty-five dollars for a single room, but that unless they have a reservation it doesn't matter because the place is already full for the night. Everyone in line seems to want to hear the message themselves. I wait my turn for the courtesy phone, wondering how far I might have to drive across the plains to find a campsite. Like everyone else, I'm desperate for a shower and a bed.

Three places turn me down before I reach the Econo Lodge. The phone rings, but in the midst of the bedlam I can barely hear when someone picks up and says something. From what I can catch, it sounds like "Piss Be Jive," a rather unexpected phrase for a motel chain's greeting.

"Sorry, uhh, Is this the Econo Lodge?" I'm trying to sound polite and shout down the line at the same time.

"Piss be jive. Piss be jive. BE JIVE MOTOR LODGE."

"Sorry," I yell. "I'm having a hard time HEARING YOU. COULD YOU SPEAK LOUDER?" I've got a finger in one ear, and I'm crouching under the counter. A phony spider plant is tickling my neck with its plastic tendrils.

"THIS IS BIG FIVE. BIG FIVE MOTOR LODGE. WE

DROPPED THE ECONO LODGE FRANCHISE SO WE COULD DROP THE PRICE. THIRTY DOLLARS HERE. YOU GOT ME?"

"Hold a room," I tell him. "I'm on my way."

Billings reeks, not just of smoke, but of sulfurous gas and diesel fumes—a refinery town. I pass through the fields of giant oil-holding tanks, and there by the Yellowstone's ochre cliffs is the refinery, jets of flaming gas shooting from the tips of smokestacks, plumes of vapor rising into the already soiled sky. Nobody is out walking the boulevards. The city streets are straight and wide, wide enough for us all to speed through downtown in two lanes, with plenty of room left over for parking.

The Big Five Motor Lodge cools its concrete heels between the bland facades of two corporate office blocks, an old-style two-level motor court whose neighbors have nearly swallowed it whole. The guy on the phone said I would see their sign, and I assumed that meant it would look like the golden arches, blazing a bright Big Five over the rooftops. I keep scouring the skyline until I turn a corner and discover a white square marked with those black letters that always seem to be missing a vowel. "Big Smiles Free," the sign proclaims, plaintively, to the multilevel parking garage that looms like the lid of a cement box. The biker crowd seems to have missed this place; there are only a couple choppers in the lot.

Inside, as promised, I get a generous smile from the older couple behind the counter. A mom-and-pop operation; I feel as if I've driven back in time to a more friendly roadside America. The radio is playing what sounds like an AM talk show; a caller is blathering on in the background about politics.

"Let me see, let me see, you are . . . ?" the man says, rubbing the furrows above his eye and fingering a stack of papers. His eyes are liquid around the edges, a bit like a bloodhound. My face apparently doesn't match the voice that just got through bellowing a reservation on the phone, which is probably a good thing.

"Oh, you just called," his wife says to me, and then, gently, to her husband, "I don't think you wrote it down yet."

"Oh yes, yes, I got you here," the man says. "I thought you said 'V,' 'V' as in Victor, that's what the problem was, see."

Some fuss and befuddlement with the key ensues. "Give him twenty-two, that's a nice room." "Twenty-two, twenty-two . . . Where's the key for that one? I set it right here. All our rooms have all the conveniences you'd expect. We're up to date here. Air-conditioning, cable television, where is that key?"

"Here it is, here."

"Oh right, you see, I set this one aside for you."

"I'm so glad I found you," I say, trying to make idle conversation while they swipe my credit card. "I was getting desperate. I was over at the Super 8 and they were full. Seems like everywhere is full." They remind me of my grandparents—there's the same cohesion of thought pattern and eccentricity, and the hint of kindness. I want to let them know that for me at that moment, just a glimpse of their domestic life is as much a haven for me as the roof over my head, but I don't know how. Instead, my comment scrapes a sore spot.

"Well, they're full, that's fine," the old man says, halting the paperwork and rising up for what feels like a stump speech. "We're doing just fine right here." He glances at his wife, who nods and smiles encouragement. "Now some people wonder why we dropped the franchise. To lower the price, that's why! You know what, the real traveler appreciates the difference."

He leans across the counter as if to blow me over with a secret, and I can smell nondairy creamer and newspaper ink and the powdery scent of fabric softener in his flannel shirt. His voice becomes husky; there's a touch of a former salesman's persuasion in his pauses. "See, those places out on the strip, they're trying for the tourists who come and stay one or two nights in the summer. That's just fine by us. You know why? I'll tell you. Because we're trying for the people who come to stay. For weeks at a time! All year long! The repeat customer. Businesspeople, salesmen. The people who come to stay, that's the key!" He steps back with a flourish of eyebrows to regard the impact of this revelation on me, and I nod encouragement. The place has my vote.

"The guy right next to you is here for ten nights. Now how many nights can I put you down for?" He's back to the paperwork, pen in hand, waiting to mark a number in the blank.

"Just one," I'm embarrassed to say.

Room twenty-two is just fine, as hygienic and bland as the chains; the owners appear to have renovated everything but the air conditioners. Mine looks like it would have wafted a chill across my uncle's bachelor pad. Inexplicably, I find I'm humming the *Batman and Robin* theme song as I search for the control panel. My face has cooled off against a burled walnut vent like this before, back when I used to bounce on my uncle's squishy waterbed, hyperventilating, while the Dynamic Duo roared around Gotham in their souped-up Lincoln. Unfortunately, vintage is not something you appreciate in window-mounted swamp coolers. I crank this old behemoth up to its shuddering maximum, but the Freon has long ago escaped into the atmosphere, and it only trickles a warm breeze into the room.

I open the door and sit on the bed, feeling exposed to the street and too tired to care. Traffic noise rumbles through the doorway, and I raise the volume on the television like a curtain. I'm hoping the tube will serve as some kind of oracle, that it will point me to the safe path through the fires, and of course, it's a ridiculous notion; the cable news is too vague. All they've got to say is that the fires are big, getting bigger, and closing some roads. A major power line is in danger near Helena. Winds are gusting, temperatures are rising, fires are jumping roads and moving closer to joining up into one massive blaze. Fifteen seconds of planes dumping water over trees and they cut to commercials. That's it. I call back down to the office, and they don't know either. They hear different reports every day, with roads opening up one morning and closing down again the same afternoon.

They tell me to call the highway patrol hotline, which gives me the bad news in detail: I-15 north, the main road heading out of Helena toward Great Falls, is closed to traffic. Jefferson City has been evacuated. Boulder is under alert. There's plenty more to talk about farther west, but I tune out the other road closures; I can only handle so many calamities at once.

Alone in the Dark

Missouri River, Craig, Montana

The next morning I get the oil changed and head to the local library to check the fire reports on the Internet. There are lots more twinkling little blazes on the incident map. They've made some progress on the fire by Canyon Ferry Dam; it's 30 percent contained, and the road north is open again. Despite the clearing to the north, the smoke here is terrible; as inescapable as a heavy fog, without any sign of dampness. No salty tang of the sea here, or scent of lilacs and tulips, no unleashed elixirs of damp earth and molten snow. No dew. It's the blindness without the tonic, a smothering that puts everybody in a foul and furtive mood.

I drive west along the Wyoming border and cross the Boulder River, a ribbon of clear turquoise rushing through piles of sun-bleached rocks. It looks like a brook, but that doesn't stop me from slowing down to appraise the possibilities as I drive past. I could fish that pool, I find myself thinking. I know just where to cast. I'm still not sold on the notion of voluntary abstention, or rather, I agree in principle, but when it comes down to it I feel like I'm a calorie-starved dieter sitting down to a smorgasbord of all-you-can-eat delights, and all I'm allowed is a side order of broccoli and a mug of tepid tea. It's peer pressure alone that keeps me from pulling over—I'm afraid some indignant angler will spot me out there and strike me down with a thunderbolt of righteous indignation. If Mike is staying off the water, I should be too.

The smoke has engulfed Livingston, and the town feels as if it's sealed in Tupperware. The bank marquee says it's 92 degrees as I drive through downtown and park near Dan Bailey's. I notice the same relics from the heyday of motorized tourism that I recall from my time in Yellowstone: the dim neon bar signs, the burgers whirling atop metal poles, the drive-up ice-cream windows. It wasn't that long ago that all this was unfashionable; back then my fellow seasonals often remarked that when unemployment hit at the end of the summer, Livingston was always a cheap option. One could scrape together a little cash, buy a ramshackle bungalow for next to nothing, and try to weather the winds and isolation of a high plains winter. It looks as if some of them decided to do just that, and then decided they needed good coffee, biscotti, a stylish couch, big-city newspapers, and so on until Livingston snowballed into chicness.

Dan Bailey's was both a storefront and a fly-tying factory when I lived nearby. It was a strange way to market merchandise; women sat in rows, fingers snipping and winding, piling up flies by the dozen. I couldn't help watching them work. Some looked sassy, like they'd be at home taking orders from behind the counter of the local grill; others peered through bifocals and seemed like they might bounce grandkids on their knees. I couldn't see any of them actually fishing. They probably hated fishing, I thought at the time. The effect was nothing like the life of leisure so frequently depicted in outdoorsy clothing catalogues; the window felt like a portal into the heart of what is usually hidden, the factory floor. The flies could just as easily have been pillowcases or car parts. I walked along the sidewalk several times just to glance in through the plate glass.

The window is still there, but the women are gone. Cardboard boxes cover the tables in the room that housed them. The boxes are full of tiny cartons, and the cartons, I discover, are filled with dozens of flies—the remnants of the production line. I console myself with bargains. In fact, I can hardly believe what I'm able to buy: they are so cheap that even I, the guy who leaves a fly on every limb, can justify buying them. It's the first time in my life that I've bought flies by the dozen. I race around and grab things up and think better of it and put them down and come back and pick them up again, until my fists are full of little boxes and packets.

It's only when I get to the counter to pay that I remember to ask what happened to the women who used to tie flies in the bargain room. The young guy at the counter looks puzzled. He's never heard of them, and looks at me as if I'm confused. Maybe I'm thinking about another store? I say I'm certain they were here—right next door where all the bargain boxes are. Let me ask the manager, he says, and stops another young guy who's traversing the store from outdoor apparel to fly-rod display. "Hey Dave, did we used to have women tying flies in here?" The question ends in a note of incredulity.

I begin to wonder if I am remembering falsely; maybe there was another fly shop down the street. It dawns on me that my last stop in Livingston was ten years ago, and that a lot can change in a decade. The clerk I'm dealing with looks like he just graduated from high school. He was probably playing dodge ball in the elementary school gym and drinking milk out of little cartons when I was last here.

Dave comes over. "You asked about the fly-tiers, right?"

"Yeah," I say, "it sounds crazy, but I remember rows of old ladies tying flies in that room over there. Nobody seems to remember them."

He appears to be at a loss for words or considering the etiquette of what he should say. Clearly, he's never seen them either. "That was before my time," he says, finally. "They've been gone for years now. We contract that stuff out."

"Well, at least I'm not crazy," I say, and leave it at that.

As we wait for the register to approve my card, I hear someone say he just fished the Boulder River and he wants to go somewhere else; there were lots of fish but they were all too small. My immediate response is consternation—I'm abstaining, he's fishing! I glance over to find a family vacation in difficulty; I'm not alone in coping with the fires. The guy looks jovial but tired; his wife looks bewildered; their son, bored. He probably figured they could all come out here and enjoy the scenery, and he could sneak away for a couple of hours of fishing every day. Instead, it hurts just to breathe, the scenery is hidden, and they have to search far and wide for water to fish.

This is the kind of parental scene that terrifies me. I can just see it: my kids detest fishing. They hit each other with my rod case in the back seat. They use my vest to wipe up a doggy accident. They want to go camping, sure enough, but only if the campground is near a water park, not a river.

"The Boulder's been fishing real well," the store clerk advises the guy. "Did you try it in the evening? We've been sending people there and I've heard they're doing well."

"I thought the Boulder was closed to fishing," I say to the guy helping me, "or at least there was a voluntary abstention."

No, he says, the Boulder is fishing real well. The other clerk counsels the family to head into Yellowstone, maybe try Slough Creek or the Upper Yellowstone. Right now they look pretty poor—they're low, and they're muddy because a recent thunderstorm churned up a lot of mud in the areas that burned during the last fires. But that should clear out in a day or two.

I should keep quiet, but I can't help myself—I know where he should go to find bigger quarry. I'd like to say that I am overwhelmed at this moment with the desire to help a fellow angler, but I'm afraid altruism has nothing to do with it. I've caught some big fish, and I haven't had a single chance to gloat.

"Bighorn's fishing well—really well," I blurt out, intruding myself into their conversation. The husband looks at me, interested but dubious; the guide looks at me as if I've challenged his authority. He lowers his voice, confides. I can still hear, but it's an invitation not to participate.

"The Bighorn can be good. But," he smiles at the guy's wife, "there's nothing there for the family. Pretty bleak all around. I think you'd be better off in the park."

He's absolutely right, of course. The father eyes me briefly, still torn; the seed has been sown. I wish I'd never said anything. I picture wife and son sitting in that dusty Fort Smith parking lot, listening to the turbines grind while Dad heads out for the hatch. For their sake, I hope the Yellowstone is fishing well and the bison herds are obliging. I shamble out with my purchases, grab an iced latte in a nook of coffee bar, and leave town, feeling like I should be punished for my sins of pride.

I drive north, through Townsend, true to its name at the edge of the empty plains, and then through East Helena where I cross a wide, warm, and weedy stretch of the Missouri. The river here doesn't seem to heed the legacy of its sources, the Jefferson, Beaverhead, and Gallatin rivers that pour their blue ribbon waters into this one channel. It seems to hearken forward to its destination, the Big Muddy, and looks like a good place to throw in a chicken neck, tie a string to a big toe, and snooze away the afternoon. Gulls and white pelicans glide over the gravel bars; swallows swoop for gnats. Matted algae is drying on the muck-encrusted rocks.

I find it hard to imagine trout downstream. The Missouri has always disoriented me; I remember my junior-high geography teacher instructing us that rivers flow every which way but north—it's a rule of the globe, she said, with the Nile serving as the exception that proves its validity. The Missouri is apparently another exception, heading north to a rendezvous with gravity at a place called Great Falls. It took me a couple years to set aside this bit of juvenile education, along with my instinctive belief that rivers get warmer as they flow downstream, in order to locate the fishable stretch of the river on a map.

Once I get out of Helena and into the ridges north of town, the air begins to clear. The sky overhead is suddenly blue for the first time in days, and the sun bathes the roadside in a tawny light that makes me think of sunflowers. Soon I'm following the Missouri north, winding through the crags of a rugged canyon.

I've heard before that the Missouri is big water, but I'm still surprised. I have to squint across the channel to the far shore. Even in this, a drought year, the sheer volume rolling down the main stem makes the Clark Fork seem small in my memory, and the Clark Fork is the biggest river in Montana when it crosses the Idaho border.

I stop in the riverside hamlet of Craig to get my bearings from the local fly shop. So much for self-reliance; I've gotten to the point where I don't even want to step into the river without expert advice. The proprietor is generous with clues. He says the river is fishing well; it's a little warm, and a little low, but the fish are coming to the surface for tricos in the morning, and for caddis late in the afternoon when the sun leaves the water. Most important, there are no voluntary abstentions in place; an angler of strict conscience might rest the fish during the heat of the afternoon, but otherwise, go for it.

Because the canyon is so narrow, all manner of transport straddles the riverbanks; the highway skirts the railroad tracks on this side, and another road traces the opposite shore. The guy in the fly shop has warned me: don't expect to sleep much unless you head pretty far downstream because the closer campsites are only a few feet from both the highway and the tracks. I head to the Mid-Cannon access, which is as close as I can get to the dam's spout of cold water and still hope to catch some shut-eye. It's situated at a widening of the canyon walls, a tiny valley of cottonwood and willow and fishing camps dwarfed by a jagged spire of rusty, raven-circled rock. There's room enough among the trees to get away from the air brakes of the eighteen-wheelers, but not enough to escape the hoots of passing trains. The tracks are only twenty feet from the screen of willow saplings where I pitch my tent.

The place is popular; I note the waders slung over tree branches to dry, the fully strung fly rods resting against tent sides, the jovial "How'd you do?" when a fully clad fisherman strides into camp. Hamburgers and onions are sizzling somewhere nearby; the chocolate Lab next door is alert to the scent even as he wags me a welcome. At first I assume the clamor of pans means that everybody is gearing up for the evening rise. The sunset is close; I frantically tie two tan caddis, wishing I'd bought a dozen in Dan Bailey's, and stuff a peanut-butter-and-jelly sandwich into my mouth along with several carrot nubs.

As I trudge down the railroad tracks, I realize that everyone else is settling in for the night. When I arrived, there were four figures casting over the runs upstream—now there are none. Even the birds have called it a day; a pair of great blue herons has settled into a roost in the cottonwoods on the other bank. I pass three guys loafing in lawn chairs along the bank, dressed in the shorts, Tevas, and fleece of an evening ashore. They salute me with raised beers; I notice chilly beads coursing down the neck of what looks to be a dark and tasty microbrew. There's a feast of unwholesome snack food on the table behind them, all kinds of chips and dips and pickles and sausages and cheesy twists and whizzes. Not a single member of the vegetable food group in sight. It looks delicious.

"Heading out, huh?" they ask, and I suspect they might invite me to stop for a beer if I show any sign of succumbing to the temptation. I nod a determined assent instead and keep the gravel crunching under my boots until I've left the comforts and camaraderie of their evening camp behind.

There's the sound of chuckling back there, just as I pass around a bend in the tracks that makes me look back, wistfully. I feel like some kind of fishing monk, passing up these earthly pleasures for my strange, nocturnal devotions. It's a western peculiarity, this lack of interest in the evening rise, born, I think, in the largesse of the rivers. Why stumble around in the dark when you can catch plenty of fish in the afternoon? I fish in the evening because I learned to fish in the East, where dusk was our only hope of a rise, and because I like to fish alone. If fishing is a form of river meditation, then nightfall is the best time to practice. The solitude at this northern latitude seems to last and last, long after the sun goes down.

I follow the tracks to a point where the river divides around several islands, hoping for a spot where the water will be shallow enough so I can get out to the bars in the middle. But even when divided, the river proves too deep and fast to cross. There's a riff of whitewater right along the bank that would be fine for kayaks, but trying to wade through it would be like trying to step out of a car going sixty miles an hour.

I keep scouting upstream until I reach a flat that stretches for nearly a mile of soft glides and lank weed beds. The tracks run along a shelf blasted into the rock; I find a path down but still have to fight my way through tangled thorns to reach the river. I slip down a chute of polished muck and emerge on the shore, scattering tiny minnows and inhaling a midge with my first breath. As I pick the fly off my tongue, I experience a dramatic change in perspective; the scale of water and sky transfixes me, makes me feel like a speck in the landscape, a water beetle scuttling along in the shallows. Instead of readying my line, I just stand there, looking up.

From the blue haze of the headwaters an osprey bears down, combing the surface with its claws. Halfway through, it plucks a miraculous fish from the water with barely a splash, like a seed squeezed from a slice of lemon. The fish is so big that the osprey struggles to get airborne; it needs nearly the entire length of the pool to gain altitude before it banks into the treetops. I can't tell if it's a whitefish or trout, but the bird's success breaks the spell; at least somebody is out fishing. I dig out my fly box and tie on one of my new caddis. A few of the naturals are fluttering like moths along the willow branches, but not enough to call them a hatch.

While I'm pulling the knot tight there's a commotion in the shallows downstream; a silver minnow the size of a mullet leaps out of the water and dances on its tail, chased by a fin-swept surge of displaced water. It's the kind of attack I associate with the stripers that ambush minnows in the salt marshes off Cape Cod, but then this river's shores seem almost tidal. Banks of silt have divided the main channel from the shallows of the streambed, and a profusion of aquatic weeds have colonized these deposits. The result is a broad channel fringed with plant life, and behind that the tepid backwash in which I'm standing. My feet have disappeared into a frothy and snail-rich carpet whose bubbles smell of boiled broccoli.

The fish herds its quarry into the bank, and when the minnows sense the trap, the surface churns with silver bodies. Amid the splashes comes a sucking sound, like an unplugged drain, and then the survivors are free. Their nemesis is prowling farther down the shore, and only a circle of bubbles marks the scene.

I cast once down there, just to see if I can tempt the predator with a little wisp of dessert after the entree, but I know he's already gone. In spite of his disappearance, he's divulged some valuable information about where I should fish. I had already started to slog my way right out to the shoals, expecting to cast as far out into the center of the pool as I could, but now I know better. I imagine more big fish patrolling the shallows, and stay put.

My first cast makes me glad I didn't march out there; my fly speeds across some outstretched fronds and drops over the edge of the bank, alighting for only a second before a violent spray of water engulfs it. The fish fights hard, stripping line out of the reel, leaping twice, and then plowing into the weeds when it nears exhaustion. I wade over and follow my tippet down into the stalks to get a look. It's a sixteen-inch rainbow, husky and glittering like its counterparts on the Bighorn.

I dry my fly and look for more prospects, sweeping aside a cloud of midges to do so. Where I go, they go too; I've grown a quivering halo of them, and they all seem to crave the tang of my breath. At least they don't taste like much. Fish are rising sporadically all along the silt beds. It has gotten darker, and the caddis have begun to weave over the banks, making excursions out over the open water and looping back to safety. There may be more of them, but they're smaller and slightly darker than the fly I'm using. It takes me a while, and several pointed refusals, before I accept that my first cast was a fluke, and that the fish have gotten more selective. I shift to a smaller caddis and rub some mud into it to make it darker.

It's the only one I've got. I position the drift perfectly above the sub-siding rings of a previous rise and manage to withstand the urge to jerk hard as the trout rises and the hook sets itself solidly. Everything goes just as it should, until the fish breaks into a run that makes the reel screech as if I have no drag whatsoever. The line spins out pell-mell, like one of those toilet rolls that with one tug unspools its entire length on the bathroom floor. I'm not ready, of course, and somehow in my attempts to slow things down a loop of line catches on the reel handle, stopping the outflow of line altogether. The tippet holds for a second as it stretches, then suddenly everything is slack. I pull in the line and clean off some gobbets of algae from the blood knots. It's time to open the emergency box.

I keep a small plastic case of store-bought dries, a gift from my parents. Inside is a selection of dries, unsullied as museum pieces, two each, including two small, dark, squirrel-winged caddis. They're perfect, but I hesitate. I've never used a fly from this box, and I've had them for nearly four years. It's getting dark now; a pale slice of moon is waxing overhead, and the nightjars are dive-bombing each other with the whizzing of bottle rockets. I don't have long to stand there looking at my fly collection. Screw it, I say, they're meant for fishing, and snap it open to pick out one of the caddis.

It's gotten dark enough that threading the hackle-covered eye has become a challenge. I spend five minutes holding the fly up to catch what remains of the light while I prod its silhouette with the tippet. Finally it dangles on a loop of nylon, and I can cast to the fish that are rising everywhere now, all along the bank. I make a short cast to the closest fish, and the moon's reflection quavers immediately in the rings of a rise. The trout explodes when I set the hook, bursting into the big run that seems the hallmark of the Missouri rainbows. My nocturnal knot, weaker than it should be, just snaps. The fish is gone. I've got to tie on another.

It takes another five minutes of groping, but I push the leader through and give it some tugs to make sure the knot is solid. Five minutes at this time of night makes a big difference; the rise has begun to wind down. It's so dark that I can't see my fly; I have to imagine its progress.

When the moonlight moves, I set the hook. The fish takes off on its big first run, just like the others, but this time I've got plenty of line already off the reel and I can play it by hand. I give up most of it, but begrudgingly, and the fish turns before it reaches midstream. Soon it's splashing just offshore, but the body is still invisible. I'm invisible too, until we get a little closer to one another. I catch a glimpse of contorted silver, and then the fish catches sight of me. It springs into the air, shining like a sword, and lands right on the tippet. The force of the landing severs the line.

I reel in, upbraiding myself for failing to realize that the fish wasn't tired. I'm happy nevertheless. Both my Adirondack caddis are gone, but at least I lost them to the forces of a fight, not by snapping them off with a hyperactive jerk of my arm. I don't have long to mourn their loss anyway, because it occurs to me that I've made a mistake. I'm standing in the dark without a flashlight, and I've got to find my way back to that slippery little trail through the brush, and I've no idea where it is. I've moved upstream quite a bit, and now the shore behind me looks like an unbroken wall of shadows.

I slosh up to the bank and follow it, hoping a bit of moonshine will betray that last muddy dip, but I can't find it. I wind up poised on a chunk of riprap, listening to the sucking sounds of the run that looked too treacherous to cross by day and that seems even more fearful now that it can't be seen. I refuse to go farther, leaping from rock to rock, teetering on the verge of a drowning.

Retracing my steps, I slow down, peering into the murk between the branches, and find what looks like a trail. The bank has eroded underneath it, leaving the tree roots to clutch air and making for a steep initial climb. I try to pull myself up over the eroded edge with rod in one hand and the other clutching the tip of a stone. I get halfway up, shift my weight to my hands, and lose my grip in a frantic scrabbling of pebbles that drops me backwards into the dark. My knees poke against the roots, and I skin both elbows to break my fall before landing on my feet. The scrapes sting, but it's realizing what could have happened, had I fallen the wrong way and busted a limb, that gives me pause. I take deep breaths and listen to the crickets. The clouds have drifted east across the moon, and the last glow of twilight has faded from the western sky. Night has truly fallen.

When I'm calm I try a different route. Immediately the trail narrows, and I begin to curse the western fishermen who trod out this worthless excuse of a path. Sure, it's fine in broad daylight—who needs a trail when the sun is shining? Why didn't anyone think about the struggles of the East Coast night fisherman? I can't see a thing; I wouldn't see a rattler if it were hanging from a branch with its fangs an inch from my eyeball. Willows have died and fallen across the trail without losing a single pointed stick; they spear my kidneys as I try to slide under them. My hands brush against nettles without knowing it. A blackberry cane claws down my neck. I have to back up, slowly, and pull it off me like a rabid cat. Two more steps and I'm stabbed in the thigh; a wild gooseberry or a bull thistle has pierced my waders.

I fight my way deeper and deeper, heaving like a bear, making a racket of snapped sticks and grunts of pain and still there's no sign of the embankment that leads to the tracks. The trail only gets smaller, until I can't say for sure that I'm following the way at all. I seem to be foundering in a wilderness of thorns. Finally I reach an impasse, a virtual cage of dead limbs. Still there is no sign of the tracks.

I stop. I'm bleeding, I'm itching, I'm afraid, and I'm pissed-off. Already the prickers I've crunched down are springing back into place, converging to smother me. I have to suppress the urge to scream like a cougar in a leg-hold trap. Be rational, I tell myself. Be rational. The tracks must curve away from here; that's the only explanation I can find. I'm not lost in here. I just need to find the path that I took to get to the river, and take it back out.

I force my way back out to the river. The real path, it turns out, is just a few almost-invisible feet farther. It seems so easy to haul myself up onto it and duck my way through the twists. There's the railroad, right where it should be, and soon I'm kicking the gravel as if that nightmare never happened.

I saunter into the lantern light of the first site, where three of the guys are still taking it easy in their chairs. I startle them, coming out of the dark like an uninvited animal. I notice now that one of them is older, with a crown of silver hair and glasses. Maybe he's the father of one of the younger guys, but he's retained their physical confidence; that's why I didn't recognize the difference earlier. He looks like one of those physicians who competes in triathlons in his spare time.

"How'd you do?" he hails me, once he can see what I am. One of the other guys looks at his watch, and the third one steps out of the shadows by the side of the camper to listen. He's in the middle of brushing his teeth.

"Pretty well," I tell them. "I caught a few." It feels like my fishing took place hours ago. They look surprised that I caught anything.

"You're out there pretty late, huh?" the father figure says, with the slightly teasing tone of one who is used to cajoling his son's awkward friends into saying something for themselves. "I'd offer you a beer, but we're just about to turn in. Got to hit it early tomorrow."

I walk back into the dark, my eyes adjust, and I find the cool shoulder of the truck door. There's my headlamp, on the seat. I turn the key and open the door and the light clicks on. It feels like I'm home.

At six, the trucks start to rumble. I groan and press my arm over my ear. My neighbor revs his truck a few times, then lets it chug along while he packs up for the day. The smell of exhaust wafts through the tent wall, where the light is still just a daub of gray. I allow myself just fifteen more minutes. Two of the trucks bounce away, and the noise subsides. I allow myself fifteen more, until a streak of pale light strikes the tent. The sun is rising. I have to get up. It's time to hustle out there and stake out a spot for the trico hatch.

The wind has shifted in the night, and a pall of smoke has blown in on a stiff breeze that has the cottonwood leaves flapping. I can feel the drought in it, the absence of dew against my skin. There's nothing to evaporate. The cliff tops are murky, the river doesn't gleam, and I can smell it again, that same old furnace. I don't see any fish rising, or spinner swarms in the air.

Along the way to Wolf Creek I pass an eddy that looks promising, where several fish are rising in the shadow of an alder stand. Nobody else is there. I almost turn around, but I can't seem to dismiss the advice I got yesterday, when the fly-shop guide told me that the biggest hatch and the best fishing are above the Wolf Creek bridge, farther upstream. I read the empty pullout as a sign that everybody else is already up there, and decide to follow the herd. I don't want to miss out.

The bridge is only a mile farther, past a meandering stretch of gravel islands where the current subsides into long golden mirrors of sky. I pass one fisherman, about the size of a midge, up to his waist where two riffles join, and then the canyon narrows. It's still just after dawn in the shadow of these cliffs, and what appears to be a feeding frenzy is underway. The pool is at least a quarter of a mile long, bubbling with rises, and nobody is fishing it.

I park the truck in a pullout. I'm still convinced that the guide is right; it's probably even better upstream, and there are probably so many fish surfacing below the dam that I could walk across their backs without wetting a foot. In my sleepy zombie state I can almost feel their slippery shoulders in motion between my toes. But I don't have the willpower to pass up this pool full of rises. I have to start fishing, right now—my hands are trembling, I'm craning my neck, my mouth has dropped. It's no longer safe to operate a motor vehicle.

I hop out and suit up, only to discover that the distance between the fish and myself is nearly vertical. The roadbed has been blasted into the side of the ridge and bolstered with riprap. There's a thin line of clay where some fool went over the edge and undoubtedly slid down to his death. It's good enough for bighorn sheep to pick their way down for a drink, but the skittering pebbles of one trial step tell me I'm not going to try it. I find myself pacing back and forth beside the truck, looking for an angle while the trout rise below, out of reach, driving me to madness.

Finally I find a culvert where the spring runoff has exposed a sequence of rocks and I can clamber down to the boulders along the bank. There are pods of fish working in the wakes behind every rock, and already the surface is coated with the papery wings and tiny black bodies of stranded spinners. Upstream a bank of weed-covered silt has formed, like the one I fished last night, and fish are feeding right along the edge. I work my way toward it, dropping my spinner into the feeding lanes as gracefully as I can.

It soon becomes clear that the fish are wary of human shadows. Or maybe they live in fear of the osprey, or the flock of mergansers that reluctantly saunter downstream, or perhaps even the pair of minks squabbling among the rocks beside me. My falling leader only herds them upstream; one by one they stop rising within reach, only to reappear in the wake of the next stone. Two guys materialize on the opposite shore, chasing the trout between the rocks too. None of us is catching anything.

Every gust down the canyon ends in a storm of whirling bodies. My fly rod is coated with them; so is the line. The mayflies patter against me with the whispering of sleet; my fleece jacket is covered with them, and they've collected in piles at my elbows. I'm blinded if I look upstream; they're stuck to my lips, clinging to my earlobes. There's not an inch of water free of them, and the fish by the bank are slowing down. Glutted, perhaps? The sun has risen over the ridge, and a line of sunshine is spreading down the slope, which may have something to do with it. The guys across the river reel in and scramble back up to their car. I've lost hope too, but I decide to watch the fish downstream in hopes of learning something I can use. They're still feeding among the rocks down there, now that I'm gone.

The trout have converged behind the boulders in groups of three or four, and their rising is peculiar. With so many flies on the water, they don't need to go down and wait for the next mouthful. They bob like swimmers doing the breaststroke, gulping a row of spinners instead of breaths, spawning a chorus of pops and slurps. At the end of a sequence their dorsal fins slice the surface film and they descend, like sharks, into the feeding lane. There they pause for a brief interlude, finding room in their swollen innards so they can float to the top for another round.

Watching them gets me thinking about the eddy I passed up on the way over, because without recourse to a net, swooping talons, or a juicy earthworm, I can't see how I'll manage to capture one of these guys. It's Schwiebert time. With so many naturals on the water, the imitation has to be exact, the drift must be timed precisely, and the leader can't cause the slightest hesitation. Even if I got all these factors in place—an unlikely feat given my talent for creating chaos—the odds that my fly might be plucked from among the thousands are slight. But things might be different downstream, where the water is fast enough to break the carpet of bodies up into flotillas, or even individual meals. There might even be the remnants of an appetite or two down there. I scale the rocks back up to the truck. I'm not done yet.

It turns out I'm not the only one with this bright idea. There are several guys fishing below the parking spot. From the truck it looks like the eddy I saw earlier is unoccupied, but when I hustle down there, thanking my lucky stars, I find another angler nearly hidden by the overhanging branches. To make matters worse, he's playing a fish! Pods of trout are churning the surface all around him while the one he's fooled stirs up mud with its tail.

There are still too many flies for me to feel confident; they clot the surface, and the trout rise with the same syncopation. I consider just packing up and pushing on, then scorn the idea. Remember those fish-less days in Michigan? How about the slim pickings in Pennsylvania, when one good rise made a morning? Hundreds of good fish are rising, and I'm ready to head for the truck? The success of the last few days has made me complacent. I need the discipline of demanding fish.

Two more waders are casting in the narrows around the bend, with two more fishing farther upstream where the river widens again. In between them is a stretch of nondescript water, bounded by willows, silt-bottomed, deep enough to dissipate the current without providing the cover of real depth. It's been left alone because it looks unpromising, but fish don't ask the fishermen for places to feed. Two pods of rainbows are working this stretch, far fewer than the multitude on either side, but enough for me.

I wade in and sink down until I'm up past my navel in cold. Dead and dying spinners coat the surface. The fish are just as skittish; they keep moving just a little farther away with each cast, feeding with the same impossible rhythm, leading me out of my depth. I feel the warning trickle down my lower spine; another inch and I'll be soaked.

I blame my retreat on the wind. As the sun nears its zenith, gusts of smoke come ripping down the canyon, roiling the surface with waves. Whatever hope I had of stealth disappears; the wind slaps my fly down among the fish, and my back casts spiral into the willows. I lose one fly, tie on a replacement, and lose it too. I have to hold onto the end of my rippling line and wait for a lull to tie on another because I'm afraid the contents of my fly box might take flight. The fish don't like the wind either; they only feed between gusts, and the lulls get shorter, the wind stronger, the chop heavier. Miniature tornadoes whirl across the surface. The rise is over. I can concede defeat. I can go.

Smoke on the Water

Missoula, Montana

It's the smoke that keeps the nostalgia at bay as I enter the Blackfoot Canyon and the landmarks start coming fast and furious. It gets thicker and thicker, as if it were the visible accumulation of time, all the days that have passed since I've been through here, the haze of an unreliable memory made real. I find myself comparing nevertheless. I cross Monture Creek—the medley of wrecked cars and tethered horses is still there. I cross Norman Maclean's stretch of big water; the Blackfoot's normally treacherous rapids have lost their thunder, but the water, tinted the powder blue of melted glaciers, doesn't look all that low to me. At least what I can see of it through the smoke.

Hellgate Canyon, where the Blackfoot joins the Clark Fork, is curiously unchanged too, all the way through the trailer parks of East Missoula. It's only as I merge with the interstate traffic and come around the side of Mount Jumbo that I notice the changes. A billboard invites me to "Sleep with the fishes tonight!" at a Holiday Inn in the town of Hamilton, near the south end of the Bitterroot Valley. I burst into a lament for lost innocence. A Holiday Inn for crying out loud! Hamilton was a hamlet of sheepherders and cowboys when I was here, that and minority-hating rebels who refused to pay taxes to the United Nations and went around town in unregistered trucks, fully armed. What happened to those kooks? Did they sell out and retire to Florida? They should be out there terrorizing the exurbs with intolerant gunplay.

Maybe it's the smoke that forces me to admit that the changes were already underway when I arrived, that the stoplights were already going up in Lolo and the bulldozers were cutting cul-de-sacs into the range, and that I was part of the fleece-bedecked, cappuccino-sipping, mountain-biking wave heading west to the last best place. I'm forced to recall my own fear of an encounter with "Freemen," the way I crossed the street at night to avoid the authentic-looking types sharing cigarettes outside the Oxford Café. In my nightmares, I kept imagining a posse of vigilantes showing up to harangue my friends and me for trespassing.

"But this is federal property," my dreamland companions and I protested from the mouth of our tent.

"Exactly," our tormentors replied, fingering their weapons. "Let the games begin!"

Places change, I tell myself, but unfortunately I'm not done with the sentimental journey yet. As I cross the Higgins Street Bridge, I crane my neck for a glimpse of the side channel where I used to stop my bike on a summer afternoon and look down to see if the trout were rising in the shade.

It's gone dry; a puddle stagnates there in a crusty white bed. Upstream is the long flat where, poking around in the shade of some cottonwoods, I discovered the spot where the sump pump from a hotel basement would periodically spurt forth a stream of cold water. The rainbows had found it too. It's the place where I came down to fish one afternoon and found a sun-leathered young man brushing his surprisingly pearly teeth. He wasn't using toothpaste, just cupped palms of urban river.

"Beautiful afternoon," he said, after spitting a mouthful back into the current. I winced at what seemed an act of faith. I thought of all the toxins and waste and disease that must be swirling now between his cheeks, and then it dawned on me that the trout lived among those poisons, and that I would be standing in the same water. Looking upstream from the bridge, I can't see that part of the river now. The smoke has faded the details, like an overexposed photo.

I drive to my friend Mike's house in the Rattlesnake, a neighborhood just outside the downtown. I find him out in the yard, surrounded by the watery arcs of sprinklers, moving hoses to a new corner of grass. At first his behavior strikes me as typically suburban, until I realize that he's not obsessing over a withered lawn—he's wetting it down, just in case.

I can see why he's anxious. Mount Jumbo fills the sky over his roof with slopes of perfect tinder, and Greenough Park drapes yellow willow leaves over his backyard fence. In a normal year, these sylvan touches would be welcome; the privacy, the views, the birdsong, all of these would be selling points. But the fires change the story. Mike's home is surrounded by potential fuel, and dry lightning is crackling overhead.

He sets down the hose so we can shake hands. He looks to be in surprisingly good spirits, although the strain of life inside a ring of fire is showing too. There's something medieval in this scene. At first I can't quite grasp what it is, until I realize it's the scale of the disparity, the immensity of the storm clouds bearing down on us coupled with our human reply, the petty trickle of a garden hose. There's no gizmo to switch off the lightning or fireproof the range. No wonder the chroniclers of the Middle Ages were so fatalistic; what can you do in the face of this, but tremble?

We watch the horizon; we sprinkle with the hose. When the thunder booms, Mike can't help but glance at the hills, his upturned face lit with the strange undersea light of the storm. Pouches of insomnia gleam like mother of pearl under his eyes. I don't think I'd be sleeping well either; instead of counting sheep I'd be watching yet another wayward ember float down to set the roof on fire.

"This summer has been hell," he says.

We go inside to escape the smoke. They've got the local news on the radio, and the smoke is the lead story. A Class One air alert has been declared for the evening, the highest level of concern. The announcer cautions us to stay indoors, avoid exertion, and carpool if travel is required. New fires have flared up, brought on by wind, lightning, and the whimsy of bad luck. A motorcycle accident near Red Lodge ignited a new blaze when sparks from the sliding metal caught some weeds on the shoulder. Before anyone could stomp out the flames, they raced up the slope and scorched several thousand acres. Now they're threatening houses. The fire situation commander comes on to say they're already shorthanded; they'll have to leave other fires to get this one under control.

There's a certain dart of adrenaline that comes with knowing we're in the midst of all this newsworthy drama. We're all a little giddy, sipping iced tea, looking out the window to see if the air looks any worse now that we know. The follow-up story informs us that due to the extraordinary fire danger, the governor has asked the federal government to close all public lands in the western half of the state. Penny laughs, exasperated. How much worse can it get?

As if anticipating the question, the announcer tells us that the closure will remain in place until the fire risk eases, which could be as late as October.

"Now you know what our summer has been like," she says.

They both look like they want to shake their fists at the sky, but they're good hosts, and they stay cheerful. Mike asks if I want more iced tea. He brings out a fishing guide to Oregon. Penny searches for fishing updates online. I'm thinking that October is two months away. There will be no hiking, no backpacking, no dog walking. There will be no fishing. I catch myself thinking about the truck; in my mind I'm already at the wheel, escaping. My relief at disappearing is, of course, a secret betrayal of this reunion. I force myself to put such thoughts aside.

Mike says he feels bad; he wishes we could hit the Clark Fork. Like most anglers in the area, he has been observing a voluntary abstention from fishing since the end of May. "I put away my rod two months ago," he tells me, "and I haven't picked it up since."

I leave town the next morning with my low beams pointing the way through twilight. It's as if the sky is a dirty rug, and someone has hung it out and begun to beat it. Ashes are floating down from the sky, silencing the traffic. My wipers brush them aside, stroking the glass like a pair of eyelashes. I've said good-bye to Mike and Penny over a mug of coffee, before they started work. Now I want to say good-bye to the river. I park by the supermarket that leans over the Clark Fork and walk out onto the footbridge. I'm not expecting anything but dry rocks and a trickle of scum. I plan to rinse away the last twinge of nostalgia with a view of the dismal river, something akin to paying my respects at a grave, before I push on into new terrain.

The river won't let me leave like that. Sure the rocks by the rope swing are bone dry, and smoke shrouds the water. Where there were rapids, a shopping cart lies tipped on its side like the skeleton of a drowned steer. But when I'm about to turn away and leave, I notice the rings of what could be a rise. I don't believe it. Then I see another swirl, and another, and pretty soon I realize that fish are rising everywhere. Along with airborne ashes, black mayflies are fluttering around me. I notice them now, clinging to the bridge spars, blowing past me in spirals of soot.

Tricos.

My rod is back in the truck. I could rig up, take a few casts, see if any big rainbows are moving . . . I walk back to the truck. Big rainbows float through my mind as I pass the airport and the big-box stores of the western fringe. Sometimes it's good to leave a river feeling unfulfilled, seeing rises you'll never reach. It means there's something there you never captured, and that you'll be back again.

Nessie

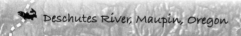 Deschutes River, Maupin, Oregon

The smoke gets thicker as I enter the Alberton Gorge, so thick I can barely see the road, even with my headlights. It has pooled up behind the Cabinet range like floodwater behind a dam. Climbing the switchbacks takes me gradually out of the depths until I surface near the summit and find myself riding into a crisp blue sky. Sunlight sparkles on the dashboard. There's not a trace of the smoke, not even a smudge of gray. The clarity of my perception amazes me. It's like I lost my glasses at the Montana border, and now, entering Idaho, I've found them again. The fir trees are suddenly bristling with needles. I roll down the window and inhale deeply, again and again, savoring the unflavored air. I never thought I'd feel relieved to leave Montana, but that's what I feel, a groundswell of liberation as I motor on into unknown terrain. No more smoke, no more nostalgia.

I'm crossing the Idaho panhandle, an area known for its rolling hills and lush forests, but not so much for its fishing. I've never even thought about fishing this country. My plan was to fish through the rugged belly of the state, try the Henry's Fork, Silver Creek, and the streams around Ketchum. That won't happen now. I may be in the same state, but as far as roads heading south go, I might as well be on another continent.

The closest river I can find on the map is the St. Joe, and the town closest to it appears to be Wallace, an old mining town just off the highway. I roam around the little downtown for quite some time, searching in vain for a sporting goods store, until I find my way to a strange emporium of art and artifacts, a boutique that sells flamboyant scarves, hand-thrown teacups and funky earrings, and, to my surprise, flies. There is, I note, a vise clamped to the counter, but the way the flies are displayed—in exquisite little gift boxes—makes me think it would be gauche to actually use them. They look like table ornaments for a nouveau western living room.

I hesitate by the window, and those few seconds of gawking cost me. Before I can scamper away, I'm caught looking. A brassy and mirthful woman's voice calls out the door.

"Hey! What are you looking for? Can I help you?"

My neck begins to tingle where the hairs are all standing on end. The social equivalent of angling is about to commence, and I'm on the wrong end of the line. I'm hooked; I'm being drawn in.

Inside, I can see the owner and a friend have interrupted their chat across the counter. I fervently wish they hadn't bothered. I'd like to offer some sport, some banter to alleviate the monotony of a shopkeeper's morning, but I'm nothing but a coarse and homely carp. Not even—I'm a glob of weeds. Just let me go. They both look like wild and powerful women, what with all the bangles and hoop earrings and the dark-tanned scoops of skin below the neckline that speak of days out rafting and climbing and all kinds of witchery.

I've been thinking about what kind of person Nicola would become if we did not become parents. There's a certain amount of liberation that comes with the loss of an ideal. She could live for herself. What would that mean? She could become wild and adventurous, voyage to places she's never been. She could write poetry and worry less about the rent, perhaps, become more powerful, more individual.

I make my bashful way to the counter where the proprietress regards me with an ironic grin. "Howdy stranger. What brings you to town?"

"Uh, Hi. Uh, I was wondering if you knew anything about how the St. Joe was fishing," I stammer, scratching the nape of my neck.

The owner gives her friend an incredulous look, which causes me to flush with consternation. I didn't want to come in. "Wouldn't you rather try on a scarf? How about that blue one over there?" Her friend nods. "It's a hell of a drive. Try a scarf."

The thought of me bouncing along on that bad road seems to inspire a titter between them. It's actually an invitation to join in, to let loose a little bit, but I'm clenched up like a high school wallflower at the senior prom—I don't want to go out on that dance floor.

"It's tough fishing down there," the owner says, her tone turning suddenly professional since I won't boogie. The St. Joe can be great, but right now, the fish are just sitting at the bottom of those long, deep runs. "You might get some action if you bounce a nymph along the bottom. But I wouldn't drive all the way down there, if I were you, unless you're ready to eat some dust. It's thirty miles of dirt road."

I scamper out the door as decorously as I can with the sound of laughter behind me. I suppose it's well deserved.

I make good time in the bright weather, crossing the vast waters of the Columbia and driving up the bluffs on the other side into Oregon. I'm about forty miles from my turn south toward the Deschutes when the sky begins to pale with the telltale smear of white. Smoke on the horizon. I start to smell its familiar bitterness, even with the window rolled up, and it begins to close around the highway again. I click on the headlights. A few more miles and the traffic slows to a crawl. The radio DJ says something about a flare-up near the interstate, and sure enough, there's a police car blocking the lanes up ahead, and a cop waving everybody off onto the exit ramp.

I pull into a gas station and watch for where the trucks are going, figuring the professionals will know what to do in this situation. The majority seems to be pulling into the truck stop across the street, coming to a halt with an ear-splitting blast of their air brakes. Waiting it out. The parking lot is full of frantic cell-phone conversations, all dueling with the truck noise, getting louder and louder with the same message: the road is closed, I don't know when it will open, I'm stuck here in the middle of nowhere, I'm going to be late.

I don't want to hang around here. I buy an iced tea inside, just so I can ask the cashier if there's any other way to travel west. He says there might be, if you drive back to Umatilla and cross the bridge back into Washington.

"But that's way back there!" I protest. "That's east!"

That's a good fifty-two miles back east, he says, and there's no guarantee that the road on the other side of the river will be open. They were talking about closing that one too, last thing I heard, because of the visibility. Might be worth a try, though.

This reply is unsatisfactory.

"Any idea when they expect to open the interstate again?"

He chuckles. "I'd be a rich man if I could tell you that. Could be this evening. Could be tomorrow morning. Who knows?"

This reply is even more unsatisfactory. Sit here waiting the whole afternoon, maybe even a whole night? Wait here in the parking lot, or in the hallway outside the "Professional Drivers Only" lounge, staring at slot machines and candy racks and hot dogs twirling in a steamy glass box? No way. I'm moving on, even if it means moving in the wrong direction.

I travel back through the same dry and rolling range with the sun shimmering in the side mirrors to remind me that every mile east is a mile I'll have to repeat. I should be squinting into those rays, or even turning south by now. The smoke fades behind me, but its absence leaves me brooding. I know we'll meet again, and I alternate between praying that the road stays open and thinking up the worst maledictions if it closes. It isn't very satisfying; whatever I've got to say, the fire isn't likely to listen.

Highway 14 is not what I would call a highway, at least by the standards of interstate travel to which I've grown accustomed. It's a narrow two-lane strip of pitted tar clinging to the bluffs along the river's shore, a back road thrust into sudden prominence as the only means of westward travel. The graders and flaggers who thought they might fill potholes in relative solitude are suddenly contending with an unbroken convoy of tardy, irritated, pedal-to-the-metal drivers. I watch one of those slow/stop-sign guys leap out of the way as a camper swerves to miss a gaping rut, and I'm so wound up and enraged that I curse him myself.

"Get the hell out of the way! Slow? Go to hell!" I charge over the rut, shocks squealing like a bad motel mattress. The car behind me does the same, only a few feet from my bumper.

In the midst of this crazy caravan I catch my first glimpse of actual flames. I've been smoking the equivalent of three packs a day for nearly a week now, had ashes fleck my hair like dandruff, picked motes of charcoal from my eyes, and yet I've never once seen the source of all this combustion. Until now.

The view is terrifying. Across the wide gray blank of the river, perhaps a mile away, the hills are on fire. Smoke boiling. Huge thunderclouds swelling up like malevolent, bloated morels. Veins of murky lightning stabbing the ground. In the midst of it all, the flames, in a frenzy, shooting up to crown the trees, rampaging through the grass. They've already burned right down to the beaches. For some reason the image of someone screaming comes to mind, a Technicolor close-up of stretched lips and straining palate invoking the horror of violation. I'm a witness to a violent crime, a rubbernecker checking out a bad accident, queasy but fascinated.

Two helicopters are swooping between billows of smoke and dropping loads of water on the flames with no apparent effect. Dwarfed by the thunderheads, they look like crickets swept up in a dirty cyclone. The fires have whipped up a gale so strong that it's easy to imagine a live ember sailing right over the firebreak, landing in a patch of sere grass, and kindling a new blaze. Looking to my right, I see it's already happened here: there are blackened patches of sage on the slopes above me where some smoldering coal leaped the great river. I was nervous before, when I thought the river would cage the flames while I shivered at the sublime ferocity of it all from the security of the far shore. Now it seems that the tiger can squeeze between the bars and come roaring down on me at any time. That screaming mouth might be mine. I curse the road people. They should have closed this road and kept me off it for my own good. Damn them. I keep an eye out for signs of a new fire on my exposed flank. Where would I go if I saw the flames sweeping down on me? I could always jump in the river, I suppose, abandon the truck to its fate. Would I grab my fly rod before I dove? Where is my fly rod? What about my vest?

After some heart-thumping moments I begin to realize that if this tiger were going to devour me, it would have gotten me by now. There's a reason why all the fires nearby have burned out. Poor fuel. Rock doesn't burn, and besides a little scraggly sage, all there is over here are the highway's graded slopes. I can thumb my nose, and the flames can rattle their cage and reach their claws through the bars, but those big cats aren't going to get me on this side of the river.

No longer concerned about being burned alive, I get back to praying that the road bosses won't close the road. I take back everything I said about keeping me off the road for my own good and express my gratitude for their decision to let me take my chances. I offer to heed the roadwork signs, even to "give 'em a brake," in exchange for free passage.

My supplications are answered, and once again the smoke fades in my rearview mirror. I cross the bridge at The Dalles, finally turning south into hills of ripe wheat. I'm not sure what to expect from the place. What is a dalle? A hillock? I'm expecting suburbs, some golden arches, but instead the golden geometries of field and shadow are rarely broken, and my road winds among these intervals of light and darkness with the Deschutes flowing somewhere far below.

Maupin is a tiny settlement devoted to rafting, the old downtown clinging to an escarpment above the river, while the rest of the town— the boatyards stacked with rafts, the tourist-trap signs hawking photos of your whitewater plunge—spills over into the basin. I make my way to the riverside through that incongruous western marvel of utterly parched high desert dropping away to reveal a lively blue tongue of water. Night is falling in the canyon. A pilgrimage of haggard and black-robed figures appears to be picking its way down between the rocks. Juniper and sage, the toughest vegetation, making a life out of drought within sight of abundant water. I wouldn't blame them if they snuck down at night for a drink.

The river has managed to hew itself a narrow bed, but the rock is still resisting. Jagged reefs rise from the depths, churning the river into white-crested rapids even now, in the midst of a dry summer. The pools are a deep shade of lapis, not the sky blue of glacier-fed lakes, but a resinous midnight blue, clear when cupped but mysterious in motion. The water leaves a black and glistening residue on the stones, an anchoring for thickets of weed that sway on the leeward side of boulders. The Deschutes is a whitewater spring creek.

I search in vain for a campsite. Each of the two riverside camp-grounds has become a colony of party-colored domes, and every flat patch of sand has been occupied. Ten people are squeezed around a picnic table eating, while another group is lounging in an arc of chairs by the beach. Their camaraderie echoes in the canyon walls. Many of them were probably strangers at the start, but they've been out bonding on the river all day, and now they're swapping stories and chinking beer bottles. One table is even singing an old Elton John song, saying goodbye to the yellow brick road. I'd like to sing along. I give the scene a long, doleful look, hoping I might discover a space if I just look hard enough. But there's no room for me.

I head back downstream to the Blue Hole parking access. You're not supposed to camp here, but that hasn't stopped somebody from putting up a tent, and it won't stop me from erecting mine. It's not a great spot to sleep; I'll be resting my head a few feet below the guardrail. But I don't have a choice.

As I bend the poles into their sleeves I keep an eye on the sunset wash of the pool. Not much is happening out there, but I catch a glimpse of what might be the last rings of a quiet rise under the alders just downstream. I'm considering the likelihood of a fourteen-inch rainbow rising in those shadows when something akin to a dolphin vaults into my startled view. It seems to hover there, then it plunges back down through the dusky ether with a frolicsome wiggle of its tail. Like a mythical beast, it leaves no wake.

It's a fish to be measured in pounds, not inches. I'd like to grab my rod and give chase, but I can't. It's not the tent itself; the tent stands easily if I can just keep my mind on it long enough to keep the pole ends in the grommets. The problem is the stakes. With all my might I can't drive the aluminum spears more than an inch into the gravel. As if to quash any notion of doing without them, a breeze threatens to roll the tent like a tumbleweed into the river. I have to track down a good-sized stone before I can finally hammer two stakes into place and leave my shelter as is, nylon puffing like a palsied lung.

By the last glow of twilight I joint my rod and tie on the usual opening gambit, a deer-hair caddis. A few caddis are indeed making their way along the shore, and the fish are rising sporadically. The river shines like mercury, and when the fish push through the surface, they leave black discs that tremble as they dissolve.

The water near shore reveals no sign of shallows, just an abrupt edge that could lead to water over my head. I lean a foot out, touch nothing below, and decide I'd better cast from the bank. I know I'll never reach the leaping porpoise without wading, but I try a double haul, an attempt to fling my back cast over the guardrail, across the road, and up into the cliffs on the other side. A fish this big demands an attempt, however pathetic it may be. The line whistles backwards in a drooping crescent and snags in the grass beside the tent. There's been no further sign of the fish, which means I can place it in the category of Nessie and other aquatic monsters that appear, dumbfound their audience, and then descend without a trace.

I settle for a soft drift down beneath the alders, although I haven't seen any sign of commotion there for quite a while either. The clouds have lost their glow. Mist blows across the water, swarming with gnats. I wait for a rise, and I wait a long time amid the antic skimming of bats. It appears the trout will not be following their lead. A few subtle rings appear far upstream, out of reach. Bat wing striking water? Probably. I've reached the point where I'm not waiting for anything but tomorrow. As I'm walking over to the tent, I hear the big one again. The splash of its reckoning with gravity echoes off the rock walls.

At one in the morning I give up trying to sleep in the tent. The walls are billowing like a parachute around me. I try to keep my weight on the three unattached corners, but it's no use; I can't sleep and hang on for dear life with the nylon cuffing me the face. Climbing out, I find a night of sparkling stars, a night that says stay up and look at me. The wind is warm with what must be the radiance of sun-baked canyon walls.

I tear down the tent and clamber up on the bug-encrusted hood of the truck, hoping to get a view of the Perseid meteor showers I've heard about on the radio. I'm wide-awake, and maybe because it's a night that beckons romance and I'm sitting alone in a canyon, I feel melancholy. Pablo Neruda claimed that he wrote his twenty love poems at night, camped out under a boat, the rhythm of the sea rolling into the verses. It's a night meant for the intoxication of early love, or the loss of it: the silent question of the river, the whistling breath of the cliffs, the willows shaking with what could be ecstasy or grief. Shooting stars make pale streaks across the sky. I recall a night full of moon out walking with the girl who would, much later, become my wife. The penumbra where we lost sight of each other. The portent of the firefly that landed on my sleeve. All that dizziness and pain; I want to tremble with it some more.

After a fireball has streaked across the sky, trailing celestial dust, I slide down off the hood and curl up in the cab for the rest of the night. I get up while the sun is still high on the canyon wall and fish upstream where the river makes a break for it in a flurry of pocket water. The outcroppings of volcanic rock are slippery with algae and pocked with holes, like old kitchen sponges. Daybreak hasn't muted the water's deep hues; its still midnight under the sheen of pale morning blue. Even now, in full light, I find it hard to gauge the depth of the currents swirling around the boulders.

This isn't dry-fly water. These rapids would have left me lackadaisical in my former float-it-or-forget-it days, but now I'm eager to fathom the deeps with a dead drift nymph. There may be schools of trout down there, jockeying for room with unidentified behemoths. Just to recall the heft of it, I give the nymph a few swings before I let it splat down near a pocket of backwash.

I'm rebuffed. The current tugs the leader through the chutes before the fly can sink. It's missing the pockets and riding the boils instead. As a recent convert, I have no sinking line in my possession—not even a sinking tip. All I've got is a collection of split shot that other people lost in the trees. I clip on the biggest, pinching it tight with a nip of my incisors, and attempt to throw it out there. I have minimal control over its flight. My rod was not built to handle this kind of load. The rig bounces off a rock, rasps through the sedges behind me, and plunges like the wreckage of the space station into whitewater.

It's still not sinking deep enough. I add another split shot. The pleasure I've discovered in nymphing is fading with every addition. It's one thing not to see what's happening, but still be able to feel every twitch, every undulation. It's quite another to throw this kind of weight around. I feel as if I'm towing an anchor.

Yet the added weight finally gets the nymph down where it needs to be. How I manage to detect a strike without the faintest discernable twitch I'll never know. The fly has just about ceased to drift, caught in the spin cycle of a pocket, and I've actually stopped thinking about catching anything. Instead I'm remembering a morning on a party boat off the coast of Maine, a stubby pole in my hands, hauling up what feels like a dead body. Yard upon yard of taut nylon until it surfaces, stunned by the depth change, and the mate reaches down and hooks it with the gaff under the gill plate. Pollock, he says, slapping it down on the deck. Big one.

It may be the gaff that makes me flinch. I raise the rod tip almost inadvertently, and the leader tenses. At first I think I'm snagged on the bottom again, but the resistance isn't dead—it jerks back. I fight the fish through the rapids, sinkers and all, and land it in the eddy by my feet. It's a redside trout, a subspecies that resulted from some long ago mingling of rainbow and cutthroat genes. I've never caught one before. Like the waters of its home, the trout is nearly black from above, with a blaze of coppery red along its sides. The black speckles of a rainbow converge into poppyseed constellations along the back, dusting even the eye with charcoal. I let it go and decide I've had enough of deep-sea fishing.

When I return to the Blue Hole, I find a guy with a hefty spinning rod launching what looks like an equally hefty assemblage of hardware out into Nessie's domain, where it rises to the surface and stays, throwing off a skier's wake. If I were a fish, I would attack this fluttering banana out of sheer annoyance. It's crude. It defies every rule of fly-fishing. I have the sneaking suspicion that it's also very effective. This guy, I'm willing to bet, can identify the beast. I sidle over.

"How's the fishing?" I call to him as I approach. His reaction is mostly hidden behind aviator sunglasses and the shade of a baseball cap advertising what could be a medical product or a muffler brand.

"We're doing pretty good," he says, keeping an eye on his lure, like he's expecting a hit at any time. "My buddy and I must have caught half a dozen between last night and this morning on these sidewinder plugs. Got two of them on ice over there that are over ten pounds easy."

I know at this point I'm going to have to reveal my ignorance if I want to know whether it's ten-pound trout, crappie, or crayfish they've been catching.

"What are they?"

"Mostly hatchery fish. But we got some wild ones too."

I try fill in the blank. "Hatchery . . . ?"

"Hatchery *fish*. You're allowed to keep them. Wild fish you have to release."

Is this guy toying with me? Intent on his lure, he seems too busy to bother. It just hasn't occurred to him that someone standing on shore with a pole in his hand wouldn't even know what he might catch in the river.

"What kind of fish are they, exactly?"

This display of ignorance finally grabs his attention. For the first time I see more than his profile. "What? They're steelhead. Steelhead trout."

I get away from there quickly. At least I've identified the leaping beast of the night before.

If there are steelhead in the river, I need to know what I'm doing. I stop at a place along the river, just outside Maupin, to find out whether the steelhead are still feeding, or if they're just ornery enough to be goaded into striking. The owner confirms the latter case. Some people think the fish have childhood memories of snapping up mayflies, before they followed the floods out to sea. Most, however, think a sex-crazed maniac responds best to a good taunting, which is why the sidewinder works so well.

He says the wild fishery on the Deschutes has suffered recently. I ask if it's due to low flows; I've just come from rivers that were threatening to dry up completely.

"When the Deschutes gets low like that, we're all dead. That's the end of the world." Water levels have never been a problem, he says, because the Deschutes wells up from underground aquifers. It's not a tailwater, and it's not dependent, directly, on snowmelt. It's more like a giant spring creek. He blames the steelhead decline on an explosion in the population of terns near the mouth. The river turns shallow and wide near its end, he says, and the smolts heading downstream don't stand a chance with all those birds swarming around. He's seen them in action himself.

I'm not sure that I can agree; I don't know anything about the terns, but I've always suspected that plummeting fish populations have more to do with overharvest, changes in climate, and changes in water quality than with predators like sea lions that have been eating these fish without depleting the stocks for thousands of years.

I decide to nap away the afternoon's nymph fishing and come out revitalized for the evening rise by driving downstream to Madras, where I attempt to satisfy my hankering for a pillow among the worst selection of snake-bit, disheveled, and downright decrepit motels I've seen. I wind up sleeping away the afternoon in the flaking stucco confines of a motor lodge with the lumber trucks roaring by on the highway and the air conditioner shuddering along on full blast. When I wake up shivering in the chilly dark and tug up the blinds, I find the window glass is warm against my palm; the sun is riding low, but the tarmac is still radiating heat like a cast-iron griddle.

The nearest fly shop is a place I'd passed on the way into town. I buy two tiny caddis pupae that are green as the chives one might find floating in a bowl of udon, and ask about other rivers. According to the map, I'm not that far from the Wood River. The Williamson doesn't look all that far either. They tell me to stick with the Deschutes; the others are farther than they look, and the fishing has been better here. Head to Mecca Flats and park as far from the campground as you can.

"Wait until the sun leaves the water," they tell me. "Half a degree is all it takes to bring them up."

Mecca Flats is a famous stretch of steelhead water flowing through a steep-walled canyon north of town. I turn down the dirt road and start looking for parking. There is none, which explains why the first few miles see fewer anglers. I get pangs of vertigo just looking down over the little heaps of dirt that pass for a shoulder. Way down there at the bottom where the sagebrush look like a crust of lichen on the slopes, the river bends still shimmer with late-afternoon light. I pass a stretch where a fallen tree breaks the current; it leans out from the bank with its roots thrown up in gnarled fingers. The break behind it looks promising for dries. There's even a little pullout, with almost enough room to squeeze off the road without falling off the cliff. But the sun is still bright here, and I can see a line of shade ahead where the shoulder of a higher peak blocks the sun. I keep going and reach the first signs of shade among the cottonwoods of the campground. The canyon widens here, and there's plenty of room for tents, picnic tables, and a full-size parking lot.

The river is different here from the spring creek of the night before; it's a freestone stream of clear but brown water, subdued into a series of long flats. Cottonwood saplings have been planted along the path, with signs tied to their trunks. I bend down to read one.

"Memorial to a fishing buddy. Please water." A rusting coffee can sits in the dry grass nearby. The tree's leaves are yellowing; it doesn't look like the sign has gotten much of a response this summer. I make a mental note to fill the can when I come back, until I notice that each tree has a sign begging for a cup of water. I can't possibly water them all.

I have to march about a mile downstream to find a stretch that's not already taken, passing shrines of human remembrance everywhere. I pass a bench where some pals sat and talked about the fishing—a plaque tells me they enjoyed the view from here. I climb down a set of pressure-treated stairs, reading as I pass the little brass square nailed to the top step. Devoted to a departed fishing friend. As I stop to read it three deer clamber out of the willows and trot into the sagebrush flats behind me, pausing to search the wind for my scent. They startle me into thinking about ghosts.

My spot is a bend in the river where an array of alder branches stands ready to greet any attempt at a back cast. Dangling among the seed cones and leaves are the spoils of lost battles: two nymphs, what appears to be a deer-hair mouse, and a handful of split shot snarled in nylon.

I've been snagged in trees so many times that the years of torment and cursing have honed my technique of fly removal into something approaching a science. My method involves using the rod as an extended arm, snaking the tiptop up through the twigs to the bend in the hook, and then shaking, gently, to free the fly. I have developed another method for retrieving flies when the leader has broken, which involves using the line like a lasso to grab the branch and tug it down into reach. This tactic works here, and I plunk two bead-head nymphs into my box. When the mouse falls, I get under it like a center fielder and catch it in my hand before it can hit the water. It's funny to think that this might be my one technical contribution to the art of fly-fishing. Not some newfangled cast, not some killer pattern, not some unique style of presentation: if I were to teach a class, it would have to be "Arboreal Fly Recovery: Advanced Techniques." I'm imagining my first lecture when I lose my own nymph in the alders on the next cast.

I capture two seven-inch rainbows that are, in my estimation, smolts, before I hear someone upstream wading to shore. It's getting dark, and most of the others have left already. I imagine the rises of something bigger than smolts in the wake of that fallen tree I passed on the drive in. There might be time, if I hurry.

After I've nudged the truck to the brink and clamped down the parking brake, I do a crab walk down the steepest portion of what amounts to a cliff and battle my way through the willows to the bank. Several good fish are rising in the wake behind the old cottonwood trunk, and several more are working the still water below the roots. There isn't much time; sundown still glows here thanks to a cleft in the ridge, but it's fading fast.

In the weak light I can't see any insects. The rises look like those of the mayfly hatch on the Bighorn—a choreographed series of interceptions.

My first cast makes clear why the others have left this spot unfished. It's impossible, with a roll cast, to get more than a couple feet of drag-free drift. I take two sure steps into the current, and then I'm flailing my arms, falling forward into a testicle-clenching embrace with cold water. It laps right up to my chin as I paddle like a dog back to the rocks, soaked, waders now a two-legged water balloon.

I don't have time to disrobe and get comfy. I keep casting, and my fly keeps dragging along the same arc, putting the fish down until it gets so dark I can't even see whether the other guys have gone. Even the river has disappeared from view, slurping blindly at the roots while it waits for the moon to rise above the canyon wall. I unclasp the bungee cord and let an aquarium full of water escape from my legs.

Something unseen starts the shaking of a shaman's gourd as I reach for an uphill rock. Shivering and bedraggled, I hardly give a damn about giving the snake a wide berth. I'm not turning around to find another path. I retract my hand and choose the neighboring rock to hoist myself up. The warning continues, a few feet away.

At the top, another car has pulled into the even skinnier spot behind me, and a guy is breaking down his rod by the light of the open car door. He looks jolly, almost giddy, smiling up at me. "Any luck?" he asks. I'm in a foul humor, ready to bite the head off a menacing serpent just for daring to rattle in my path, but I try to disguise it with a show of civility. No, I tell him. I couldn't get much of a cast down there.

"It's tough. You can get them closer to shore sometimes; some days are better than others. Did you try that eddy just upstream?" No, I say, there were a couple of guys already there. I was down below, and I fell in trying to get a cast near the tree.

"Oh yeah," he says, "I always fish the upstream side, away from the tree. I hate that run below the log. You can fool them down there if you're lucky, but you can't catch them. I don't know how many times I've hooked a good fish and had it go right for that submerged log. Snap! That's it."

"How'd you do tonight?" I ask. "You must have gotten here really late."

He chuckles. I can tell he's really pleased about something, even though I don't know him and can barely see his face. I don't like that. I want someone to commiserate.

"You got that right," he says. "I literally had about ten minutes. Just got back from a business trip. Came out here. Figured I'd get maybe one cast. Just one cast."

He still hasn't answered my question. The punch line must be big. He extends his arms to suggest something ample in between.

"Best night I've ever had, and I come here a lot. This is my favorite hole." His hands rock up and down for emphasis, as if he can't quite believe them himself. They're so far apart, a yardstick would be too skimpy to span them. "One cast. That's it. Been fighting that fish all this time. Half an hour. Biggest fish I've ever taken out of here."

"Wow," I say. To myself, I continue: *Lucky you. You've caught Nessie, and I've been catching smolts and enjoying a nice cold swim. There are times when I just run out of the desire to keep going, when I despair of ever catching anything but smolts, and you, sir, have delivered such a blow. Good for you.*

"Biggest fish. I'm talking really big. Amazing." He's beaming. I'm happy the dark disguises my expression. I feel compelled to torture myself with one more question.

"What'd you get him on?"

"Adams. A little Adams."

Adams! Now that really burns me up. An Adams could be any old bug—he wasn't even matching the hatch! I can't take it anymore. He asks if I'm staying in the campground—he's planning to set up a tent down there. I say no, I'm heading south. He offers me some parting advice just the same, probably because I can't hide the lemon pucker in my face. "The secret to this place is to fish upstream of the campground. The access is tough so there's less pressure." It's what they told me in the fly shop in Madras, the advice I failed to heed until it was too late. I wish him a pleasant evening, get out of my waders, and take off so I can sulk in private.

This is the nature of my journey, I realize. I show up, I don't know the water, and I don't catch anything much. Meanwhile, the persistent guy who fishes here all the time—he knows where the big ones lie. He can spend ten minutes and catch the biggest fish of his life. I want to stretch my arms in amazement like that. I want the fish to keep getting bigger as I get farther west. I want the fates to line up in my favor the closer I get to home. But catching the big one, like getting pregnant, has only partially to do with luck.

I'm so busy feeling dreary that I make a wrong turn and come to my senses after a twenty-mile voyage out into the darkness of the Warm Springs Reservation. I realize I haven't seen the faintest marker of human habitation for miles, not a single light in the blackness outside the window, and the gas has fallen below a quarter tank.

There is no traffic. I make a U-turn right there and barrel back to the river canyon where the one gas station is now closed. It's touch and go all the way to town with the fuel-gauge needle finding the bottom and staying there. I'm forced to consider whether empty is an absolute term. Are there gradations of empty? There's a motorist's platitude: when the gas gauge reads empty, you've got about a gallon in reserve. I put it to the test.

Sliding into bed, my once-frigid flanks scarlet from the blast of a hot shower, I find those elusive fish are still rising among the tree roots of my darkened mind. There's fuel for fishing yet.

Ice Cube

Williamson River, Collier Springs, Oregon

I haven't seen my wife in what feels like a lifetime of miles and motel nights, and suddenly it dawns on me that the moment when we'll see each other again has arrived. Tomorrow morning she'll be stepping off the train in Chemult, a moment of drama I've suppressed. There have been times, particularly since I left the Dakota plains, when I fantasized about driving all the way back to California without stopping, just to see her. I put her out of my mind instead. I camped, fished, cooked, and complained, and now I'm unprepared. Flowers. I should have gotten flowers. Where can I get my hands on flowers at this time of night in a town full of beat motels? My last chance at a florist was somewhere back in Washington—not a sufficient excuse for arriving empty-handed at the station. I sleep fitfully, twisted up in the floral quilt, trying to recall if there were any late-summer wildflowers blooming by the highway that I might snatch up into a ragtag bouquet. I don't remember seeing any. The red numerals of the digital alarm clock blaze in the darkness, counting off the hours in fifteen-minute increments.

Trains and flowers figure prominently in our history. The renaissance of our relationship dates back to the moment when she arrived from England at a train station in the south of France, where I wish I could say I was waiting with a bunch of flowers. Unfortunately, I was late, or, as I like to think, her train came early (it seems absolutely impossible to me that I might have been late for an event whose every detail I had fretted over for days), so that I had to search for her among the pandemonium of the evening rush hour. We hadn't seen each other in several years, but we had been trading letters across the Atlantic in a furious epistolary romance. Now the longed-for moment had come, and I couldn't find her. Commuters thronged past me in a blur of gabardine raincoats, skirts, suits, and scarves. I trailed, and nearly approached, first one blond-maned figure and then another, none of whom seemed to fit my memory and all of whom retreated up the stairs into the darkness. I finally found someone who seemed as bewildered as I was, standing with a bag in the shelter of a pillar, scanning the faces that rushed past. Her hair was longer than I expected, fluffed out in golden tresses over her shoulders. It's an awkward thing to approach someone in a place where everybody is scrupulously avoiding eye contact. Nonetheless, I approached, unsure whether to hover there until she turned or tap her lightly on the shoulder. She looked smaller than I remembered, and I hesitated, slowly stretching out my hand, pressing my fingertip down into the cloth just firmly enough to say I was there. She turned. It was her.

Nicola likes to say that the moment she knew—knew despite all the ambiguous verbiage—that we were destined to be more than friends occurred on the climb back through the old town to my apartment. It was here that I mustered the courage to take off my backpack, saying I'd forgotten I had something for her, and remove a bouquet of sweetpeas I'd bought at the market earlier in the day. Sweetpeas, not red roses: I'd agonized over that. She pulled back the plastic that kept them from getting crushed and inhaled their fragrance. She gave me a kiss.

She's on another train now, and I'm coming to meet her empty-handed. I scan the sere grass along the shoulder for any sign of flowering—all those weeds went to seed a long time ago. Meanwhile my old friend the battery light has chosen this moment for a full-time warning. I shift up, I shift down, and the light stays there, a dismal orange. As soon as she arrives, I'll have to get a mechanic to take a look, if I can find one on a Sunday morning. Things are not going well.

The Chemult station is little more than a bus shelter looking out at an expanse of sighing pines. I climb the steps to the platform where little boys are romping and their parents are scolding them to keep back from the tracks. A train is coming. We see the nose of it in the distance, hear the drone of its wheels. I compose my face while the parents grab on to little limbs, one of which is poised to chuck a stone.

"Drop it. Now!" the boy's mother barks into his ear. He clutches it in his naughty fist, not letting go, dawdling his body from his pinioned arm. The train blares at us, then shudders past, bound for elsewhere. Mom releases her grip, and the kid uncoils himself and chucks his stone onto the tracks.

My mask of joy and pleasure fades into an expression of bafflement. I follow the dwindling behind of the caboose, wondering if I'm in the wrong station. As if reading my thoughts, one of the dads sets down another little scamp and tells me that was the Seattle train. Our train is an hour late. "That's a relief." I say, "Better them than me."

If Nicola misses the flowers, she doesn't show it. Her train brays the air horn to announce its coming and then chugs to a halt in a crescendo of metal shrieks. The steward kicks out the stairs and hops down. One by one the passengers duck their heads and come down the steps into the sunshine. There's none of the sterile dullness of waiting at an airport terminal—it's grand to watch everyone drop their cases for a round of hugs and pats on the back, and now I don't need to make up a face because I'm smiling as I see her nudging her backpack out the door. She hasn't seen me yet.

Sometimes she'll ask me what I see when I see her walking down the street toward me. *What do I look like to you?* Of course, I'm never able to say because I'm usually too immersed in quotidian details for that kind of perspective, until now. I've been gone long enough that I feel the distance linger in my gaze, so that I see her as I might a stranger, a small woman hoisting too large a bag with an arm still muscled from her dancing days and speckled like a quail's egg by the sun. She tucks a flaxen lock behind her ear to keep it from her eyes, and the motion reveals her face. Something visceral twists inside me as all trace of objectivity vanishes.

Would you still fall in love with me if you saw me now?

How can I answer? I've already fallen.

The steward helps her down. He's hustling; they're trying to make up time. She finds my face in the crowd. The instant of recognition makes me feel sick with pleasure, as if I'm careening down the track of an old rollercoaster, knowing I'm safe and yet not so sure. All the physical signs of terror are there, open floodgates of sweat, pulsing blood beats in the temples, tickles in the throat. She comes toward me, blushing, searching my eyes in the gaps between people and then looking down to keep the emotion in her face hidden until they pass. We're both beaming.

"Hello," she says, and slides the strap of her pack off her shoulder.

After the train pulls away, we stow her gear and get in the truck, ready to ride off into romance, until I turn the key and remember the battery light. Actually, it reminds me with a flickering pulse that doesn't look healthy at all.

I tell Nicola the bad news as we ring the bell of the garage across the street. Nobody comes at first. While we wait I have a vision of Mephistopheles scrambling into a blue jumpsuit out back and rubbing his greasy claws. "Cash or credit?" he practices as he zips up, while a cash register zings in the background. "Cash or credit?"

The mechanic comes out, a young guy who looks surprisingly guileless; a bit hungover, maybe, with disheveled hair, but the kind who spends his spare time tinkering in the guts of an old Mustang. I tell him the saga of the light's intermittent appearance and its sudden refusal to go away, and he says he can diagnose the problem with a simple test. If you take the clamp off the positive anode and the car dies, it's the alternator; if the truck keeps running, it's an electrical problem.

I start the truck. He wrestles off the clamp, and the engine sputters and stalls away. It's the alternator—a big, expensive part, as far as I know.

"You're lucky," he says, reading my grimace. "You could have been stranded somewhere, real easy. You've been running down the battery for who knows how long. At some point you'd have turned the key and . . . zippo."

I think about just how terrible a blow to romance that would be, stuck on the roadside, miles from the nearest habitation. I count my blessings. The unlucky part is that he can't fix it. Doesn't have the part in stock and can't order it because it's the weekend. All he can do is charge up the battery and send us to Klamath Falls.

Klamath Falls is an hour south. The road into town is lined with tire stores, auto body shops, and fast-food joints, and we find a parts store with a reconditioned alternator easily enough. Getting it installed is another matter.

"Who can we get to do this?" the guy helping us asks the others behind the counter. They shake their heads.

"Larry?" Somebody nods. He calls Larry; there's no answer.

"How about Bill over at Trimline?" He tries Bill; Bill's out too. He shakes his head. It doesn't look good, he tells us, it being Sunday and all.

"What about Kevin? I saw him earlier. He was in here." He calls Kevin—answering machine. I'm beginning to think we may have to spend the first night of our renewed acquaintance in one of the dire stucco motels I spotted along the highway.

"What about Doctor Dan?" someone calls out from the back office. "Yeah," our guy says. He seems to hesitate before picking up the phone, just a fraction of a second, but I catch it. "I think he could really use the business," the first voice continues.

"I think Doctor Dan is a good bet," our guy tells us, cradling the phone to his ear, but his pause worries me. What's wrong with this doctor? Why does he really need the business? Why is he the last resort?

The doctor is in. Our helper tells him the story, and they agree on a plan. "Okay then, they'll be waiting in the lot," our guy says, hanging up and turning to us. "You're all set. He's on his way over here."

"We could meet him there, at the garage," I say. "We're not broken down or anything."

"He works out of his truck, so he doesn't mind coming to you. Just give him the part."

"Oh. Okay." I weigh the part in my palm, as if looking at a ball of steel might reassure me. What kind of mechanic doesn't have a garage? My wallet rubs uneasily against my thigh. I'm seeing Mephistopheles again, driving his own vehicle this time, a veritable torture chamber on wheels. Misfortune and woe, I fear, are on their way over.

We see him coming in an old ice-cream delivery truck. I'm looking for the devil behind the wheel, and at first I'm convinced I've found him. Doctor Dan squints at us from his seat, measuring us, and I fear it's the look of a small predator—ferret, coyote, some frisky and blood-thirsty bundle of sinews and fangs that has discovered us like baby mice in a grassy nest. Then he grins and hops out into the sizzling glare of the parking lot.

"Hi folks!" he exclaims, proffering a grimed and powerful hand. "Hot out here, huh?"

He's smaller than I expected, but swollen with muscle around the shoulders like a wrestler or, with his fresh crew cut, like a navy roust-about. He's brisk and friendly, charging around the truck for a look, tossing the part on the seat of his rig. He asks if it will start. "Well, all righty," he says, when I answer in the affirmative, "Why don't you follow me over to my place? There's some shade over there. At least over there you folks can sit down while you wait."

I'm starting to think Doctor Dan doesn't seem so bad, but Nicola still looks troubled. I follow her skeptical gaze to the message printed on his T-shirt, which I hadn't bothered to read.

"Police Officer!" it exclaims, next to a pointed gun. "Lay down on your back and do what the nice officer tells you!"

Oh boy. Doctor Dan sees us both looking scandalized, and he cranes his neck down to read his shirt himself, as if he needs to discover what's emblazoned on his stomach too. I see him working through the pitfalls of this awkward situation as he stares at the lettering. Should he say nothing and hope we'll drop it, or should he explain it away? He chooses the latter, and I admire him a bit for it, beginning with the impish, boys-will-be-boys grin.

"What? You don't like my T-shirt?" he asks Nicola. She shakes her head and purses her lips in obvious disapproval. "Ah well. I thought it was funny. It's just a joke, folks." She's not appeased. He shrugs and rubs his bristly flat top, lost. What can he do? It's not like he can take it off. I decide to intervene by motioning toward his van. "Why don't we follow you?"

On the way over, Nicola gives me an earful about Doctor Dan's disgusting T-shirt. "I know," is all I can say. I can imagine Doctor Dan tolling his own series of wrongs about uppity tourist women, and it makes me nervous. I'm sensing one of those situations that can go badly wrong, offenses taken, a whole chain of dominoes falling. I don't want Nicola to yell at the doctor. I don't want the doctor to say something lewd or snide in reply. I just want the alternator replaced, for a fair price.

"I don't want to go near his house," Nicola says. "I don't trust him."

"I know. I don't like it either," I say. "But we have to. Let's just let him fix it so we can get out of here."

Doctor Dan's stucco bungalow is for sale, but he hasn't done much to spruce the place up. Everything but the sign's red lettering has aged to some shade of beige: the walls of the house itself, the trim, the dusty windows, the tiny square of parched straw, even the low chain-link fence that surrounds it all. It's the kind of place where a bad-tempered rottweiler would feel right at home, gnawing someone's limb on the porch. The front door is wide open to the living room, and there's some scuffling going on in the darkened space beyond the arm of a couch. Dan gestures vaguely toward the doorway.

"Go ahead and have a seat. It's just me and the boys here."

The sweep of his arm could be stretched to include two folded lawn chairs leaning against the house. I look at Nicola. I don't think she even imagined going inside. She looks appalled, maybe even frightened. There's an aluminum baseball bat lying on the ground, presumably dropped there by the boys but looking vaguely suggestive of violence. I pull out the lawn chairs and set them down in the shade of a drooping box elder whose leaves are turning beige for lack of water. We sit down to wait.

Doctor Dan doesn't appear to enjoy being watched, but that's too bad, because soon we're not the only observers. First a young guy in a baseball cap and a black heavy-metal T-shirt comes out to peer under the hood. He has an unlit cigarette between his lips where the whiskers are just beginning to thicken.

"You got a light?"

Dan's having none of it. "You shouldn't be smoking yet—you're too young!" He looks to us for approval, eager to show us that he has principles. A model citizen. The young guy looks at us too and stiffens into a more manly posture.

"Yeah, right. You could have told me that when I was seventeen, maybe. Come on, I'll let you have one too."

Dan breaks down and fishes out a lighter, with an apologetic shrug for us. "You kids," he says, and sticks one in his mouth and lights it.

Before he can pick up the wrench again, another guy pulls up in a red monster version of my own truck and leans out. He's older, with a moustache of thick silver bristles and the shadow of a white cowboy hat disguising most of his features. "What you got there, Dan?" He decides to watch too, leaping down from his truck as if it were a saddled bronc. Soon the young man's friend joins the trio, who also lights up and leans his backward baseball cap under the hood.

"Give me some room here, fellas," Dan says, throwing us an exasperated glance to let us know he's thinking of our needs. "I got people waiting here."

The guy with the red truck squints into the shade at us too. "Buddy," he says, kicking one of the tires, "these are Firestones—they've been recalled. You oughta take these over to Schwab. I just got four brand-new tires for free, no questions asked."

I nod and grunt an assent. After the T-shirt, I'm wary of any conversation. "Maybe you're right."

When the guy sees I'm going to stay quiet, he turns back to Dan and punches him in the shoulder, which makes Dan lose his grip on the bolt he's trying to loosen. His vise grip skates across the manifold.

"That's right," the guy says. "I got my money back, and I didn't even have to bring my gun or my dog." Dan snakes a sideways look at his friend; with the cigarette clamped between his lips, it's hard to tell if he's smiling or snarling. The other three chuckle.

The Doctor gets the old alternator off and sets it on the curb. Then he pokes around in the back of his truck for another set of wrenches to tighten the belt around the new part. He's finished his cigarette, which allows him to chat with us between tugs on the wrench.

"That place you went—they're bad news. They don't like me there because I caught 'em cheating me. That's right. They tried to cheat me, and I caught 'em at it. This is the first referral I've had from them, since . . . hell, since last year."

When he says "cheat" he doesn't raise his voice, but his eyes sparkle with a venom that seems more deadly for its subtlety, like an adder coiled in the toe of a shoe. Like they say, it's the silent dog, not the barking one, you have to worry about. I tell him that they went through several other names before they remembered his.

"Doesn't bother me. I've got plenty of business from the other shops in town. You know, they cheated me again with you. I mean, not cheated me, but just the same, they could have called me before you bought the part."

"Why's that?"

"I get a discount on the part. I sell the part to you retail and pocket the difference instead of them. I would have made forty bucks on this here part. But, no, they don't call me until after you bought the part, so they get the money."

"That's bullshit!" says the guy with the truck. The teenagers whistle at each other as if to say they know what they would do if somebody tried it on them. They'd be breaking heads. One of them gives me a suspicious look.

"I'm sorry," I say, "we didn't know. Maybe there's some way we could take it back and let you buy it or something."

"Nope, it's not your fault. It's just the way it is with them. They're cheats. That's why I always go to the other place."

We retreat into silence for a moment, watching him finish up. He sets down the wrench, grabs the part with both fists, and tries to pry it into motion, as a test. It stays put.

"You're all set, folks!" he says. "Start it up!"

I turn the key and wince as the sound of unlubricated metal teeth gnashing against a whirring rubber tongue explodes from the engine.

"Whoa! Hear it reefing that belt!" Dan shouts. "Turn it off! Off!"

I turn it off and give the Doctor a "What-the-hell-was-that?" look.

"Man, your battery must have been low! That's okay though—it won't happen again."

I'm not convinced. I'm recalling the clerk's moment of hesitation, the whole "He-could-use-the-business" tone of things. It occurs to me that there may be reasons why they stopped recommending Doctor Dan, and they may not involve accusations of cheating. Does this guy, working out of a truck in his front yard, know what he's doing?

"You sure?" I ask, trying my best to suggest that it's not a lack of faith in him, just anxiety that's prompting the request. "How about I start it just to make sure?" I turn the key, and the belt screams again.

"Turn it off!" Dan yells. He grabs his wrench. "This thing's supposed to be self-tightening. Step aside, men!" He climbs up on the bumper to get some leverage and groans a full arc more on each bolt with his neck veins bulging and his face squeezed red like a blood-bloated tick. "That's gonna do it. Try it now!" He's panting as I turn the key and the engine proceeds through the normal grumble of notes.

"That's that boys!" He slaps his hands together as if to brush off the dirt, although the grease on his hands isn't going anywhere. He's back in hyperactive terrier mode. Before I can get out of the truck, he's slammed the hood shut and is poised with a pen over a work order. The others scatter at this sign of money about to change hands, as if such a transaction demands privacy. The teens head back across the street and duck inside.

"Take it easy!" the cowboy shouts before he rumbles off on his new tires.

Their departure seems warranted, for the Doctor has gone kind of funny. He seems shy all of a sudden, and although his pen is poised to write, he hasn't put any numbers on the sheet. His head is tilted slightly, like a cat peering into a mouse hole. When he darts a glance my way, the look I discover there is calculating, the look I feared from the start. It's Mephistopheles.

I brace myself to argue over an exorbitant price, worried that he'll try to keep the old alternator that I can take back to the parts store for a fifty-dollar refund. He rubs his mouth, looks at a torn cuticle, and works the joints of his free hand in slow circles. He can't seem to write anything until a shudder comes over him and he exhales something diabolical. Its departure seems to liberate his fingers, and they scribble a price, quickly, as if to get it down on paper before the devil can get back inside. He holds it up to me, mute. It's scrawled so badly I can barely read it. A crooked four and a twisted zero. Forty dollars, for the labor.

"Don't let me forget to give you the core," he says. The words don't come easy, but it's clear that Mephistopheles has lost. Doctor Dan is an honest man after all.

I pull out the cash, and he pushes it into the front pocket of his jeans. Then he dashes over to his van to find the cardboard box and slides the broken part into it. I feel bad all of a sudden, as if he's purposefully undercharged me, just to show that he's no cheat. Wouldn't a mechanic in a garage charge more? Fifty dollars for an hour's labor? Sixty? It wasn't his fault that his friends came out to watch and jabber. Plus he got stiffed on the part discount.

"I'll put in a good word for you over at the store," I tell him as he hands me the box. I set it on the seat. He shrugs, as if to say he's above their dishonorable ways. We get in the truck. It's just about time to say good-bye.

"Where'd you say you folks were from?" he asks, just a final bit of friendly chatter before wishing us a safe and pleasant journey.

"The Bay Area. You know Richmond? It's near Oakland."

"Oh, geeez!" he says. The news blows him a step backward. "How can you folks stand it? I went there once, Oakland. Drove into town and suddenly there were all these black people coming up right to the car . . ."

Stop now, Dan! I'm thinking. *Don't go there!* Nicola looks like someone has just jabbed a finger in her eye. She's grabbing her forehead and wringing her temples. But Dan won't stop.

"All these black faces staring right in the window. I turned right around and tore ass out of there and never went back!"

Enough Dan! Stop right here!

"You couldn't drag me back there. How can you people stand it with all of them around?"

"We like it there," Nicola says, cradling her brow.

Dan gets the message. He's about to add something, but he stops himself and swallows, more of a gulp really, as awareness of what he's done spreads across his features.

"Thank you for your *work*, Dan," I say, wondering if he'll catch the emphasis and whether it's too subtle to convey my ambivalence. If he could have just kept his demons at bay for a couple minutes more we'd have taken his side. Now it's not so simple.

"Well, you folks have a good trip," he says, and bends down for a wrench as I start the engine. We set off through the dappled shade of the street, letting Dan recede in the rearview mirror, getting smaller and smaller as he gathers up his tools.

"We're not going to recommend him," Nicola says. "No way."

"Well, okay," I say, not wanting a battle on our first day back together, "but he did help us out, and he didn't take advantage of us. We could mention that." I have a long list of rationalizations—that he's a product of his community, that he's a single father, that he didn't know enough to keep his scurvy views to himself, that he's down on his luck and maybe getting more business will help him change his ways, but really it all comes down to gratitude. We're on our way thanks to Doctor Dan, and he didn't stick it to us. The fact is we've been rescued by a sexist bigot.

"Yeah, Doctor Dan is great, as long as you're not female or black, or Jewish, probably, or Asian, or . . ."

"Yeah, okay, I got it. If they ask us, we'll say he did good work, but that the experience was not for everybody. How's that?"

"The experience was not for anybody."

"Okay. If they ask, we'll say he did the job. That's it."

Nicola nods. She's staring out the window at the fast-food signs. This is definitely not what I had in mind when I arrived at Chemult station. We need to get out of here, fast.

She waits in the cab while I run inside with the part. The guy we dealt with earlier is gone, replaced by a new woman who rings up the credit without even asking who did the work. She doesn't know about Doctor Dan, and when it comes down to it I don't offer his name. "You have a nice day," she says, handing me the slip. I leave with the credit slip and no questions asked. That's it: don't ask, don't tell. The whole moral quandary has ended with a whimper.

Nicola doesn't ask me what I said, but I tell her anyway. Reaching for my seat-belt clasp as she continues to stare out the window, I feel like I deserved at least a few more hours of heroic grandeur without a test of my mettle. Don't we earn at least a day of heroic proportions after a long absence? I feel craven instead, pierced in my Achilles' heel, a blundering failure of an Odysseus, but what was the alternative? A consciousness-raising teach-in in Dan's withered front yard with the "boys" gathered round like cigarette-puffing apostles of enlightenment? All I asked for was a fair price for an automotive repair, and that's what I got.

"I didn't say anything about him," I say, "Good or bad. They never asked." The words taste like the gruel of defeat. We drive most of the way back in silence.

I realize as we set up camp in a Forest Service campground above Collier Springs that I'll have to hope for a chance at redemption in the next couple days. That may mean taking a hiatus from fishing. We spend the next couple hours in the tent getting to know one another again. We cook a dinner of baked beans and rice pilaf. Tame chipmunks slink up to the picnic table to investigate. A Steller's jay shrieks in a pine bough, hoping for scraps too. Little kids ride their bikes up and down the dirt road, shouting for their parents to watch and skidding to throw up a cloud of dust.

The sun is filtering down through the trees, fading into evening. I shouldn't go fishing; things are fragile. I say I'm just going to walk over and take a look, just a look. I'm not going to fish.

"You can fish if you want. I don't mind."

I try to appear reluctant. Well, I say, I don't really want to, but maybe I should. Clear my head. I haven't fished at all today. Yeah, maybe I should, if you really don't mind.

"Don't go out there forever. I don't want to be sitting here alone in the dark."

I say I'll go for half an hour, max. That's what you always say, she says. I yank on my waders and slide my feet into my gruesome sneakers and clomp over for a kiss good-bye. There's mistrust in her eyes, and a warning. If I let her down this time, there'll be hell to pay. I tap my watch. I'm going to set the countdown on this, I say. Don't worry, I'll be back here in thirty minutes. Thirty-five minutes tops.

"You said half an hour."

"Right, thirty minutes it is. I will be back here in thirty minutes, I promise." I turn and clomp away across the campground, stripping out line as I go.

"Don't be late!" she calls out to me before I head down into the ravine.

Thirty minutes is a blink of an eye when it comes to fishing. I've broken a lot of these promises; however, I'm always careful to include the word "about" in case I forget to look at my watch or the fishing gets good and I see just one more perfect run, one more imperative rise. This time I omitted the "about" because even if Moby Dick is rising around the next bend, I intend to be back on time.

The river makes it easy for me. The Williamson here is a slow brown trough of algae-slick stones, the water foaming like cappuccino where it falls through riffles. Tiny fish are pricking the surface when I arrive, tiny enough that they might be tadpoles coming up for a breath or crane fly larvae testing the air before they hatch. Fifteen minutes elapse and nothing happens, except that two guys with their rods already broken down hike up the ridge to the campground. I cover a long, still pool, knowing it's in vain, in exactly eight minutes. That leaves me seven to hike back. I may even be two minutes early.

Nicola is reading in the tent when I arrive. She looks up, startled by the squishy sounds my shoes make as I kick them off by the door. I tug down my waders, using the tent for balance, and unzip the screen to poke in my head. "You're back!" she says.

"Of course I am! You think I'd stay out there with you here?" I climb inside and sprawl on my bag, luxuriating in the way the tents feels cramped, leg against hip, arm brushing shoulder. We spend the rest of the evening looking for meteor showers by the light of a full moon, clasped together in our bags. I don't want to sleep; even with the candle blown out I can see the moon's glaze on her eye when she blinks. It's a chilly night, and her sleeping bag is far more ample than mine. I curl myself along the length of her body like an inchworm, and still the cold seeps in along the zipper. She's slumbering soundly long before I nod off with my fleece hat covering my ears.

I let her sleep on as dawn begins with the croak of ravens. Whispering an explanation in her ear, I slide my pants up inside the warmth of the bag and slip out of the tent. She's liable to be tired, I figure, so this morning is my window of opportunity. It's a quarter past six; I can fish at least until eight and be back in time to wake her with a cup of freshly brewed tea.

I decide I don't like fishing the morning rise—it's too cold and brutal a sacrifice. My jeans are clammy, my fingers are stiff, and my breath pours forth in a great flume of condensation. I drive downstream to the picnic area with the heater on full blast, through a mist that has congealed, potent and frigid, under the pines. The mist is thickest over Spring Creek, the turbulent jet of turquoise water that turns the Williamson into a major-league trout stream.

As I walk down to the bank I'm imagining another Yellow Breeches scenario, with the fish congregating in the ribbon of colder water flowing down from the mouth of Spring Creek. I wade across to the opposite shallows and strip out line, searching for a pocket, a backwater, a depression in the gravel, anything that might harbor a fish. Usually I like three or four false casts before I release the line, but I've had nine or ten before I just let go and shoot the line through my fingers. The entire riffle seems devoid of structure larger than a baseball, and the pool below is no better, a pond devoid of clues. I stir up nothing larger than a water strider.

Off in the distance I can see the branches of a flood-beached tree, and the water glitters down there in a way that suggests a small cascade. The suggestion of faster water is all I need. I set off down the bank, following a deer path where I can, bushwhacking the rest of the way. It's tough going, and the sweat begins to roll, my feet plashing in their own little baggies of sour water, salty driblets stinging my eyes. As I get closer I can see the reward—there is indeed a pitch in the streambed, and the water foams, freshly poured.

Only after I have navigated the last great barrier—a wall of dead willow spikes surrounded on three sides by a deep, beaver-haunted moat, do I come into the clear and find a false-casting threesome already splashing their way into position. They must have arrived while I was pushing, back first, through the brush. A bakery truck chugs past behind a scrim of trees, and I follow it to the pullout where their jaunty red SUV is parked under a cottonwood. The highway is right there.

The tree provides the only expanse of broken water for as far as the eye can see. There's nothing to do but go back by the path I've blazed and try fishing the chilly pools of Spring Creek, where some legitimate aquatic insects are actually hatching. A few crane-fly-sized midges spiral in a helter-skelter path over the surface, caddis dodge along the shore, and what appears to be a small yellow stonefly scrambles off a rock into flight. Further encouragement comes in the form of a sign tacked to a tree that states there is no limit on brook trout. Death to the unnatural! I could use a horde of eager brookies about now, no matter what their size. The water itself has that sapphire hue of a supercooled substance, vodka that has sat in the freezer until it's as cold as ice but still makes an aqueous swirl in a shot glass.

I step out toward a carved reef of clay where the water appears to be a couple feet deep. My foot drops and keeps searching for bottom. I'm swimming yet again in six feet of water, and the shock seizes my lungs in a single abrasive gulp.

After I've floundered to shore, shaken the spray off my hair like a wet Lab, and wrung out my sleeves, I keep right on shivering. It's still a cold morning, and now I'm soaked and my stomach is empty. How many baptisms will this voyage require? I find myself wondering. Haven't I already reached the point of total immersion, submerged myself already in the rhythms of countless pools? Must I drift like a log, die like a salmon, to complete this journey?

This place is fished out, I sputter to myself. *The picnic people have caught them all.* I hustle back to the truck, where I catch a glimpse of my face as I back up to turn around. My lips are gray, like a wad of chewed-up bubblegum.

Back at camp, I tear off my wet clothes and force my fingers to clasp the buttons of a dry shirt. Our neighbors are breakfasting around us, and I try to keep the truck bed between my naked limbs and their view, for modesty's sake. They can still see my head jerking up and down in an obvious struggle.

"Daddy, what's *he* doing?" a little boy at the nearest picnic table asks between mouthfuls of egg. He points me out and the father, who along with the rest of the adults has been pretending not to look, now looks at me quizzically.

"He's *changing his clothes.*"

"Why is he *changing his clothes?*"

"I don't know why he's *changing his clothes.*"

"He's funny, Daddy. He's funny."

After I've managed to get the waist of my jeans snapped, I solve the mystery by draping my soggy clothes over some nearby branches where everyone can see them dripping. Nicola is still drowsing in the balmy cocoon of the tent, oblivious to my encounter with cold until I press the frozen ham of my palm to her bicep in an attempt to rub a greeting. She writhes and cries out at my touch. "You're freezing!"

"I forgot. I'm sorry. I fell in the river."

"Let me see your hands," she says, and compresses them between her own. They feel like they're melting, deliciously at first, then painfully, sizzling with tiny pricks along the nerves. I let them remain until they feel like they're glowing, then set about making some breakfast.

I feel not a single pang when we cross the Wood River, bound for Crater Lake and a break from fishing. I'm ready for a respite from these devotions, this ritual bathing in cold, turbulent water. I feel no urge whatsoever to pull over and throw a line into what appears to be a smaller version of Spring Creek, winding slow and blue through cattle country. In fact, the water source for the two rivers is probably the same, and we're headed for it: Crater Lake, the caldera of a dormant volcano. The lake, surrounded by a ring of peaks, has no natural outlet. The water seeps through underground fissures, gushing forth in springs when it reaches the valley floor. Just the thought of another Spring Creek immersion trickles down my spine like snowmelt. Some other time, I say to myself, some other time.

We climb into the pines. A caravan of campers leads the way upward to a view of the wind-ruffled turquoise lake, and a busy parking lot. After finding a campsite on the rim, with a sense of buoyant space beyond, we sit on a log and watch the ravens riding the thermals. Tomorrow, we decide, we'll hike, but today we'll just watch, lounge around, and doze.

"I can't get past the money. It seems selfish, self-indulgent, to spend that much on something we want but don't need."

She's right—it's a lot of money, and insurance won't cover a dime of it. We put twelve thousand dollars on the table before we begin, win or lose. That's a down payment on a house. It could buy us a new car. It'll wipe out our life savings. The thought of spending all that money and being left with nothing is almost impossible to bear. It's harder for Nicola. She grew up in England, where the national health system covers everything. Spending money on health care is something only wealthy people do. But is it an indulgence? Ecologically, I suppose it is—it's not like the human species will go extinct without our offspring. But isn't there an imperative here, something we can't suppress that will lead us to the brink of spending all we have on the chance? That doesn't feel like indulgence to me, but it is a gamble.

"I feel like even if we do get pregnant, we'll be punished for doing this somehow."

That red light flashing in the car—I see signs of devastation everywhere myself. I am one of those prepare-for-the-worst people. I envy those people who just carry on, take the good and the bad with equanimity. They must live longer.

"I think we'd produce a good kid, though, you and I. I think we'd be good parents. I can see us with a little one. The three of us."

The kids (they like to put several eggs in at once, to maximize the chances that one will implant, which often leads to multiple births) should not get my big ears or pointy nose, I feel like saying. But what if it actually worked? Our child might inherit my pessimistic tendencies, but an avalanche of brightness would bury those, because I would no longer be the same man. I would have to believe in the possibilities of life, if we succeeded, if we placed this bet, and the mystical powers that be blessed us. I use the word "bless" with caution—I hear it too much around town. But it seems appropriate to circumstances like these. Nicola has been buying children's books and furry little bears for years, things ostensibly for other couples that she can't quite give away. She has a drawer for these items. It's an act of faith I want to honor.

"We can't worry about the money," I say. "It's just money."

"I know. So now you want to do it?"

"I'm running out of reasons not to, I guess. I want to do it, then I get scared, and I don't want to take the risk. I want it to go away. I don't want to have to make the decision. I'm excited, then I'm scared."

"Me too."

The afternoon drifts away like that, and when the shadows are spilling into the canyon we head down to the lodge. It's been a long time since I've been anywhere more civilized than a gas station, so there's plenty for me to see. We sit in the leather lounge chairs as the sun goes down over the lake, and again what startles me is not the water but the space, the bowl of sparkling and translucent light. We look down on a string of tiny magpies winging their way to shore, as if we were riding a cloud.

Of course, the people captivate me too, like a pageant of well-groomed, well-fed, and well-rested performers streaming by in all their elated, bored, giggling and grouchy finery. Nicola has actually packed for this kind of occasion, and she looks refined in her heathered fleece and pearls. I look a bit more rustic in what amounts to my least-dirty clothes, a nylon shirt soaked in the Deschutes and left to turn crispy on a picnic table, and a pair of chinos I've been avoiding because of a rather large hole in the crotch.

There's talk of golf and the stock market around us. We sip our

Caldera Amber Ales, munch on little circles of toast plumped with a dollop of eggplant pate, savor the Gruyere in a bowl of French onion soup. There's a fire snapping in the fireplace, and we bask in the warmth, lingering long after dark to keep warm. I'm dreading my sleeping bag; the weather service has predicted a low of 35 degrees near dawn. Already a chill sweeps into the great hall whenever someone steps outside on the deck for a look.

Only when we're ready for sleep do we drag ourselves out into the dark, marveling briefly at the crisp view of stars. Crisp because unencumbered by water vapor, haze, carbon dioxide—all the insulation that keeps us warm and alive after sundown. We're closer to the void of space. I put on all the layers I can find—flannel pajamas, long johns, fleece vest, with the hat in reserve for later, and slide into my bag, wishing fervently that the zippers on our sleeping bags matched.

"You'll stay warmer if you're naked," Nicola says. "That's what you're supposed to do."

"I'll get naked if I can sleep in your bag with you."

We try that configuration, and others, before conceding that I'm going to have to go it alone. Her bag is meant for smaller folk; my buns are toasty, but my shoulders, right down to the middle of my back, are bare to the elements.

"How about we share my bag?" I ask, a little plaintively.

She snuggles her bag right up to her chin. I can see she isn't coming out of there until morning. "No way."

I spend the night with my head crammed down like a turtle, basking in my own breath until I run out of oxygen and little flashbulbs start whirling across my eyelids. I have to emerge at regular intervals throughout the night, filling my chest with arctic air, and it isn't long before I make a solemn pact: my first deed upon returning home will be to go out to the store and buy a new sleeping bag, a thick one. Total overkill. A zero-degree bag. No, an eight-below-zero bag. No, an Everest-style mummy sack that fluffs out like a blubbery walrus. And lots of those little bags of magic chemicals that radiate heat after you squeeze them, to put down around my toes. Lots of those. I dream of a warm bag the way a starving man dreams of feasting.

Angling for Invertebrates

Hot coffee. I can smell hot coffee, the aroma of some neighbor's mug curling up in little twists of steam and wafting in through the door of the tent. I want some, right now, and I don't want to have to get out of the warmth I've spent all night gathering and hoarding in my bag to make it. I refuse to begin the day with my hands immersed in the ice water of some spigot, filling the pan with water. I'm not going to search for the matches and fumble with the fuel pump on the stove for fifty awkward strokes. I want the warm mug in my hand.

I nudge Nicola and sell her on the idea: brunch inside the lodge, with glorious views of the lake and somebody placing platters of hot food in front of us. She agrees readily, as long as we can take a shower first. She doesn't want to go in there with me looking too scruffy.

I've managed to travel most of the way across the country without setting a bare foot on the concrete floor of a campground shower stall, and with good reason. I hate them. I hate the way the line of unshaven and half-garbed men forms outside the mildewed plastic sheeting. I hate the foul smells that rise from the stalls next door. I loathe the wreath of black hairs that ornament the floor where my T-shirt, inevitably the clean one, falls from its perch on the single clothes hook. And most of all I detest the incessant demand for dimes and quarters, the way the hot water begins to taper off as a warning just before it cuts out altogether. Where am I to attach a coin purse to my naked thigh? How am I to grip a dime with soapy fingers, and how find the slot through a lather of shampoo?

"Do I have to?" I ask. "Couldn't I just wash my face, clean up a bit?" I flick my hair around a little bit in a gesture of grooming.

"You need a shower." She gives me a look that says, believe me, you *need* a shower, don't fight me on this one. I know better than to quibble. If my armpits and nether regions *need* a soaping, so be it.

Between us we have five quarters. I give her three, which means I'll have about one minute and thirty seconds of hot water in which to immerse myself. Curiously, there is no line in the men's room—the place is empty and the mirrors bear no trace of their usual morning steam.

The reason for the absence of a crowd soon becomes clear just as soon as I have disrobed, hung my clothes on the hook and tiptoed around a gruesome band-aid to put my quarters in the slot. I stiffen for the impact, and behold, it comes—not the steamy torrent I expect but a mortifying plume straight from the well. The cold lambastes my backside, and I squeal in horror like a guinea pig, nearly sliding to my knees as I duck out of the way. I've forgotten my biggest gripe against campground showers. They're always served by a little, itty-bitty tank that can handle maybe one, maybe two showers in an hour, so that unless you rise in the dark before everybody else in the place and hustle down there, you will plunk your coins into the meter and be rewarded with a blast of liquefied snow.

I grab my clothes and escape the stall. Even the spray is cold, like standing near a waterfall. As I dry off I can hear my money frittering away with the ticking of the meter. I have a choice: I can get dressed, unwashed, or I can follow a hunch that leads to a hot water tap on one of the sinks.

As I suspected, the water from the tap is piping hot. The only obstacle to bathing, other than the fact that the sink is too small for me to climb into, is that the taps are those annoying press-down kind that make it impossible to even wash your hands because one hand must always be pushing down on the tap to keep the water coming. There is also the issue of etiquette, since it's not normally the rule to caper around naked in front of the sinks, splashing water on your gonads.

I make my move furtively, listening for the crunch of gravel outside. A wad of paper towels, a dash of soap, some water on the floor, and it's all over with no one the wiser, except that I decide to push it and wash my hair in the sink too. Towel around my waist, I'm leaning over, suds sliding down my brow, when I hear footsteps. They come closer, too close for an approach to the women's bathroom. I rinse furiously in an attempt to avoid embarrassment, but I'm too late. The door whines open. I hear the outdoor sound of a breeze in the pines, and I wait for a grunt of disapproval.

"Hel—lo! What are you doing in there? Are you almost ready?" It's a very familiar voice.

After breakfast we decide to take a hike along Annie Creek, which in addition to stretching our legs and offering the sights and sounds of the high country will also provide the chance to throw a line. I'm ready for a timid encounter with shallow water, nothing that's going to dunk me over my head, just a small, safe, late-morning encounter with water.

We scramble down a series of switchbacks to the floor of the caldera where the stream babbles over its bronze gravel like another stream I know, Pebble Creek, in Yellowstone. The meadows look much the same, lush and spangled with wildflowers, and so does the water itself, the shallow riffles and grass-lined runs, even the few deeper pools behind downed logs. The undercut banks are similar too, and those of Pebble Creek are crowded with cutthroats, some of them surprisingly large.

Casting to the tail of the first promising run, I'm pondering a potential dilemma of riches. To land a single fish on Pebble Creek meant scattering dozens more, some that might be larger and make me regret setting the hook. Will the trout here be chasing each other to get my fly first?

After nothing responds to my offerings, which include both wet and dry menu options, I stride up to the hole, hoping to frighten the fish into showing themselves. My shadow looms across the surface. By now the water should be heaving with the struggle of too many bodies for too few hiding places, but there's not a flicker of a fin down there. Just to be sure, I pick up a stone from the center of the riffle. The underside swarms with a rich stew of wriggling and crawling tidbits, suggesting this rock stays underwater all through the seasons. There's plenty to eat.

I fish through the next pool, and the next, and stomp up to the brink of each one after I catch nothing. My feet get wet, but I don't scare up any signs of fish. Nicola is romping in the meadow, busy taking pictures of the sunlight gleaming on the wings of bumblebees, of shooting stars and buttercups, and of sparkling water. She looks a lot more joyful than I feel.

"There are no fish in here!" I announce to a stand of young fir. They sway indifferently. I have reached a kind of epitome of fishing as art form, a completely unnatural act of faith. I am fishing, and there are no fish. Whatever solace there is lies in the extremes of the imagination. I think of all those months with the basal thermometer, charting the temperature rise and fall that marks ovulation. Sex as a practice of precise timing, not spontaneity. And then the disappointment. A grasshopper launches itself into the air with the sound of a baseball card ticking against bicycle spokes—another indifferent, ludicrous sound. I crank my reel in reply, pulling the fly in all the way to the tiptop, and set off through the greenery to join Nicola. We roam around aimlessly in this basin, and as I'm looking up at the sky or bending to inspect a blossom I begin to realize that my world has been flowing into an ever more narrow defile for quite some time, a canyon replete with the echoes of rushing water, with mayflies dancing and the husks of their youth glued to the branches of willows. All that I love about fishing, but the walls of a canyon nevertheless.

We just sit for some time, holding hands. The smooth pressure of her fingers feels new to me, makes me notice the calluses on my own palm. The sensation of just sitting there, leaving time to the bees and the breeze, is a novelty too. Things happen without drama. The bark presses its scales into the back of my thighs. A plane draws a chalky arrow across the sky. A woodpecker thrums a log in the distance. We get up without a cue, when we feel like it, and teeter across a logjam to a gravel bar where we can splash around. There is no good time to talk about what we want to do.

"It's a lot of money for a 40 percent chance," she says, looking through the viewfinder of the camera. "You sure you want to do it?" She's feeling me out—how much do I really want it? Twelve thousand dollars is a lot of money.

"I don't care about the money. What about you? Have you thought about it?"

"I'd like to make a little someone who looks like us. That's what I want."

"That's what I want too."

The water feels like a different medium now that I'm not wading slowly against the current, searching the depths. It's just water, clear and cool, playful as a fountain on a hot afternoon. We're on our way back up the trail when I remember my fly rod, leaning where I left it in the shade against a tree. I have to hustle back to find it.

Later, as we hike the last legs of the trail, I pause to read the caption of an interpretive sign: "Annie Creek's cold, clean water is home to an abundance of invertebrate life, including crayfish, mayfly and caddis fly larvae." The painted crayfish on the sign appears to be clapping its claws in pleasure, and even the mayfly nymphs seem to be scuttling with happiness over their stone, because there's not a single set of predatory jaws patrolling this billboard. As I suspected, Annie Creek has no fish; I've been fishing in a stream that doesn't even contain vertebrates, let alone trout.

"Who cares? I'd rather spend the afternoon with my wife than a trout."

"Do you wish I was a trout?" She's smiling, but it's brittle. "You could hold my fin." What if we don't succeed? she's asking. Will I go on roaming like this, looking for some kind of reparations for the child who is missing at home?

I nearly left my fly rod under a tree—that should be proof enough! From now on, I want to say, we will make these trips together. But there's no way to prove that now. I squeeze her fingers, bend down to her face so that there's nothing to be seen but the two of us.

"Of course not," I say. "Who'd want to kiss a trout?"

Good-byes

Upper Sacramento River, Dunsmuir, California

Truth be told, as we pass the road sign that welcomes us back to California, I'm gripped by a fantasy of home so strong that I can barely see the road. It takes me on a virtual tour of our house, lets me lounge on the couch, inspect the tomato plants I stuck in the ground, brew a pot of green tea in the kitchen while a breeze from the backyard soothes its way through the screen door.

It's all less than a day's drive away now, and the on-ramp beckons, especially when we drive into Dunsmuir and the only room we can find—a "Honeymoon Suite"—hasn't been remodeled since the days when my dad's hair flowed over his shoulders and his snug jeans ended in bell-bottoms. I know the '70s have come back into style—but not these '70s, not the rust and ochre plush carpet, not the bedroom set with the dresser carved to look like a Spanish treasure chest filled with doubloons. Certainly not the partition between bath and bed, fashioned in a series of yellow and green circles to look like a case of beer bottles stacked on their side. Junkyard rust, the stale pool in an unflushed urinal—this color scheme is the reason the '70s went out of style in the first place. This is not trendy.

Why am I feeling this visceral repulsion? Why not just stretch out on the bed with the lights dimmed? Because my stomach flops around like a beached carp just thinking of the juvenile embarrassments associated with this decor: doing "the Hustle" in the living room when my babysitter let me stay up and watch some Disco Fever dance-a-thon; donning a *Planet of the Apes* costume and looking out at the world through the eye slits of an erudite orangutan mask; wiping out on my Big Wheels and sitting on the couch with an ice pack on my scraped upper lip. My parents had this very same furniture set!

The owner has a point, however, when he argues against camping in the park down the road. The midnight train could be late, hours late, and wouldn't it be nicer to roll over to the bed stand and call for an update instead of waiting down at the station for hours on end? It could mean the difference between a good night's sleep and sitting awake in the car half the night.

"What's the chances they'll be late tonight?" I ask him.

"You're better off asking what's the odds they'll be on time. That'd be about once in a blue moon, as far as I can recall."

His pessimism proves correct. After snoozing in the dark for an hour, I call from bed to find out that the train is running two hours late. The agent says they're trying to make up time on the way; we'd better get there in an hour and twenty minutes, just to be sure. Pillowed and warm, I'm more happy than I would have been had we driven to the station for this news, but it's not like I can just switch off and go back to sleep. We know we should sleep, but we can't do it.

"Try repeating a mantra," Nicola says, "like Ommmm. Ommmm. Ommmm."

"Ommmm. Ommmm. Ommmmm."

"No! Not like that! To yourself!"

We tussle with the sheets to keep our feet covered. We groan. We curse Amtrak. I count sheep until they start bawling as they leap the fence. The digital clock emits a faint hum, and occasional trucks rumble past on the freeway. Sometimes I think I sense the river flowing on through the oaks and boulders at the edge of the lot, a susurrus that trickles under the door to my ear. Finally it's time to get up.

The station looks deserted, but we're not alone. Tired faces lurk behind dark car windows, smoldering in a stew of wrath, cigarettes, and late-night radio. There's no waiting room, but the switching station, lit by fluorescent panels and smelling of old newspaper ink, has a few swivel chairs between the file cabinets where the engineers can wait, and a couple of the overnight operators are still bent over papers and sipping coffee. The radio crackles with unintelligible reports from all over the line. There's a motto over the door: "No job is so important, or service so necessary, that it demands a compromise in safety." I wonder when and why that went up.

The train is still running two hours late, last they heard. We can sit and wait inside if we like. Nicola shakes her head. Too bright for two in the morning. We go back to the car.

Half an hour later we hear the unmistakable grumble of an approaching engine. It blows out a breathy toot, then trumpets like an angry elephant. We look at each other with surprise. Is this it? Maybe they did make up the time after all. Our neighbor seems to think so. She gets out and drags her bags up to the platform in what seems a vote of unwarranted confidence, or desperation. She stands beside them expectantly, a small, stocky woman in red flats and a pink dress that reaches her calves, while her companion stays slouched in his seat, baseball cap drawn over eyebrows. We stay put too. And watch the train roar by without a pause, a long chain of cargo and boxcars, with the backdraft clutching at her hair and blouse.

She shakes her fist at first, raving soundlessly into the thunder of the wheels, and when the caboose arrives she leaps out into its wake. Only as it recedes can we hear her. She's hoarse. "Pinche mothers! Chingate!"

She glares at us. If we had believed, had gotten our bags out there, maybe our train would have come. But no, we just sat there and brought the wrong train down the tracks. She wheels the bags back to the side of her car, and growls as she opens the door again. "Make up the time! Porque lo creo? Hijo de puta! Five minutes more and that train will be even later than they said!"

She glares at us again, this time challenging us to disagree so she can rip the door off and tear our lungs out. I shake my head to say it's unbelievable, but true. She's absolutely right. Five minutes more and they're even later than they said they would be. I think she's going to get back in her car, but she's not done. She goes back to the tracks and stands right in the middle with her hands on her hips, peering into the northern darkness, defying the malevolent train to come and get a piece of her, to come right now and run her down. When even this gesture fails, she stalks back to the car.

Half an hour later there's a rap of knuckles on Nicola's window. She's long since locked the door, but the noise, and the face pressed close, startles us both. "It's coming!" the woman says, her eyes like beads of mercury. "Right now!" Car doors slam. A trio of shaggy youths plays hackeysack by the stairs while a green-haired girl watches. We hear the bellow of the horn, and a single light grows to become the snout of an engine. In a flash it has stopped, thrown open the doors, and loaded everyone aboard. After all those slow minutes, there's barely enough time to say good-bye, to clarify the place of fishing in my life, to reassure and redress.

"Stay safe," I say, "I'll be home soon."

"Come back to me."

"Off we go folks! All aboard!"

We wave at each other through the window until her train disappears into the night, headed south along the river.

All night I dream about the woman in the tracks and the train that killed this river. One morning in August 1992, a train came down the rollercoaster that follows the Sacramento through a narrow canyon. In my sleep I feel the pendulum of their sway, back and forth, straining outward and then recovering, except this time a rock has fallen into the tracks and come to rest just right for misfortune, or a buckle in the track has caught the weakest wheel, and the cars begin to keel. There is no recovery. They keep going, the weight of one dragging the next down. Down goes the load of Japanese sedans, the pallets of redwood planks bound for Oakland lumberyards, the refrigerated crates of red delicious headed to the supermarkets. When the catastrophic bangs of their dismemberment subside, something else becomes audible in the hush: the quiet splash of herbicide as it drains from the fissures in the tanks and runs down over the rocks into the river.

In my dream, the woman stands in the tracks and shakes her fist at the carnage that has kept her train from coming. When she opens her mouth to speak, I wake up; she's conjuring dead fish from the river, and I'm frightened by the bloated corpse of a trout drifting toward me. I sit up in bed and turn on the light. I can still see, at least. That trout had worn away its eyeballs, and it seemed to want to fill its sockets with mine.

Sitting by the lamp is the source of my nightmare, the glossy brochure I decided to read in bed, thinking it would help me forget the station and fall asleep. All the details of the disaster are in there, in clinical summary—the massacre of thousands of fish, the sterilization of eight miles of river, the legal settlement that established $14 million as the price tag for lost resources, the slow but surprisingly vibrant recovery of the stream. The settlement money paid for the brochure. I flick it off the table to the floor where I can't see it, and shut off the light.

Not surprisingly after the night's events, I miss the morning rise. The sun is dry and hot under the cedars, and the truck cab is already a sauna. As I'm packing up, a guy in wet waders crosses the lot, headed for the cabin behind my room. I call out an appeal to him as he gets close, and he pulls his polarized sunglasses down to his collar and comes over to talk.

"Not bad," he says, in reply to my query about fishing conditions. He still has that Zen mist in his eyes. The river has the power to make an ordinary face, with its splotches and sags below the cheekbones, take on the shine of mesmerizing water. He's been away, and something of the river comes back with him. He offers the technical details of the morning, evading what he probably couldn't explain if he tried.

"I took a couple on a Prince nymph dropper with a sparkle caddis on top. Three split shot to get it down."

He tells me he comes up here from down around Fresno every summer to rent a cabin and fish this stretch of river. I tell me where I've been and where I'm going, hoping he might have some helpful hints for the rivers to the south. He doesn't. He's never fished Hat Creek, or Burney Creek, or any of the other famous waters just down the road, although he's heard about them.

"Hat Creek below the pump house—that's *holy water!*" he says, with real reverence. "Yeah, that's the holy water."

I want to ask if he remembers the spill. Did he fish that year, or the year that followed? It feels too gloomy, a dose of ammonia for someone who's still in the moment. I stick to asking about where I should fish, but he starts to wake up all on his own.

"You got to get up earlier if you want some action!" he jokes, the words elevating in volume as he releases them. He nods toward the patch of sunlight that's already cooking the pavement and waits for my excuse, a comical skepticism toying with the corners of his mouth. I can see he suspects I deserve a good-hearted ribbing. Was I out partying all night, like he would have been at my age? I almost hate to disappoint him with my excuse—no, I wasn't out closing the bars, I was waiting for the train to show up.

His face falls. It's a legitimate defense.

"Oh geez! That outfit! They'll sure keep you up! They get here before dawn?"

Barely, I say, barely.

"Well, there's always the hoppers. They like it hot. I hear they've been killing them on hoppers down by the sewage outflow. You want to watch your step down there, though. Rattlers. They like it hot too."

I decide to leave the sewage waters and rattlesnakes for a last resort. The botanical gardens are just around the corner, and I suit up in the shade of massive live oaks. Other migrants are just waking up too, stretching their limbs after a night in the back of the Econoline van with Oregon plates. A frizzle-haired woman, her face still puffy with sleep, folds back the paisley curtains while a bearded guy with no shirt and sun-browned shoulders rummages in a cardboard box for silverware. A collection of talismans dangle from leather thongs around his neck. I feel like I've wandered into the private rooms of an outdoor hostel, especially when the white-maned fellow at the next picnic table pauses in the midst of chewing to greet me with a chilly stare. The Jif-and-Wonderbread sandwich waits in his tattooed paw while his tongue continues to work a bit, as if my presence is an unpleasant taste. I salute him with a nod and escape to the river.

The Sacramento roars through a caravan of smooth gray boulders, treacherous and beautiful. Look away from the live oaks and bay laurel and big leaf maple for a moment, imagine instead the green twigs of hickory and ash, basswood and alder shrouding the banks, and this could be an eastern stream—big, cold, and spritzing in topaz over the cobbles. Water hovering jets of bubbles, grottoes excavated under the duress of spring—I recognize these waters. What I don't recognize is the film of algae greasing the rocks. One hasty step and I nearly take a butt-first ride down the back of one chunk of granite, with more slick chutes beckoning just below. My sneakers simply will not stay put; I have to wedge them into crevices to keep from falling over. I put a hand down on dry rock to steady myself, and it's immediately clear why the dragonflies aren't landing—the surface is hot enough to cook flesh.

The stretch through Dunsmuir is catch and keep, and its tumbling water is best suited to hardware. Above the rapids I find a rare stretch of riffles. Bear's breeches, their leaves like a giant glossy version of rhubarb, dangle over the water, deepening the dark possibilities for cover. The railroad tracks bend close here; I can smell the creosote of the ties and hear the crackle of locusts as they flutter over the gravel bed. That's why they were killing them on hoppers downstream. I look in my fly box for something big and compelling, something with a come-hither wriggle. What I find is the skunk, still limber in it rubber legs even after all those smolts. It may look like a white-legged cricket with a bleached Mohawk, but it's got the motion of a locust kicking itself back to shore.

A ten-inch rainbow agrees. On my first cast it beats the skunk to a twirling leaf and snaps it up, leaving a wake through the shallows. I work my way through the shade, trout attacking from every nook. For a chance at the skunk they'll come a great distance, a dark streak through the water; they'll even leave the shade and splash recklessly. But only once. One good look at the skunk is enough.

When I've reached the whitewater and searing midday light of the next run, the response ends abruptly, but it's left me with a vision. I see trout leaping with abandon at the sight of a thick wad of deer hair and a pair of long enticing legs, preferably brown—a big crunchy locust.

Ted Fay's is the second-oldest fly shop in California, and Ted brought fame to the place by being the first to popularize the short-line nymphing method I learned on the Little Manistee. He's no longer around, but the current owner knows the river, and he's got quite a selection of rubber legs. I choose some that are not just beige like a locust's limbs but sparkling with red and green glitter, a grasshoppery number if I ever saw one. The owner says the fishing is slow, especially up at Ney Flats where the fish have seen everything twice. Downstream there's more bank action, but the water gets warmer as you go.

I set up camp near Sims, under a stand of young fir, not far from the river and the roar of the highway. The glare of the afternoon sun makes fishing unthinkable. After a nap in the stultifying tent with the mosquitoes at the mesh imploring me for just a small drink of blood, I get up for the evening rise. The river here is much larger, sprawling into long, shallow runs that look like they probably heat up in a hurry. Most of the big boulders are gone, too; a few remnant behemoths remain in place upstream, but most of what I can see from the road is granite, jumbled like mismatched china at a garage sale. I watch the flow from the bridge, stooping now and again for a handful of the sweet and oozing Himalayan blackberries crowding the footings. The seeds crunch like gravel against my teeth, making me think of bears. According to an old newspaper I found in the railroad switching station, a frisky black bear broke into a Dunsmuir home last week, snuffling around while the lady of the house sang in the shower. She emerged, toweling her hair, to find a shaggy figure with berry-stained paws perusing the contents of her kitchen cabinets. He'd had enough of the bittersweet tang of berries, apparently, and, after stripping a few canes clean, so have I.

Every bridge has its daredevil pitch of riprap, broken beer bottles, and tossed-aside night-crawler cups, and the fly-fishing-only section is no exception. I take my life into my hands and slide down through the brambles and head for midstream, waving my rod overhead like the stinger of a scorpion, on alert for any sign of activity. If I were a trout, I'd clamp my jaws around one of these fat locust numbers. Tepid water surges around my thighs, getting warmer as I near the shallows of a long central bar where the stones are still warm from the sun. The river has split in two, with faster, deeper, and, hopefully, slightly cooler water against each bank.

Above the concrete vestiges of an old bridge the river strikes a different pose. It's left its old freestone bed high and dry for a fling with deep and murky meanders. Clay erodes from its incursion into the bank, leaving the roots of a box elder hanging over the whirls of a long, slow run. It looks like dry-fly water.

I crouch among the clover and ragweed stems, their dry pods tickling my nose, and watch the water curl like the buds of translucent flowers and disappear into the smooth belly of the clay-bottomed run. I know the fish are there, an invisible presence in the margin between mud and stone, waiting to emerge from the shadows of the cutbank to feed in the relative safety of dusk. They're liable to be vigilant, ready to bolt at any sign of clumsiness. The soft stipple of the hopper's deer hair dampens my fingertips. I consider changing to something more delicate, particularly since a few tiny sulphurs are shooting from the surface like sparks, but there's the drone of the crickets to consider, and the rasp of abundant grasshopper wings. Not everything near my nose is an old bloom. Multifaceted eyeballs are watching me. Mandibles are washing one another with tobacco juice. Antennae quiver in response to my breathing. In their honor I decide to risk one cast with a hopper.

The first strike catches me off guard, coming as it does within a second of the hopper's landing, as if the trout saw it coming through the air and dashed under it like a fly ball. I haven't even grasped the line yet, and raising the rod tip to set the hook only throws slack over the water.

The hopper drifts a little farther on the next attempt, under scrutiny perhaps, but even the skeptical fish can't resist the shoreward twitch of rubber legs. Two seductive strips and an open mouth chugs it down. I'm ready with the hook this time, and although the line tightens in a figure eight around my wrist, I subdue the fish after two dangerous leaps. One look at its face and I know why the hook held this time—it's a fifteen-inch male with the hooked beak of a cormorant. Plenty of bone and gristle there to fasten a hook, even a barbless hook.

The final mad scene of the evening has begun, and it's taking place on the other side of the run, where the mayflies have come down to mate in a flurry. Small fish are pecking the surface, and between them, close to the bank, is the signature heft of one good fish. I've got five minutes of light before true darkness, and the bridge is half a mile downstream by water. The situation could be worse than the Missouri; I've remembered my headlamp, but there's no trail to find.

Visions of another immersion, this one in the dark, midstream. I've been here before. I should play it safe and get moving, but of course the fish rises again, and I promise myself just one cast. I actually get the leader through the eye of the sulphur, clinch the knot, and send the fly out there in record time. Magically, the lunker responds, sipping my dry as it coasts along the bank.

I battle it into nightfall, an epic of reel-singing runs and and deep bows of graphite, until I can't see it, can only follow the power of its resistance from one end of the run to the other. I'm in up to my waist, disappearing into water darker than the sky, when the fish washes to the surface, spent. The flashlight I could use to see it is zippered away in a pocket at my back, and without it this capture feels strange, less a triumph than an invitation to mysticism.

I talk to the water all the time, urging an imaginary underwater gentleman to rise for my fly and cursing him when he refuses me. Bringing the catch to the surface always breaks the spell: a fish struggles there, glittering with scales, starving for bugs, and incapable of conversation. Without the light, the impression remains that I've hooked someone who can talk. I wade ashore, dragging this being along beside me, and bend down to grope for my fly in the glistening blur of its face, feeling the dark orb of its eye upon me, watching my hands. The hook, nestled in the membrane above the lip, comes away easily.

"You're free to go," I mutter. There's no reply, of course. The face floats there for a moment, regarding me, then twists into the water, immediately gone.

Headlamps, as I suspected, are little help with submerged stones. My toes are bruised from multiple stubbings by the time I reach the bridge, and my sleeves are soaked from saving myself from worse. The camp-ground is spooky. There's none of the camaraderie of a family establish-ment, and no sign of the order imposed by a host, just the lights of way-side strangers scattered in the dark and the thunder of air brakes and heavy loads on the freeway. The moon is rising over the canyon, and I can hear the crickets, but just the same when I hear the crackle of what could be fireworks—or could just as easily be gunfire—I fear that now, on the verge of my homecoming, some meth-addled, sinister face is going to appear at the tent door as soon as I put my head down.

I sit in the truck and look at the atlas, trying to gauge the distance to any motel on my way south. They're all too far, and it's too late and too crazy to get on the road now. *Don't be ridiculous,* I tell myself. *This place is no worse than anywhere else, even if a great horned owl is hooting back there. Yes, it's an owl, not a Satan worshipper.*

As the ghoulish face fades, I realize what I'm fearing most is disap-pointment, a kind of spiritual death. I'm afraid we'll do all the shots and procedures, and the IVF won't work. We won't get pregnant. Or we'll get pregnant, and then there will something wrong with the baby, and we'll have to decide whether we want to go through it all again, or give up on the thought of producing our own offspring. I'm almost home— I thought I would be better prepared by now.

I get in the tent and keep the candle flickering until I finally muster the courage to blow it out. I'm sleeping here, with my Buck knife for company, as best I can.

Searching for Holy Water

In the morning it's hard to remember what all the fuss was about. Sunshine makes everything seem harmless and cheerful. The toilets flush, and the latrine even has a stained glass window, which is hardly government-issue decoration. Some creative soul must have taken a shine to the place. Could it be that a secret artiste dwells in one of the old 12-cylinder pickups with the gun rack over the seat and the whitetail stag leaping across the side of the camper? Could it be that what I thought looked like a meth lab was in fact an open-air studio? It all seems possible as the light filters through the needles and I crunch some raisin bran without the benefit of milk.

Coming down through the mountains on the twisting road, I pass Lake Shasta, drowned valleys spreading out like the arms of a milky-blue octopus, but miss the dam, reputed to be the highest in the country. The lake makes me think of all the rivers to the west that I won't be fishing—the Trinity, the Eel, the Van Duzen, the anadromous waters that have been dammed, drained, and silted up until they've become almost empty, beautiful ghosts of themselves. Most of them are closed to fishing.

In Redding, I turn east toward the Modoc plateau, heading away from the fast-food strip into the hills of golden grass and valley oaks. On the northern horizon, Mount Shasta glows, a pink mound of impossible snow. Having come down thousands of feet, I ascend again to five thousand feet, then drop a thousand to Burney, a lumber town of neon motel signs and burger joints. Groves of cedar and Douglas fir tower over trailer parks, branches filling the sky, and Shasta, the sleeping volcano, is invisible. Yet the signs of kinship with Crater Lake begin to pour forth here, in the springs that fill Burney Creek, then the Fall River, with the icy blue blood of the Cascades.

I'm not sure whether to put Hat Creek in that category. What I find in Cassel is a concrete-lined canal, weed balls rolling with the sluggish current into an expanse of barren pasture. A dirt track runs along the canal, and an entire battalion of worm dunkers are plying their trade along the length of it, bobbers and juicy gobs dangling incongruously from the tips of fly rods. I can only stare at them, recalling the look of divine awe in the face of the guy in the motel parking lot yesterday. This is the holy water?

Above the culvert, and a weir, are a couple of particularly emphatic "No Trespassing!" signs. Electricity hums through nearby transformers; the dusty morning air tingles with it. I ask a senior-looking gentleman who seems less absorbed in the progress of his worm where I might find the fly-fishing-only section.

"That's Clint Eastwood's ranch across the street. I think that's fly-fishing. You got to be staying there, though."

That explains the ferocity of the postings, but a celebrity guest ranch is not the place I'm looking for. "Well, actually, I think I'm looking for a different place. It's kind of, well, I think it's called the Holy Water."

"Never heard of it." He waves his arm down the dirt road. "There's a couple more pump houses downstream. Maybe it's down there."

I pass two federal campgrounds, stark industrial sites carved into the willow flats, and lose sight of the canal as the road winds up over a ridge. On the other side, down in the valley, is a factory complex of some kind, a series of evaporation troughs, or some kind of series of chemical baths. Only as I get closer does it dawn on me that their product is my quarry, or at least the simulacrum of it: they're growing trout. Crystal Lake Fish Hatchery, the sign says, pointing right through a high chain-link fence.

I don't feel the need to see the doings at Crystal Lake. I can see the riparian brush of the creek winding along the outskirts of the valley, and a dirt track bears left toward it. I take it. Half a mile closer and I begin to get a bad feeling. I can see the cell-block windows of another pump house ahead. I arrive at the end of the road to find the barbed wire, warning signs, culvert, and concrete spillway, the same electric buzz. I have to visit to the hatchery.

There is a place where the water springs cold even during the dog days of summer, where small trout swarm and lunkers cruise the shallows, fearless of human shadows. You won't find the banks trammeled by waders, or the air filled with the hiss of lines; nobody fishes there. To believe in this concrete simulacrum of every angler's dream, this citadel of pellet-plump, illicit fish flesh, you have to be ten years old.

On a sultry August afternoon, I stood with my fellow conspirators under a ragged stand of sumacs, outside a chain-link fence whose top strands of barbwire were festooned with mummified night crawlers and rusting spoons, the failures of other poachers.

Morale was already low. We had pedaled our bicycles for miles before realizing that we should have brought drinks or money with us, and had then spent the rest of the journey scouring the roadside for beer cans to return for the deposit. We gathered enough for one can of cola. Now the soda was gone, the cicadas were thrumming the humid air with the staccato pulse of a heat-stroke victim, and the hatchery outlet was nowhere in sight.

"Where is it, Barilla?" Danny had the crappiest bike, a three-speed stuck in high gear, which forced him to pedal like a maniac to build up momentum for even the smallest hill. He hadn't enjoyed the ride. Jake didn't say anything. He wormed his tongue around the rim of the soda can and handed me the empty.

I had promised my friends nirvana. I had no choice but to march through the hatchery gates, toward a pickup loaded with a brown mound of pellets. Schools of hungry trout thrashed in the pools beside me. I could see the driver, an old man with silver hair and a green uniform, leaning on a shovel, watching me. As I got closer, I realized he was scowling at my hand with a mixture of sourness and incredulity, as if he'd just bit into a spoiled lump of luncheon meat and was wondering where to spit.

I looked at my hand. There, dark with the sweat of my palm, was an oblong tube of cork, and protruding from that was a length of amber fiberglass, fretted with chrome guides. It ended in a dangling, feathery fluff in which a hook, though small, was clearly evident. I fought off the urge to throw it into the bushes. It was too late for that.

"I wasn't fishing," I said, hoping that if I said it forcefully enough, he might buy it.

He looked me over. The capillaries across his cheeks were mostly broken, so that his face already assumed the flush of what could be rage. I got ready to run. "I didn't think you were," he said finally. "Since you and I both know there's no fishing allowed in here."

The pellets made a breakfast-cereal crunch as he pushed down on the handle of the shovel. He flung a load of them into the air so they fell like hail into the dark swarm of fish.

"Actually, I was trying to find the stream that's below the hatchery. I came in here just to ask where it is, not to fish in here or anything."

He sighed. He looked fatigued and a little impatient, like the weary bus driver who always has to wait for the same late kid every morning.

"I'll show you. But we don't let many escape, you know. I don't expect there's any in that little stream worth catching." He tossed a last scoop into the water. The surface boiled again with bodies. "All right, come on, hop in," he said, pointing to the passenger's seat. We wound our way through the troughs and little waterfalls, heading, it turned out, toward the very stretch of fence where my friends waited. We passed the lunker pool, and I leaned out the window and yelped like a beagle. "Wow! Look at that one. Whoa! That one's even bigger. A huge brookie!"

"That there's a tiger trout. Half brown, half brookie. Pretty rare."

Imagine hooking one of those suckers! If I worked here, I told myself, I wouldn't be able to help myself. I'd have to fish that pool.

"You like to fish?" I asked my driver. He chuckled and rolled his eyes, disgusted by the idea.

"Ho boy, no! No, no, no! When you do what I do for a living, the last thing you want to do is go fishing, believe me!"

"Not even for the big ones, like that?"

"No, no. I feed those guys every day. Why would I want to feed them on my own time?" He laughed again, but it seemed to me that he had lost something he preferred to dismiss, and I made him aware of it. He must have gotten this job because he liked trout and he liked being outdoors, and now his hair was silver and angling seemed trivial, an artifice indulged by children. He was waiting to retire. What would it take to kindle that enthusiasm again?

We were approaching a locked gate. I could see Jake and Danny watching us with worried faces. They had their bikes ready for a quick getaway. The hatchery man ratcheted the truck into park and left it running. He unlocked the gate and pointed. "This is it." I picked my rod out from the dusty pile of fish food and slipped through the gap.

"Now don't let me catch you trying to get over this fence! You won't make it, and we'll call the cops on you! You'd think those other idiots would learn, but they don't, they don't." He gestured toward the collection of hardware strung out along the line, then turned away, signaling good-bye with a nudge of his green cap.

"I thought you were totally busted!" Danny yelled to me. They had thrown down the bikes and were running, fighting through branches and nettles, in their hurry to hear my story.

We were standing on the creosote spars of a railroad track, near a small culvert where the stream ran beneath without sign of its crossing. We never would have found it.

"He said you can fish here?" Jake asked me, pointing to the orange "No Trespassing" signs stuck to the fence on one side of the tracks and nailed to every nearby tree on the other. Everywhere we turned a sign was telling us to get out or face the consequences, except for the line of track beneath our feet.

"Well, he didn't say we couldn't. I don't see any signs on the tracks, do you?"

A glance at the stream proved that the hatchery man was wrong about one thing already. In the shallow, sandy wash below the tracks, a trio of trout finned in time with the current. These weren't minnows of the sort born in a stream like this, the kind of brook a ten-year-old could leap across without wetting a sneaker. These were giants of the kind normally stocked in the big rivers—eighteen-inch, pellet-chubby rainbows!

I feel vaguely nauseous as I walk along the hatchery walkway and smell the cloying and persistent odor of fish. Is it the egg-frying heat of the concrete making me dizzy? Is it the belly-up brookie, or the ones sporting a pink garland of fungus from the wounds on their sides that make me sick? Or is it the sight of the industrial hand behind the magic curtain?

When I walk into the doctor's office, its simulated coral reef helps me forget about all the technology behind the visit. Here it's all on display: concrete, water, fish flesh, and nothing more, no attempt to hide the artifice that will produce the semblance of stream-bred trout. Can I imagine the stainless-steel vault where they will store our embryos among the thousands of others? Life suspended in a frozen world. Perhaps they stack them in rows of test tubes with numbered labels, and wraiths of liquid nitrogen dance around the gloves of the technicians when it comes time to pull someone's potential offspring out.

A tour is in progress by the lunker pen, a woman in uniform sweating profusely as she describes the trout-rearing process. I stand at the back and watch the fish follow every twitch of her hands, as if they held pellets. Two kids, a little girl and a slightly older boy, are bored with listening to numbers and size classes and are pushing their faces into the folds of their mother's shirt. "This is the last one," she says, handing each a coin. They scurry to what looks like a parking meter at the end of the trough. Pellet dispensers: A dime for a few, a quarter for a handful. The gator-jawed giants swirl and nip at each other with approval as the children toss them in, a few at a time, while schools of the unfed riot nearby.

I catch sight of an osprey circling above, mesmerized no doubt by the sight of such easy prey and baffled by the lengths of wire strung overhead to foil any attempt at capture. The tour guide sees me and lifts an arm to point, exposing a dark swath of perspiration beneath.

"That's an osprey, a fish eagle. Wouldn't he like to get in here! That reminds me of the time a pelican flew in the gate when someone left it open. It swooped down and grabbed one of these big fish. The fish was so heavy the pelican forgot what it was doing and crashed right into the fence. Knocked itself out cold. There's this bird lying there on the concrete, and a fish flapping around! Before any of us could get over there though, the pelican wakes up, grabs its fish, and flies out the gate!"

We were ready for those hatchery giants swaying in that tiny stream. Things are bigger when you're younger, and these fish were enormous, longer and thicker than my forearm, and smart. Danny cast first—with his twenty-pound test and feather-duster fly. The trout ambled downstream to some goldenrod to watch us. Their wakes made tiny waves slap up over the bank. It was my turn to cast.

We felt the trembling in our feet before we saw it. There in the distance was the dragonfly's brow of a locomotive, getting larger without appearing to move.

"Train. We better get off," I said. I pulled in my line. I knew it was futile anyway after Danny's performance.

"No shit. But where?"

Danny had a point. There was no place to go without trespassing. The fence hemmed us into a sliver of lowland that might just allow a boxcar to grind off our noses. The other side was wide open, but adamantly forbidden.

Jake jumped first, down into the milkweed and monkey-flower on the wooded side. We scrambled after him and waited as the train rose to an enormous bulk and the clang of the wheels began to make everything vibrate, even the leaves. We could see people inside the engine, arms pointing us out, a flash of teeth. Then the boxcars were rolling past, pulling us closer with their whirlwind of empty mouths, making us dizzy, battering us with noise.

A gaggle of workers had gathered on the scaffolding of the caboose. We thought they intended to wave—they were pointing us out as if they meant to hail us. Didn't they always wave to kids who stood by and watched them pass, under the assumption that all kids wanted to grow up to be an engineer like them? We were finished with the train and fire truck phase, but they wouldn't know that.

There were three of them. As they got close I could see their faces, all ruddy with sunburn, squinting ahead into the sun to get a look at us. I could see the lumps of taut muscle in their arms, shifting under tattoos as the train swayed. It occurred to me that it might be boring to ride a train all day, and that we were something different along the line, entertainment. Even as I prepared myself to smile and salute, I could see that the kind of wholesome entertainment I was expecting to provide wasn't what was on the program. They weren't smiling.

"Hey! You kids! Get the hell out of there! Get off our property!"

"You bastards! I'm calling the cops! Run! Run!"

"We're coming back! I'm gonna kick some ass!"

One of them, a grizzled ruffian whose engineer's cap was snugged down to his ears to keep it from flying off, was clambering hand over hand down a steel ladder. He swung his way down with the confidence of a treetop monkey, right down to the brink of the wheels, where he held on with one fist and leaned out with the other palm open as if he intended to try snatching one of us by the scruff of the neck.

Jake already had his hand raised to wave. He lowered it uncertainly. I felt my own hand falling, searching the air behind me.

The guy's paw drew close, grew stubby fingers that spasmed in the air, grabbing for us, all attached to the hideous, snarling face of an adult baboon in full territorial display.

Like a film without volume, no audible sound came from us as we staggered backwards; no sound could rise over the crashing wave of locomotive noise. My hip caught on something that gave way suddenly, and I felt myself falling, my hands sinking into wet and clammy soil. I lay there stunned with the grass blades pressing my face, wondering whether something would begin to hurt. From the ground I saw Danny leap straight into the high bush blueberries, saw them sink under him and then spring back, shuddering. Jake had fallen too and was crawling past me on all fours to the protection of the bushes.

The caboose passed us by so quickly that had I not been casting a fearful look over my shoulder, I would have missed it. With a final violent flourish our tormentor swung himself out at us, both feet leaving their purchase for a mock roundhouse kick. He wasn't even close, but the gesture was clear enough: he had kicked our asses.

"You little shits! Can't you read? You're trespassing!" they howled as they pulled away. "We're coming to get you! You better run!" Run! Run!" Their shouts and laughter faded with the muffled sounds of the receding train.

"Fuck you!" we yelled in unison, offering them our middle fingers now that they were far enough away. "Go fuck yourself!"

We were all heaving, as if we'd just sprinted the length of a football field. I wiped the mud off my hands and looked at my friends, who were as stunned, scared, and pissed-off as I was. The pale little boils of nettle stings were erupting on my arms.

"What are we gonna do?"

"Let's throw a bunch of shit on the tracks so they'll derail next time." Danny said, pushing up an ancient Schlitz can with his toe.

The very thought of a terrorist strike against the monkey man terrified me. I imagined him picking up my spoor from the junk we heaped on the trestle and tracking me down to my house.

"Do you think they're coming back? Maybe we should get out of here."

"Nah," Jake said. He was trying, with little success, to wipe the grass stains from his knees. "They were just trying to scare us, the assholes. Let's fish in here. They can't stop us."

"You mean go in the woods? What about the signs?"

"Fuck it! I don't care! Let's see if they can catch us."

"If they catch us, we're dead meat," Danny said.

"Come on, Barilla," Jake said, and he ducked under the blueberry bushes. I could hear his footfalls scuffing through the leaves on the other side of the posted sign. Danny followed. I came last.

The tour is ending. "Any questions, folks?" she asks us. Someone asks where they let the brood stock go. What's in the pellets? When there's a pause I clear my throat and ask her where the fly-fishing-only stretch is located, which discombobulates her at first.

"I'm not sure. There's Rising River, that's Clint Eastwood's place. I know that's good for fly-fishing. And you can fish at the pump house just down the road. Anyone can fish there."

I don't want to do it, not here, but I have to say the words. "What I'm looking for is a place called the Holy Water."

A guy in suspenders and a white ten-gallon hat has brought along a bag of peanuts in their shells. He cracks one in the awkward silence and pops the nuts into his mouth.

"I've never heard of such a place," the woman says. "There's a wild trout section. That's below Pumphouse Number 2. Maybe that's it."

"That's it! That's the one! Pumphouse Number 2!" From now on I can stop calling it the Holy Water and avoid sounding like a lost pilgrim. There's something incantatory about the words *wild trout,* even in the Babel of angling. Yet I have to wonder if this adult fascination with the authentic is healthier than the child's delight in the artificial. These hatchery fish only disappoint if you are looking for the mystic quality of the wild.

Below the railroad tracks, it was dark and cool among the forbidden ferns, but surprisingly open. The bushes grew along the tracks like a tall hedge, and behind them there was little to disguise my red T-shirt, or Danny's yellow shorts, unless we crouched down. Worse yet, the woods ended in a backyard, presumably belonging to whoever scribbled their signature at the bottom of the posted signs. The brook meandered along the edge of the lawn, curved around the side of the house, and ended in a cattail-ringed pond not much bigger than an above-ground swimming pool.

"They can see us," I hissed. There was nobody out on the screened-in patio, but that didn't mean there wasn't a face lurking in the dark behind the window glass. Some irate homebody could be getting his shotgun down from the rack right now. That didn't seem to bother my cohorts. They were joking around and snapping sticks like this was their own backyard.

"Maybe that guy on the train owns this house," I offered finally, after failing to move them with more rational appeals.

"Good! Let's catch all his fish before he gets home," Jake said. He wasn't even crouching. Danny stood up too, giggling.

"Get down, Frazier! They can see your shorts!"

"Shut up, Barilla! They can hear you!"

Danny, declaring that whatever disease he might catch didn't matter if he died of thirst, vowed to drink right from the brook, and he was stooping down to lap some from the nearest pool when two enormous wakes sped away from his face. A giant rainbow nearly beached itself on gravel as it splashed sideways to escape into the next run. What had looked like dark lengths of driftwood now appeared to be in faint but perpetual motion, with barely enough water to cover a dorsal fin.

"Look at that monster! And that one there! Holy shit! This place is loaded!" Danny had forgotten his cold drink and was galloping around in search of his pole while Jake popped up again for a better view. I tugged him back down.

"Keep it down, you guys! Come on!"

"Don't worry, you'll get your turn," Jake said, creeping forward with his rod to where two great rainbows lay in wait. "This is just like fishing in the hatchery."

I wasn't so sure the fish would respond. I assumed they must be in the stream because the pond was too warm; whoever owned this place must have stocked them in the spring when the water was cold. They must be stressed out, I thought. They won't be hungry.

My pessimism was interrupted with a yell, loud enough that whoever lived in the house could have heard it in the shower. "Got one!" Sure enough, Jake's rod was bent to a hoop, and his battered old reel was relinquishing spurts of line.

"Keep down!" I cautioned him, which had no effect whatsoever. He leapt up and battled his fish in plain sight, while the rainbow made a racket of its own, slapping its tail, vaulting into the air, and landing with a concussive smack. I winced with every explosion and kept my eyes on the house.

Once Jake had horsed his prize into the ferns and smothered it with a full-body hug, it was Danny's turn. He insisted on moving even closer to the house in search of new water. Jake and I hung back, watching his yellow shorts slide through the greenery until he was out of the ferns and onto the grass of the backyard.

"Well, I guess we'll find out if anybody's home," Jake said. The odor of fresh slime, too sweet to be called a stench but pungent as raw garlic, hung over him. His arms glistened, streaked with blood and wisps of leaf. I envied him. He had broken a forked stick and jammed it through the gills so he could hoist the dead but still supple body into the air. Now it hung from his side like an unsheathed machete.

There was a commotion downstream, and a splash. I assumed Danny had tripped and fallen into some muck; I waited for him to let out a curse.

"I got one! You guys! I got one!"

I hustled over there in spite of myself. This I couldn't believe without ocular proof. It was true; Danny was tethered via his nylon rope to another struggling behemoth, his first trout on a fly.

He didn't exactly play the fish, since he didn't relinquish any line. Rod bent to the snapping point, he held on through a cyclone of splashes. Somehow the hook held. When the rainbow paused to re-assess its tactics, Danny surprised it with a trick of his own, hauling it up onto shore with a quick jerk backward. There he grappled with it, the battle remaining in doubt until the trout bounced its last and lay there gasping. Frazier had caught a trout.

He stood to display his catch, hugging it to his chest, oblivious of the slime smearing his shirt. Before we could respond to his "Check this sucker out!" we heard the thud that made us all cringe, a car door slamming somewhere nearby, probably around the front of the house. Jake and I bounded back into the shadows and took cover. Danny didn't follow us. He was still out there on the lawn in his bright yellow shorts.

"Frazier, you dickhead! Come on!" I nudged Jake to yell something too.

"Fraze! They're home! They'll see you."

"I need to find a stick."

He was hunting around in the undergrowth, picking up branches and tossing them aside as too thin or too rotten or too short. He attacked a maple sapling instead. The fresh wood refused to come away clean, hanging on with a twist of fibers, so that our discussion of what to do next was punctuated with the thrashing and wrenching of branches.

"I'm ready to split," he said, "just as soon as I get this stick." Jake said he was ready to take off too. It seemed I was the only one interested in hanging around. I couldn't ride home like this, with those two guys gloating the whole way, their handlebars laden with trophies and mine ingloriously empty.

Danny had his stick. "What about that guy coming back here? Like you said?"

Jake nodded, reeling in the end of his line. "Yeah, they're home now, dude. We better split."

The house was as silent, the windows as dark, as before. But someone was in there, fixing a snack in the kitchen, slumping on the couch in front of the television. Could the ape-man be back from work already?

"I'm going in," I said, picking up my rod. "You guys can take off if you want."

It's a white-hot afternoon when I arrive at Pumphouse Number 2, the so-called Holy Water. The last two pumps I visited withheld all but the silent dregs, but here the generators have unleashed a torrent that sweeps down in a violent sheet of undulant white crests. Only one other worshipper is in attendance, slogging a nymph through the first pocket water downstream. He's beyond the last of the oaks that shade the banks. There's no sign of shade for miles beyond him, just dry grass, shimmering in the heat.

There's a sign near the trees describing the restoration of wild fish here. The fishing was bad, so the government took action. They removed the "wild" trout to a nearby hatchery and poisoned the rest. Seven tons of "trash" fish were removed from 3.5 miles of creek, a weir was constructed above Lake Britton to keep them out, and then the trout were brought back from the hatchery. Seven tons. Of what? Green sunfish? Pike minnow? Squaw fish? Having just come from the hatchery where the wild fish would have waited, I don't like the sound of these manipulations. This isn't what I mean by wild.

I pull out a stool and the half-gone carton of milk I bought in Burney. I still have some Pecanariffic cookies, and I munch them one by one from their plastic tray, easing each of them down with a slug of warm milk, watching the river for signs that I should fish. The lone fisherman gives up and drives off instead. Before his dust has cleared the parking lot, another big Suburban bounces down and halts in the shade beside me. It's the guy with the peanuts. He has a fishing license dangling from the lobe of his cowboy hat now.

"I see you found the Number 2 Pumphouse," he says, and cracks a nut. He keeps the truck running so the air-conditioning will keep the family—wife in front, daughter and two slumped boys in back—cool. They look out at me through the tinted glass, wanly, like refugees.

I'm remembering the ride home from the hatchery. I had my fish hanging down from the handlebars as the cars passed. People craned their necks to see us as they passed, three kids on bikes, three large trout brushing their knees as they pedaled up hill. It was a long, thirsty ride. I set down my bike in the lawn by the front steps. My fish, hanging from a stick, was as stiff and inert as a baguette. The tail was dusty, the eyes were glazed, and the flanks had lost their sheen, but I kept the body close, as if it was a limb I'd lost but couldn't bear to part with.

I watch two acorn woodpeckers inspect some dead bark while I finish my last cookie and polish off the milk. The sound of electricity has been with me all day, and, holy or not, I'm suddenly tired of the zip in the air, the magnetic tension of it all. I fold up my stool, toss the packaging in the barrel, and drive away from the holy water, leaving it unfished.

A Last Pair of Sirens

Pit River, Cassel, California

The stretch of Hat Creek I know crosses the highway in a picnic area. I've never seen anyone fishing there, and because it's only a quarter mile to the Pit River, I've never stopped to fish its languid channel myself. I pull into the picnic area now because I feel some sense of obligation to test the waters. At least here it looks like a spring creek, pale as bone in the shallows and blue as bleach in the depths, like the stretch of the Wood River I passed without stopping.

A family has interrupted their picnic to all have a go at fly-fishing from the well-mown turf of the shore. First the father casts, badly, then the son tries, with a serious look, and catches some grass behind. His sister tries, and finally the mother takes the rod, giggling, and nearly tosses the entire outfit into the water. Everybody pauses to look as I come swishing down the bank in my waders, my Australian brim cinched over the flaps of my blue Legionnaire hat, my eyes hidden by sunglasses, and my vest bristling with odds and ends like a giant, overloaded pocket protector.

I climb above a cliff of powdery chalk where the highway cuts through the ridge. From the trail I can look down through the oaks on the strange juxtaposition of two rivers, one placid, nibbling away at the limestone, the other brawling through a series of rapids, both within half a mile of the other. In the Hat, tiny trout, no longer than my hopper, dart and wriggle over the patches of sand, five feet down. The backwash and spume of the Pit looks more appealing. I decide to drive the half mile.

Several trucks are parked in the circle of baked mud that passes for a parking lot on the bank of the Pit, where I've never seen anyone before. I wonder, as I step out into the coyote thistle, if I'll have to share a pool. Maybe the fishing is really hot right now. I can smell the river, the fecundity of it, the broth of cannibals and sun chasers, scavengers, and murderers that was missing on the creek next door. Ketchup and fresh-shucked corn, that's what Hat Creek smelled like.

On the crusty stones at my feet, recently relinquished by the river, lies something else, something human. It's still half-submerged in a plush carpet of algae. I prod it with my foot, and the handle of a net— not the cheap aluminum kind, but the hardwood, heart-shaped cylinder favored by fly-fishermen—emerges. The lacquered wood still shines, ready for resurrection. But the net has gone native, the green goo writhing with creatures that don't need much oxygen. I wonder what happened to the owner. On a big river like this, one misplaced step and you would probably wind up looking like this net. It feels like bad luck, thinking about the hand that lost it. I leave it there.

I know this river well enough to know I don't understand it at all. It's too big, too fierce, and too cloudy. Dries skim over its back, get pummeled, and drown. Nymphs disappear and don't come back. I follow the cracked tar of an abandoned road to the one place I know how to fish, a side channel where the river, having already divided once, breaks again around an island before relinquishing all its force in the dead calm of Lake Britton. The side channel looks like a truncated creek, a short stretch of riffles, a pool beneath an uprooted but still-living oak, then the vanishing into bigger water again. It's a place to begin; the bearings are clear, and there's no danger of drowning, although there's no chance of a giant inhabiting the place either.

To fish it I have to wade out to the island, a feat I've managed before, although the water seemed shallower at the time. The current hisses around my thighs. I concentrate on my feet, nudging each one firmly forward before lifting the last, until I've crossed the worst. Arroyo willows have colonized the island's rocky shores, mixed with the stems of white-flowered clover that the locusts like. The stones themselves are remnants of the last time Shasta or Lassen erupted, born of some ancient lava flow that spilled like hot chili, hit the water, and cooled. Then the river went to work, breaking down the lava deposits, tumbling them into chunks, polishing them until they were round, and finally piling them up on this bed. For now. It's not over. They're only resting here.

Dark as ash, sometimes red as brick, the stones are petrified sponges, riddled with holes where the molten rock cooled before the gas could escape. I know I shouldn't, but I pick one out to take home with me. If I can't keep fish, at least I can collect a stone—it will be around long after every trace of me is gone. In addition to the stippling of the ancient bubbles, this one has a round disc sanded into its side like an eye socket, the action of one piece of gravel whirling around the same circumscribed arc until some flood jarred it loose. I leave it there for now and approach the first pool where the choppy riffle subsides into a deeper eddy.

Despite the shallower water, it's still tough to pick out the best holding places, since the rocks are just visible in the cloudy water, like chunks of brownie in a mouthful of milk. I cast the hopper down and across, letting it swim through the rough water as if kicking hard to make it back to the island. Something flashes behind it, missing, nothing visible but a silver flash of scales. It could be a rainbow, but for all I know it could be "trash," a lunker chub. They may have wiped out the ghetto fish on Hat Creek, but nobody mentioned the lower classes of the Pit, and I have the feeling they're plentiful.

After five minutes of casting, there's no more water to cover upstream, and I put the fly back over the fish. This time it doesn't miss, and I set the hook. I expect a period of taut mystery before I get a look, but the fish settles the question of its species immediately with a walk across the surface. It's a burly twelve-inch rainbow with tiny fins, an adolescent swimming through what is probably its second summer of abundant meals. I release it and fish through the rest of the side channel without success as the water slows to a virtual halt.

Beyond is the murky bayou of the lake. Having traversed the rapids upstream, entire trees, branches and all, hang suspended here, going no farther, at least for now. A great blue heron takes flight from a white-stained trunk as I approach. I'm clueless at first, confronting what looks like flood damage, a neighborhood drowned by a failed levee.

Only when I've surveyed the length of it do I notice a strand of current that follows the near bank, skirting the whorls of submerged roots and rippling into the shadows of some overhanging oak branches. Where a bit of translucence meets the darkest shadow in a virtual cavern of branches, I see a rise, a quiet peck of some tiny morsel, long observed and leisurely consumed. There's a pause of decorum, then another delicate rise. This is a fish of substance, a fish with table manners.

My hopper, the Coney Island chili dog of the dry-fly universe, is out. I need something to tickle a gourmand's palate, the insect equivalent of a baked goat cheese, sprinkled with toasted hazelnuts, drizzled with a varietal olive oil, topped with a golden raspberry coulis, and served on a bed of organic arugula, grown locally and harvested this afternoon. My fly box is not the place to look for such delicacies. I select a vintage flying ant. After all, it was Edward Ringwood Hewitt who, after observing trout exhibit a marked preference for ants even during a heavy mayfly hatch, discovered their superior flavor by munching a few himself. He found they offered a decidedly spicy burst of flavor, which he attributed to formic acid and which I, not having tried them myself, imagine resembles a crunchy little jalapeño pepper.

I strip out line, curve my wrist for a sidearm shot under the branches, and release, right into the clutches of a swamped tree. This Creature from the Black Lagoon proves vindictive when disturbed, its scabrous arm rising up to snap my entire tippet, then sinking down again with my fly. The confrontation terrorizes the fish. There are no more rises.

On my way back I pick up my souvenir. I want to keep both hands free for balance, so I stuff it into the nearly empty lumbar pack I brought along to carry my water bottle and zip it shut. It just fits, like a really heavy laptop. Halfway across, in the serious water, I realize this is not just stupid, but a dangerous folly. Wasn't it Virginia Woolf who filled her pockets with stones to drown? Here I am with thirty pounds of rock strapped to my back in the middle of a ferocious riff of whitewater. If I go down, that rock will make sure I don't get back up.

But it is a nice rock, a real novelty. And that lumbar pack—if I fell I could always unbuckle it with one move . . . and I'm already halfway across. Two more carefully secured footings and I've crossed the stiffest resistance. I've got my souvenir.

Back at the truck I get out the stool and peel a bruised banana in the shade. I push my waders down around my ankles to cool off my legs, which, since I'm wearing shorts, makes me look like I'm taking a crap. I don't think it matters. I'm hidden from the road, and the valley stretches behind me for miles without any sign of habitation or movement. There's only one other vehicle left—a conversion van, so there's nobody to see me.

As I take a glug of hot water from a gallon jug, wishing I had a tea bag to flavor it, I hear laughter coming from the river. Over the tips of the star thistle I watch two rubber dinghies bob to a halt by the bridge. Two figures, one a spiky blond, the other scarfed in a red bandanna, splash to shore and tuck the boats under their arms, coming toward me. They look to me like teenage boys, and although I should pull my waders up, or step out of them, I'm just too lazy to bother. They won't care.

When they get closer I notice that these boys have breasts, that their brown arms are covered with tattoos, and that the bandanna is actually a ponytail, dyed the scarlet of a macaw. They aren't teenagers either; there's the weathering of past summers etched into these faces. At the point I make my discovery, of course, they can see me too, an unsavory figure lurking in the shadow of the truck with his pants down and a half eaten banana on his knee. It's too late to pull up my waders without indicating that they shouldn't have been down. I freeze in a pose of nonchalance, shifting a little in my seat so my fully zipped shorts will be visible. I salute their approach with my jug.

We exchange hellos. They look cold, lips blue, skin taut with goose bumps. I try not to look like I'm staring at their tattoos as they tug open the van's sliding door and towel off their hair, although I notice "Linda" in capitals across the blonde's shoulder along with a red rose and a posse of gremlins and cherubs. Even more fascinating are her extremities; she has a letter on every knuckle, spelling out something I can't read, something like "right" and "wrong." When she kicks off her water booties, a winged skull appears on top of each foot. Every time she moves her toes, the tiny bones ripple, and the death masks appear to mouth something macabre. My ranger friend would have loved to meet these two; he could have spent all day decoding their insignia.

"Did you drive all the way from Massachusetts?" the redhead asks, once they've started to warm up. I'm glad she's said something. I could feel the ten feet of space between their van and my stool getting smaller and more awkward between us, with me sitting there watching their every move because there isn't anywhere else to look except my own embarrassing lap. I say I left Amherst about a month ago, on a fishing trip.

"I'm from Newton, originally."

"Oh, right!" I say it brightly, hoping she'll say more, since Newton means nothing to me except the place where the Peter Pan bus stops on the way to the airport in Boston. That's it, that's all she's got to say about Newton. She asks me instead how the fishing is, and I say I haven't really started yet.

"I'm waiting for it to cool off," I say, hoping she'll make the connection to my waders. "It sure is hot out here."

The blond woman leans into the van to stuff the boats into the back, her skulled feet clutching the dusty step as she shoves things into place. I can see her frowning out at me occasionally through the smoked glass, checking me out for some reason.

"Where did you put in?" I ask her friend. I feel dismay at my own fearful forays into the current. These two don't even have life jackets, let alone a proper raft, and they've come from the canyon upstream, which I always thought was Class V whitewater. She waves her arm toward the summit, where three pipes elbow into the mountain. As far as I know, it's at least a mile drop into the gorge from there.

"Up above. We're testing it out for another trip."

Somehow they have come through without drowning, laughing and full of adrenaline. They stayed afloat and enjoyed the ride. I should probably say something like "cool," or "rad," to suggest my envy at their bravado. Throughout the trip I've caught sight of these fleeting figures who are anything but matronly. Might I have passed these two on the road to Sturgis? Where are they going next? There is some other life out there for Nicola and me, but what is it? I know people who don't have children—they have dogs instead. How they dote on those surrogate canines, training them, reprimanding them. I don't want a terrier for a child.

There must be some life less extreme, less potentially tragic for us, than Thelma and Louise surfing the rough water of the Pit. Something a bit more definitive than "I'm from Newton" might have helped me.

Now, because I can't decode their appearance, the craven, unvarnished truth issues from my lips. "It looks pretty hairy up there to me. Jesus, I'd be scared shitless coming down those rapids in a boat like that."

"It's not so bad," says the blonde, bouncing back into the conversation and scuffing the skulls into a pair of flip-flops. She jingles the keys at her friend, and they exchange glances. Now I feel really awkward. They've got some important secret to share, and my presence has reduced them to gestures. I sink deeper into my chair, succumbing to the futile notion that by making myself smaller I might become less intrusive.

"Time to head." They jump in the van, crank it to life and circle me to turn around, plumes of yellow dust rising in their wake. They stick an arm out to wave, drive fifty feet around a bend, and stop, turn off the van. The dust subsides. It takes me a few seconds to realize that they're changing out of their wet clothes, and that they probably wanted to do that back here but couldn't because yours truly was sitting here with his pants down and didn't have the decency to give them some privacy. I get up immediately; the idea that they thought I was some kind of peeper makes me want to bawl: *I'm no peeper! These are waders! I had shorts on!* Standing up, my shorts reach my knees, uselessly demure. I could stroll around the lot naked now, without a single witness.

I decide to explore the upper reaches of the canyon, not to recuperate my manhood, which feels soiled more than squashed, but to find some new water. Down a serpent of dusty switchbacks I descend, winding up at a no-fee campground where I get the feeling that real drifters have set up for the season, their fire pits mounded with burnt bean cans. Clothes sway on a line between two cottonwoods, and caged chickens peck in the dust between the tires of a van.

I pick my way through withered brush festooned with wrappers and discarded winter clothes, glad that the campers seem to have packed up their valuables and gone to town for the day. I can't hear anything over the boulder-pounding cataracts of the river. All the hoarded snowmelt of spring is being spent now, it seems, to swell tomatoes in the Valley. Would I wade in here? Never. Would I hop in a little rubber dinghy without a life preserver and ride the standing waves? Not in a million years.

There's no trail along the shore, just a landing scooped out of the poison oak where the wayfarers come to wash dishes. Downstream, accessible from another trail, is their bathing spot, an immense tub of echoes and churning water. The current looks less ferocious by shore, but how deep is it? Ten feet? Fifteen? Deep enough to dive, probably. There's no sign of a bottom in that churning water.

❧

I start preparing to leave before I've really decided to go, and suddenly I'm aware of the rituals I've developed—turning the knobs upright to unlock the cap, raising the glass door, and dropping the tailgate with a clang to sit down. I do it all slowly, kicking off my sneakers one at a time so I can stand on each one without getting my feet wet or my waders dirty, feeling the perspiration on my legs cool. I slide the rod into its case, take off my vest, pile the waders and sneakers near the ground cloth and the souvenir stone.

I stop at the parking lot below the bridge and walk down to the river, just to make sure I'm not missing anything. The sun has descended to the treetops, leaving most of the river to shadow. A few tan caddis have emerged to take advantage of the change, but the most visible addition to the evening air is the squadron of mosquitoes that appear immediately, in formation, to attack my head. One makes a stealth approach to the nape of my neck, drawing blood before I strike it dead. It's the only sign of an insect meeting its end in the vicinity. After I get tired of listening to the crickets and watching the feathery genesis of mist, after I've slapped most of the first mosquitoes, and their reinforcements have arrived, and still there's not a single rise, I feel justified in leaving. I trek back to the truck and get on the highway, bound for home.

I wind my way back through the forests of Burney, studded now with the glowing eyes of deer, and reach Redding, where the hot air of the valley stalls, cooking slowly with all the fruit-fly aromas of food left out too long, the smell of tomato canneries pumping out sour steam, of melons fermenting in the fields. The big tractors are plowing by the light of a single powerful beam across the blackness of tilled earth, their dust smothering the highway. I drive through prune, pistachio, and almond groves, and the billboards tell me I've passed the olive capital of the world without stopping, missed my chance for cheap nuts and bargain fruit by the bushel. At Woodland I make the turn west through the Coast range, the air cooling as I get closer and closer to the sea. Rolling down the steep grade above Vallejo I see those salty waters again, the Suisun Bay flats, and the hills of the East Bay lit by the sparkle of innumerable lights.

It's nearly midnight when I pull up the street and park in front of our house. It's hard to turn off the truck. I can feel the road calling to the fast-twitch muscles of my imagination, telling me to keep goading the truck onward across this continent and the next, while the rest of me sighs with bliss: *You're home.* I'm ready to sleep for days in my own bed, to shower when I wake, to pull clean clothes out of a folded stack in the dresser. I'm ready to open the door of the fridge and forage in the cold, to eat half a pint of ice cream and save the rest for later.

But the bills, and the shoebox full of junk mail? And the broom, the washer and dryer, the dish rack, the daily monotony of routines and things-to-do lists? You could shed those like a snake rubbing free of an old skin. The world is always new, down the road, around the bend, across the border.

We just got started, boy! Come on—Apache trout! The mountains of Mexico—you ain't fished those yet, you lily-livered . . . Montana Slim, who has no place here.

I unlock the front door and find I'm unexpectedly eager to review those accumulated catalogues and outdated magazines. What special offers did I miss? Do they know they're offering gold and platinum to a vagrant? I rifle through the envelopes, hunting for one worth opening before I realize what I'm doing.

Nicola is asleep. I notice she's made the bed into a smooth tableau of comforter and folded-down sheet, and that she's pulled the covers up to her chin. She's sleeping as she always does, on her side, with her hands curled by her mouth. She breathes a welcome as I find her face with my lips. I stroke her hair where it thins at the temples. Sleep makes her lisp. Come to bed, she says, and drifts away again. There's a womb of pillows and fluffy down bedspreads beside her, but I'm not ready for it yet. In a minute, I say. She replies with a small animal assent.

Before I can sleep, I have to take a tour of the rooms. They look the same but smell different; cool and clean, like a lawn mowed yesterday. There's none of the springtime paperback mustiness now. I sit on the couch. I turn on the new lamp Nicola said she bought in a sale. New shadows play on the living room walls, but it's out in back, where the shoots and seeds I planted have matured into a jungle, that I find the signs of time's passage.

Spring was ending when I left, and now it's late summer. The three tomato starts have clambered over one another and, for some reason that's undecipherable in the dark, begun to wither and die, branch by branch. I can't find the cucumbers because the zucchini, once a tidy rosette of leaves, has coiled itself like a python over every available surface. The unpicked squash look like green cordwood. Nothing looks like it did. The garden has gone on without me.

I'm ready for bed. Teeth scrubbed, face soaped, I slide naked under the sheet into that soft, drowsy dream. I cup my arm around Nicola's waist and press my face into hair. I'm home.

Little Fish Finale

Yuba River, Penn Valley, California

I sit in the backyard thinking about salmon smolts and the many ways there are to reproduce. Their birth must feel quite different from ours, egg mixing with milt in the running water, outside the body of the parent. They go through all the undulations of development while lodged in the gravel. The river becomes their mother, until the spring surge sweeps them out to sea. Their first gasp of salt water must feel like an accident, but they learn to breathe salt water, to swim through depths more profound than any river pool, to traverse the wide barrens of the oceans until they look nothing like the slender finger of flesh they once were. But the taste of the riffle where they were born is imprinted on their memory, and they always return to that same stretch, or die trying.

To come home completely, I should have a river I call home, where the pools feel as familiar as the rooms of my house. The tour that ended in the garden should have led out along a path I know so well I don't need a light to follow it, out through nettles and forget-me-nots, or sagebrush and boulders, to the water flowing past in the dark. The sound of that water would orient me to home again.

I don't have that kind of river here, living as I do on a peninsula between two bays, hemmed by the smokestacks of chemical plants and refineries on one side and the licks of salt water on the other. I feel the lack of it daily, an inability to chart my way through the seasons, and certainly this journey doesn't feel complete, even as I replenish my limbs and salvage some order in the garden. I find myself wondering whether it's still raining on the Delaware, whether the thunderstorms have ceased in Pennsylvania, whether it's rained some relief for the Clark Fork. I can't bring myself to unpack anything more than the stones I've collected along the way, arranging them like the talismans of a riverbed on the concrete of our patio. Even the cooler still has hot water sloshing around in it. I need to visit one more river, and the closest I have to a home is the Yuba.

I've fished the Yuba a number of times, and although it's a couple of hours drive into the foothills and therefore still a stranger to me in many ways, I've formed some bonds with those waters. Wild trout still flourish there, and native steelhead come home to spawn. It's the river where I first encountered the primeval scene of wild king salmon spawning, that ecstasy of decay and sex that complicates any identification with seafaring salmonids.

We have made our appointment with the fertility doctor. In the end, we have to take the plunge into the unknown—trying to get pregnant feels like the natural thing to do. I've discovered that beneath the veneer of technological wizardry, the body's workings remain mostly undefined, mysterious. The advances of the lab do not dispel mysticism—they inspire a deeper version of it. What are the long-term consequences of the injections? What will improve our chances of conception, or deny them? The answers are vague. The doctor recommends maintaining a positive frame of mind. Relax. Envision positive results. A friend buys us a box of raspberry-leaf tea—good for the female reproductive system. Nicola buys a large paper egg to hang over our bed. We build a little shrine with candles, start to develop an invocation, a prayer we can repeat. Fates and growth mediums, deities and specialists in scrubs—we will be weaving these elements together over the next few months.

I might be skeptical, if these rituals weren't the main chance for me to get deeply involved in a process over which I have little control, like stepping into a river and starting to cast. Physically, there isn't much for me to do. Nicola is back on the pill, resting her ovaries. In a month or so she'll begin the injections. Hopefully a number of the eggs will all ripen at once. They will remove them. They will become embryos, some saved, some implanted. If the process works, we will know the exact day of conception. Usually the doctor adds two weeks to the gestation period to account for the indeterminacy of ovulation and fertilization, but we will be able to count forward from the day of conception to the day of birth.

~

The first kings are back in the river when I arrive. Black as rubber boots, they drift along, on patrol for each other. Death has already begun to mushroom along their once-sleek sides, but most are still vigorous, dueling with one another over stretches of cobblestone. I avoid them, as usual.

The Yuba flows through the gravel spoils left behind by the Gold Rush, when the riverbanks were blasted away with hydraulic cannons. Below the Highway 20 bridge the river courses through vast wastelands of gravel, deep enough to be scooped up by bulldozers and sold. Upstream the canyon closes in on a series of deep pools, and as the pools get deeper, the ledges steeper, and the poison oak smothers the trail, the fishing improves dramatically. I usually walk upstream for a mile over the stones to a single willow that spends most of its life submerged to the tips of its branches. The river has set to work on undermining the roots, scouring a hole beneath the branches that is easily over my head, forming the only refuge of substance in a quarter mile of fast water. Because the willow will not budge, it has collected a necklace of washed-up stumps and drowned limbs.

I know there will be trout here. Smolts abound on the Yuba, young steelhead with a yen for dries and a penchant for somersaults, but there are always bigger fish holding under the willow. Everybody knows it, which is why every season a new collection of lost flies gathers in the branches, a ripe crop with nobody willing to harvest it until I come along and, dancing nimbly along the edge of the hole, pluck them all.

The only question I have as I hike upstream is whether someone will already be fishing there. On a busy day the lower pool will be taken, and the willow is next in line, although for many people it isn't big enough water to last an evening. As I round the bend, I see two rods in motion in the pool above and another guy scanning the edge of the long flat beyond. The willow is free.

In the midst of an August heat wave, with temperatures rising to near triple digits in the valley, I don't plan on seeing a hatch. I'm ready to begin with my usual repertoire: tan caddis to stimulate the appetite, then a nymph if it fails to please. I'm about to pluck the scruffy caddis from its compartment when I notice a dimple in the shade of the branches. There's another dimple downstream, in the wake. A smolt leaps like a swallow to snatch something, something small. I find one riding the current near shore, a blue-winged olive, tiny and new to the terrestrial world. It feels like a gift, a happy and successful end to my journey.

I find a small olive dun left over from the Delaware and make a short cast, snubbing the line so the fly will glide under the branches without getting tangled in them. The fly drops, rests for a moment, and a fish rises. I miss the strike. Nothing unusual there. There's plenty more under there, and I don't even think I pricked the first. He'll be back again, I tell myself. This is going to be good.

I'm so intent on reading the water that at first I don't recognize the problem with my casting. Every time I throw a back cast, it feels like I'm catching something behind me, some tree branch or grass stem. But there's nothing growing back there, just a stretch of small stones.

Am I imagining this? There's no obvious explanation. The rod looks fine—the tip is still there; the guides are all there. I try another cast and again feel as if I'm trying to flex an arm full of broken bones. "What the hell is going on here?" I demand of the evening sky. The trout keep right on rising. I notice that two guys have rounded the bend below me and are fishing the marginal water down there. They're probably waiting for me to finish, hoping to stand right here. Otherwise, why wouldn't they go behind me, cross the river, and keep on going to the better water upstream? *I'm here until night falls,* I want to tell them, *don't wait for me,* but when I try to demonstrate my resolve with an-other cast, the result is the same: slack line coiling around my feet.

The answer appears when I twitch the rod. Actually, I do more than twitch; I cut the air in front of me in a frenzy of frustration. The rod should feel like a bullwhip; it should whistle like one. But there's no torque because the graphite is shattered where the two sections join. The pieces fit together invisibly when the rod is straight, but under stress they part like the fibers of a snapped twig. After several thousand miles in the back of the truck and a marathon of rivers, my rod has buckled under the strain. I have no choice but to vacate my position. The other fishermen slide upstream; I see them casting to the willow before I disappear around the bend.

Given this devastating turn of events, I could quit and drive home.

My rod is broken, my spot taken, and night is coming on fast. I've had plenty of fishing this summer, enough to fuel a winter of dreams. Yet I'm not finished—I still have my old rod; I still have flies; I still have some time and some water to fish. It's not the best rod—I got it for my tenth birthday, and they haven't made one like it for twenty years. I have no idea what modulus of graphite powers the blank, but I do know that it has survived all the abuse a ten-year-old can muster, and no amount of whipping has ever cracked the ferrule.

I cut the fly from the new rod's leader and fasten it to the old one. A few false casts reveal the difference between the two rods; the old one is neither as graceful nor as powerful. I won't be able to cast as far, and I'll have to compensate with the muscles of my forearm.

In the midst of my false casting I pause, wondering whether I should bother. A moldy king slashes the surface, chasing another with lust-sharpened teeth. The line swishes back and forth over my head. I'm not a salmon fisherman. My only option is to fish the pocket water below the bridge, a stretch I know to be brimming with small fish making their way down from the spawning grounds where they were born. There's no sign of activity below the pylons, just the roar of the side chute breaking against boulders. I choose that blank and unpromising water. Why not embrace the obvious? After thousands of miles I'm home again, fishing the water I know. I make my first cast, taking pleasure in the ritual motion, in the feel of a rod I've known since childhood, in the reply I know is coming. I want to catch one small fish before nightfall. Only one. I'm a smolt fisherman, after all.